ORANGE SKY, RISING WATER

NICHOLAS WALTON

Orange Sky, Rising Water

The Remarkable Past and Uncertain Future of the Netherlands

HURST & COMPANY, LONDON

First published in the United Kingdom in 2025 by
C. Hurst & Co. (Publishers) Ltd.,
New Wing, Somerset House, Strand, London WC2R 1LA

Distributed in the United States, Canada and Latin America by Oxford
University Press, 198 Madison Avenue, New York, NY 10016, United
States of America.

A Cataloguing-in-Publication data record for this book
is available from the British Library.

ISBN: 9781805264156

Printed and bound in Great Britain by Bell and Bain Ltd, Glasgow

www.hurstpublishers.com

To Luca.
Thank you for taking us around the Netherlands with you.
We learned a lot and loved it.

CONTENTS

The NETHERLANDS

1. Emmeloord to Urk
2. Westenschouwen to Vrouwenpolder
3. Hoek van Holland to Delft
4. Den Burg to 'T Horntje
5. Bijlmermeer to Amsterdam Centraal
6. Baarle-Nassau and back again
7. Nijmegen to Arnhem
8. De Kuip to Delfshaven
9. Fort Ében-Émael to Maastricht
10. Oud Wassenaar to Madurodam

Terschelling

Vlieland

Waddenzee

Emden

Groningen

Leeuwarden

Groningen

Harlingen

Texel

Friesland

Assen

Den Helder

Drenthe

Emmen

Noord-
Holland

IJsselmeer

Urk

Hoorn

Kampen

Alkmaar

Lelystad

Flevoland

Zwolle

Overijssel

IJmuiden

Almelo

North Sea

Haarlem

AMSTERDAM

Schiphol

Apeldoorn

Deventer

Enschede

(Den Haag)

The Hague

Scheveningen

Amersfoort

Gelderland

Zuid-Holland

Utrecht

Hoek van Holland

Delft

Gouda

Arnhem

Rotterdam

Utrecht

Nijmegen

Dordrecht

GERMANY

s-Hertogenbosch

Zeeland

Breda

Tilburg

Noord-Brabant

Bergen op Zoom

Baarle-Nassau
Baarle-Hertog

Eindhoven

Duisburg

Essen

Vlissingen

Antwerp

Düsseldorf

Mönchengladbach

N

Ghent

BELGIUM

Leverkusen

BRUSSELS

Limburg

Cologne

Maastricht

Aachen

Bonn

0   40 km

Key to maps

—— Walking route	⌇ Roads	⤜ Water feature
● Start/finish of route	—— Railway	Beach or dune
■ Place of interest	------ Ferry	Park
----- Belgian border	⌇ Coastline	Urban area

INTRODUCTION

In July 1886 the blue-collar workers of the Jordaan district of Amsterdam gathered for an illegal eel-pulling event. Competitors manoeuvred their boats underneath a live and very slippery eel that had been strung up above what was then the Lindengracht canal, and attempted to tear down its slithering body. The activity was similar to *ganstrekken*, where horse-riders in Limberg competed to pull the head from a goose's body. As the goose was dead this was only outlawed this century. But because eel-pulling involved a live eel it was already illegal before the events of July 1886, and this prompted the police to move in. Two days of politically-tinged rioting followed, known as the *palingoproer* (eel riots). Twenty-six people died.

I mention this because the Netherlands has a long history of rioting that does not necessarily fit with the peaceful international image the country now enjoys. The Jordaan also saw the potato riots of 1917, where anger over food shortages and the sight of boat-loads of potatoes for export exploded into street fighting and looting that left nine people dead. Amsterdam's ugly coronation riots of 1980 saw a militant squatter movement engage in running battles with military police as Princess Beatrix was being crowned Queen. More recently the nation's farmers

1

pioneered the use of massed tractors as an offensive weapon, something that has been copied by their agricultural, muddy-booted brethren across Europe. And in 2021 hundreds of teenage beachgoers were involved in fights that involved glass bottles being merrily chucked at heads. There are plenty of other examples, old and new.

Back in 2020 and 2021 the Netherlands was facing another rash of riotous behaviour. Much of it was directed at the various restrictions and diktats of the government's Covid-19 policy, and some of it was fuelled by simple boredom. At my young family's home on a *binnenstad* canal in the lovely old town of Delft the police called at doors and pinned leaflets to bicycle racks. The riots, they said, were heading our way, led by groups of agitators in much the same way that murderous bands of soldiers rampaged across Europe during the Thirty Years War. We were advised to take bicycles indoors, stay away from uncovered windows and prepare to make extensive insurance claims.

As it happened, the riots largely passed Delft by. But elsewhere the violence and mayhem was real. Policemen were attacked with weapons, buildings were vandalised and set on fire, and countless bicycles were thrown into canals. This all made it clear that not everything in this little corner of Europe was as we, or many others, had come to expect.

What had we come to expect? There is a Dutch comedy skit by a group called *Klik Beet*.[1] A party of Dutch people, dutifully dressed in hi-vis jackets and carrying packed lunches (doubtless cheese sandwiches), are in a bus on their way to a protest. They digest rules such as a strict noise limit of 95 decibels, and have pre-applied for a permit to destroy one bus shelter (although they carry protective glasses and a dustpan and brush). They even give a lift to a grateful member of the riot police. The protest leader gives a little pre-demo speech about how they want it to be a memorable and enjoyable day out. At no point does anybody mention wanton destruction, physical violence or eels.

My family had moved to Delft after several years in Singapore. On the morning we arrived, the three of us wandered along the Delftse Schie canal in the June drizzle, delirious with jet lag and congratulating ourselves on having moved to such a captivating little town. From the first Vermeer-tinged views of this mini Amsterdam to the ultra-efficient registration as Delft residents, Dutch reality fitted neatly with the Dutch brand we had in our head. It was friendly, outgoing, efficient, courteous, low-key, safe and deeply, deeply civilised. In 2024 the national statistics agency declared that this country had the second highest standard of well-being over 23 indicators in the EU, beaten only by Sweden.[2] We liked it.

For such a small country there is also an awful lot to like. We were lucky to travel far and wide across the Netherlands, both before and during the Covid-19 restrictions, and saw most corners of the country. We walked the cobbled streets of the small towns and villages that are the gems of the Netherlands, from Harlingen to Brielle, Veere to Elburg, Valkenburg to Gorinchem. We scrambled over intricate star-shaped fortifications and watched dairy cows dance as they were reintroduced to outdoor fields after a winter in a barn. I piloted an imperious *bakfiets* cargo bike over cobblestones and cycled alongside my young son on his school run. I started each day with an invigorating swim in the lake at Delftse Hout and set off crazy amounts of New Year fireworks with friends. My wife and son developed an undying passion for *friet* with gloopy truffle mayonnaise, while I had my photograph taken at the Vaalserberg, the country's highest point.* We stayed in campsites, hotels, treehouses and riverboats.

---

* The Vaalserberg is 322 metres high.

We forged enduring friendships, both Dutch and foreign. It is a fabulous country in which to live.

The Netherlands can also feel comfortingly familiar to British people: Amsterdam's canals, the impeccable spoken English, those windmills, the love of sandwiches. The English in particular can be seduced into thinking of the two countries as siblings, intrepid protestant maritime nations mirroring each other across the North Sea. The Glorious Revolution of 1688, when the Prince of Orange was grafted on to the Royal Family as William III, was the ultimate expression of this.* In part of the English imagination the Netherlands is a representation of what we could be if only we were more civilised, more liberal, more efficient and far, far better at languages. In truth, other than the second half of the seventeenth century and umpteen drunken city breaks, there are more differences in history and temperament than similarities.

Just as fans of illegal eel-pulling would have known, there is more to the Netherlands than its civilised image suggests. Easy charm and plain talking can morph into gruff confrontation over minor matters such as a principled reluctance to pick up dog poo. Strangers sometimes felt a curious compulsion to tell us why they disagreed with us, or simply volunteered that we were wrong about something. When we drove on the motorway we were alarmed by the ultra-aggressive drivers that swung recklessly off slip roads on to the motorway as though they were channelling Max Verstappen.† Once I made the mistake of honking my horn at a reckless middle-aged driver who responded by braking inches from my front bumper at 120 kilometres per hour. The Dutch—at least some of the Dutch—have an edge.

---

* William III was King of England, Ireland and Scotland.
† Max Verstappen is a multiple world champion Formula 1 driver, sometimes criticised by (non-Dutch) racing fans for his recklessness.

So when the elections of late 2023 plonked the far right populist firebrand Geert Wilders and his Partij voor de Vrijheid (PVV or Freedom Party) in prime position to form the next Dutch government, it was eyebrow-raising but not surprising.* His victory was as Dutch as dressing up entirely in orange and dancing madly to techno music. It was as Dutch as watching some eel-pulling and then having a nice riot.

However this is not simply a book about there being a different side to this remarkable country beyond Rembrandt, Cruyff and high levels of tolerance for narcotics and prostitution. To understand the Netherlands you first need to delve into *what it is*, which is something of a geographical and socio-political miracle. The more you understand that miracle and how it has come about, the more fragile it seems, the more susceptible to the challenges that the rest of this century will bring.

The title of this book, *Orange Sky, Rising Water*, speaks to that miracle and those challenges. When my family made that move to Delft we lived in the attic of an old brewery on Koornmarkt, full of oak beams as broad as a man and reeking of history. As the glorious days of our first summer started to be blown away by gusty autumnal winds, my wife and I would sit on our balcony, pour a glass of wine and stare into the darkening heavens. When the clouds scudded low across the South Holland sky just above us we noticed that they developed a strange orange glow. At first we thought it must be some kind of reflection from the lights of

---

* The PVV won 23.49% of the vote and went on to form the next government with the centre-right VVD (15.24%), the NSC, which focuses on good governance (12.88%), and the BBB farmers' movement (4.65%). The leftist Groen Links/PvdA won 15.75% of the vote. At the time of writing Geert Wilders has pulled the plug on this coalition, frustrated at his inability to shift the deal on immigration and other priorities. Further elections are expected in late 2025.

Rotterdam, just off to the southeast. But no. We soon realised that it was actually the reflection of the thousands of gigantic agro-industrial glasshouses that blanket the countryside in this part of the Netherlands.

That literal orange sky and those glasshouses were part of a Netherlands that we were only just starting to recognise and understand. Despite the lush grass and willows and dairy cows immediately outside Delft, we were not surrounded by a bucolic green patchwork of polders and forests. In the Netherlands, especially in the west, every square inch of land has to work for its living, whether as hyper-productive dairy farms, cleverly-planned urban spaces, or indeed glasshouses humming with calibrated horticultural growth. The Dutch have built their success on productivity, doing a lot with very little. That orange sky is the result.

And rising water. The great rivers, the canals, the marshes, the criss-cross of polder watercourses, the shallow mudflats of the Wadden Sea, the capricious North Sea clawing away at those long, sandy coasts. The rain. Water is ever present, catching the light, drawing the land together and linking it to the outside world. Water defines the Netherlands, in its geographical essence a delta for continental river systems, not unlike Bangladesh or Louisiana. It occupies a soggy and fragile corner of the Eurasian landmass where by rights humans should struggle to gain a foothold alongside the frogs and coots.

There is no escaping the fundamental fragility of this geographical inheritance. For the Dutch, water is a dynamic and potentially destructive force that needs to be controlled. Over hundreds of years the Dutch have arm-wrestled water to forge the physical country that we see today. Land has been wrenched from the waves, and marsh has been turned into fertile pasture and light industrial estates. This has resulted in the most extraordinary landscapes where water and land meet and probe and dance together: take a look at Achterbos or Aalsmeer on a satellite map. Old paintings of the Dutch landscape glow because so much light was being reflected by the copious amounts of surface water. The need to put that water where the Dutch wanted it and not where it wanted to be led to the building of those famous Dutch windmills, largely used for pumping water rather than milling grain. It remains an ongoing process: an entire province was added in the decades after the Second World War, and whenever there is a land use question to be resolved somebody will suggest grabbing a bit more land from the sea. The overall result is a country that sits flat and sometimes unnervingly low behind its fortified network of dykes. When you land at Amsterdam Schiphol airport you pass sea level and carry on descending for three more metres.

Engineering, the physical control of water and where it is, is only half the story. The other half is how the Dutch have organised themselves, harnessing their collective energy to unlock extreme economic and geopolitical vibrancy. The Netherlands rose to become a pocket battleship among global powers, among commercial powers, among artistic and cultural powers. In more recent decades this unpromising delta has reinvented football and become a crucible of technological invention and agricultural productivity. The Netherlands has also forged as distinct an identity as any nation on earth. How many other countries can be instantly conjured up with the mention of a single colour? It has achieved all this with a relatively small population and very limited supply of dry land.* It would fit into the United States well over 200 times, or be

---

* Currently it is just over 40,000 square kilometres with a population of around 18 million. Like other countries its population has fluctuated throughout history; unlike most other countries its size has grown over time through land reclamation rather than conquest.

their 42nd largest state. By many measures you can count it as the most astonishing country on earth.

But time—and the incoming tide—waits for nobody. The water is rising. Can this near-thousand-year record of controlling the water and building an extraordinary country continue? Two of the most striking impacts of climate change will be sea level rises and extreme weather events. Both are mortal threats to the Netherlands. Meanwhile the intensive, productive way in which the Dutch have fashioned their country under its orange sky is creating extreme environmental pressures. This flat river delta is used to facing down nature, but the next decades promise an epochal challenge to the Netherlands' physical existence.

There will always be engineering solutions, but the Dutch need more than that. Will that socio-political underpinning, the famed polder system of consensus and constructive compromise, continue to support the engineering solutions that keep Dutch toes dry? Although rioting over eels and potatoes is a time-honoured Dutch tradition, there are now signs of friction, fractiousness and visible discontent that may undermine the foundations of Dutch success. Even if history registers Geert Wilders' impact on government formation as little more than a brief and unserious interlude, his modern brand of populism combining right wing anti-immigrant sentiment and left wing spending promises will continue to find an audience. In time could the Covid-19 riots, the tractor protests and Wilders' electoral success be seen as cracks in the dyke?

This matters, because past success is no guarantee for the future, especially for the Dutch. Their country is simply too fragile. China or Britain or Italy could royally screw things up for years, often for generation after generation, and would survive in one way or another. The Dutch do not have that luxury. If they screw things up in the face of rampaging climate change impacts, then they face being washed away into the North Sea. Its miracle simply needs to continue, then continue, then continue. There is a lot at stake as the water rises under that orange sky, and that means there is a lot to understand.

My first aim is therefore simply to explain why the Netherlands is such a remarkable place. I want to bring it alive, show what it is like physically, and introduce you to the lives and voices of some of the people who live there. Second, I want to tell the Dutch story, dive into its extraordinary history and show why this continues to shape the Netherlands today. Third, I want to lay out why this particular moment is so critical for the Netherlands, and why the challenges that it faces are so acute.

To do this I want to show it to you by walking across it. I have split this book up into ten individual walks. Each of them places you in a geographical location, a landscape, whether blissfully rural or hauntingly urban, historical or modern, coastal or buried deep in the Dutch hinterland. The walks are not a simple tour around sights, like some saunter behind a tour guide wielding a raised umbrella and a headset. Each one shows you something about the Netherlands, raises questions, lets you see the country and the people and the issues.

I have loved walking since I was a child growing up in New Zealand and Northeast England. When I started working as a journalist I realised it was the perfect way to understand how a place worked. Walking shows you geography and shape and scale, and the corners that you miss if you scoot by in a taxi. It exposes you to people doing everyday tasks, to their routines and frustrations, to their interactions and the infrastructure that guides them. It lets you feel the energy, watch them as they buy and sell and chat and laugh and get annoyed at each other. It is journalism at walking pace, teaching you to take time, look at things, measure distances properly, see how the land and buildings and the city fit together.

This approach works well with the Netherlands, because geography is so central to understanding the country. The first walk is in Flevoland, a seldom-visited new province of reclaimed land. However that is not the main reason why the first walk heads across the tulip and potato fields, then along a dyke towards the town of Urk. This walk exposes you to the other side of the Netherlands, as far away from grand central Amsterdam as it is possible to go. Instead of liberalism and crowds, Golden Age museums and chubby tourists, you see a planned new town and the heavy machinery of farming life, along with the town of Urk, full of fishermen and religious hardliners. There are no cruise liners, stag parties or Instagrammers.

The second walk is all about geography. It is across Zeeland, where those continental river systems spill out into the North Sea. To understand the Netherlands you need to understand the power of water, omnipresent and omnipotent, whether filling those mighty rivers, canals and ditches, or scouring the beaches and dunes along the coastline. It also introduces the engineering solutions that the Dutch have found to manage water—in this case the extraordinary Delta Works—and the polder model that underpins it.

The setting for the third walk is just to the north, from Hoek van Holland to Delft, through Westland, the heart of the Dutch agro-industrial complex. It is a netherworld of eternally-lit glasshouses and enormous agricultural processing facilities, dotted with old cottages and farming magnate McMansions. This orange sky walk is about the intensive Dutch miracle and its environmental cost.

Further up the coast is Texel, the largest of the Wadden islands and the location for the fourth walk. This one is historical, and centres on how the Dutch turned decisively outwards in the sixteenth and seventeenth centuries to become an unlikely imperial global superpower. The waters off Texel are where fleets gathered before striking out into the open sea, seeking fortunes in Java and the spice islands, or the slave plantations of the Americas.

The fifth walk brings us back to mighty Amsterdam, the brimming capital of that superpower and now a global tourist centre to rival any other. This walk brings up two of the challenges that the Netherlands now faces: its relationship with outsiders, whether cruise ship passengers or remnants from that erstwhile empire; and its relationship with the burst of extreme liberalism that took root in the city in the 1960s and 1970s.

After Amsterdam we go deep into the countryside of Noord Brabant, and the chance to play hop-scotch across an absolute mess of borders, enclaves and exclaves. This sixth walk is not about the relationship between the Netherlands and Belgium, but about the serious crime wave that is eating away at the fabric of Dutch society and its institutions. Noord Brabant may seem sleepy and bucolic, but its location between Rotterdam's vibrant port and the Belgian border has placed it right at the centre of an international narcotics business that has sparked a dramatic Dutch crime wave.

The seventh walk ends in the city of Arnhem, the location of the most famous military episode of the Second World War on Dutch territory: *Operation Market Garden*. This seventh walk starts at Nijmegen and is focused on how those dark years of defeat, occupation and liberation helped to shape the modern Netherlands.

The eighth walk is across the Netherlands' second great city, Rotterdam, in so many ways the antithesis of Amsterdam. In part, this shows the rebuilding of the country after the Nazi occupation and how the economy rediscovered its vitality. Even more, this is about one of the key social and political issues that the Netherlands faces in the twenty-first century, and the one that Geert Wilders has built his political capital upon: immigration.

The other great change after the Second World War was how the Netherlands' perception of its place in the world shifted from global imperial power to medium-sized European stalwart. That is why this ninth walk is in Maastricht, the birthplace of the European Union. Is the formerly marauding global power now too parochial, and have the Dutch lost confidence in their ability to influence the world?

Finally we walk from the Netherlands' most expensive street in Wassenaar, down the beach towards Den Haag (The Hague), where international schools and expat communities sit next to deprived Dutch working class communities and virtual immigrant ghettos. Is the Netherlands quite as egalitarian as it believes itself to be, and what does this mean for the future of this country?

Together the chapters should give you a good idea about why the Netherlands is quite so remarkable, and what it faces in this era of climate change and fractious politics. This is not a history book, so if you want more details about the constitutional arrangements that underpinned the Batavian Republic I am sure you can find them elsewhere. I have approached this book as a journalist, so history has been used to embellish the Dutch story just as a Dutch mother uses *hagelslag* (chocolate sprinkles) to embellish buttered bread. Inevitably there are areas where the history crosses over between different chapters, so I have included a time line of major events. I have taken a leaf from the *Big Book of Dutch Tact and Diplomacy* and been blunt with some of my opinions, at the risk of incurring the wrath of a small and cantankerous minority. I apologise in advance for any offence caused: I have formed my opinions honestly and diligently, and know that I do not have all the answers. Criticism of certain aspects of the Netherlands is made in full knowledge that the country gets far more right than wrong. (As a joint British/ Italian citizen I am more than aware of this.) This book is fired by my respect for and wonder at this amazing country and its people, and my enduring happy memories from the terrific four years when we lived in the Netherlands as a family.

As a bonus this book will also give readers the outline of ten extremely interesting day walks that are visually compelling and satisfying to complete. (For my previous book on Singapore I explained the country by walking 53 kilometres across the entire country in one day. Although some readers have replicated that walk, I hope each of the ten for this Netherlands book are more accessible and less exhausting than 53 kilometres on hard concrete on the equator.) If you want something more visual, I have produced a series of short videos from each of the walks, available on YouTube, along with audio podcasts. Full details of all the walks, including downloadable maps, are available on my website.[3]

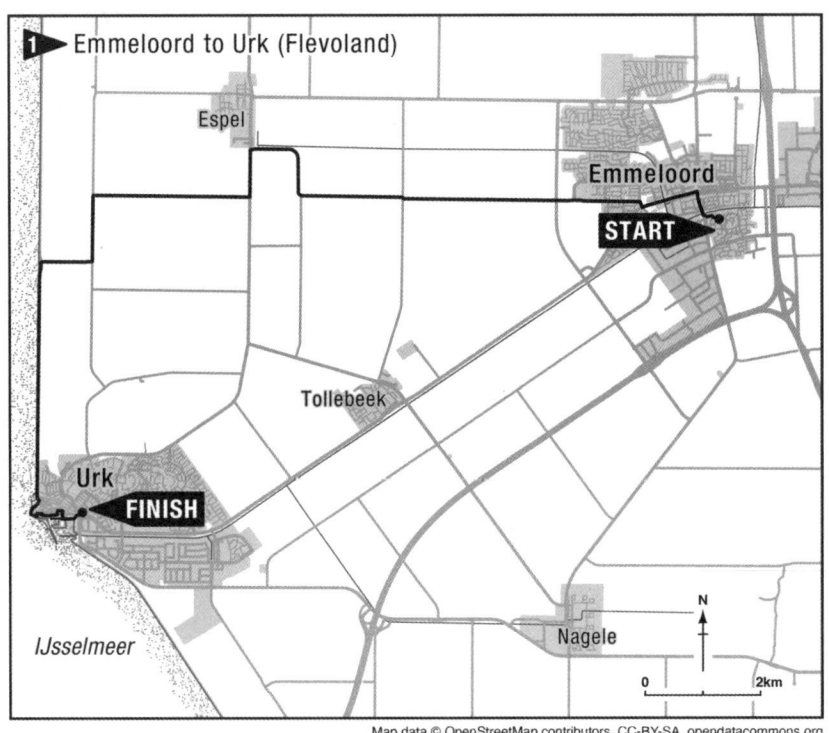

Emmeloord to Urk (Flevoland)

Espel

Emmeloord

START

Tollebeek

Urk

FINISH

IJsselmeer

Nagele

N

0   2km

1

EMMELOORD TO URK
(FLEVOLAND)

This walk starts in Emmeloord, right in the middle of the northern half of the province of Flevoland. Both the province and the town were built in the decades after the Second World War, so they are full of straight lines and angles and easy to navigate. Head out from the centre due west on the road marked Korte Dreef and Urkerweg, and at the roundabout just after the small hospital turn right, then left again on Drostlaan. This road will take you out of town in an almost entirely straight line. After nearly six kilometres you will have a slight detour to the north before resuming that trek westwards on the Ankerpad. When it hits the Westermeertocht turn left, then right onto the Schapenpad between fields and wind turbines to the sea. Then simply head directly south with the IJsselmeer on your right, until you reach Urk. This fishing port used to be an island before Flevoland was claimed from the sea, and is the end point of this first walk.

* * *

It felt like we were not meant to be there, as though we were gate crashers from a different dimension. People noticed that we were speaking English, that my wife was a suspiciously Latin brunette, and presumably that we were several centimetres shorter than even the shortest of the locals. When we parked up there were no foreign number plates on display, and a healthy babble of crunched consonants and swollen vowels filled the air. We were outsiders at a peculiarly Dutch—or shall we say Friesian—event. We were off to see a bit of *fierljeppen*.

My wife had heard something intriguing, a snatch of conversation. But although the tourist information was stuffed full of brochures and posters for 1,001 other things to do in Friesland, there was nothing about *fierljeppen*. So she asked. The ladies behind the counter were taken aback, and almost denied that the *fierljeppen* world championships were due to take place just along the road from Akkrum. But then they smiled and scribbled down a direction on a piece of paper. There would not be many signposts advertising the event.

The air of concealed mystery made it feel like we were off to see some cock fighting, badger-baiting, or even eel-pulling. But *fierljeppen* is not nearly as illegal. It literally translates as 'far leaping', and is a sport born of living in fields obstructed by multiple ditches and channels of water. It is a longitudinal version of pole-vaulting, and we were off to watch the world championships in a purpose-built *fierljeppen* arena.

The idea is simple, and the fields that surrounded Akkrum gave clues about the *fierljeppen* logic. Many Dutch livestock fields resemble peculiar mathematical board games, with fingers of water probing deep into a grid of grass peninsulas. For the cows this is just like being in a normal field but without the need for fences; single gates shut off individual islands of grass from other parts of the watery maze. The problem for the farmer is that they may have to negotiate a series of ditches and water channels to get directly from A to B on their farm. The solution, rather than an improbable succession of costly bridges, is a pole. Using that they simply vault across the channels.

Over many years this has evolved into a fiercely competitive sport. The *fierljeppen* arena that was hosting the world championships centred on a long rectangle of water. On one side was a succession of earthen mounds that culminated in a wooden platform on the edge of the water. On the other side was a sandy landing beach. Beyond that were rows of expectant *fierljeppen* enthusiasts on deck chairs, sipping plastic glasses of Heineken and negotiating the glutinous splodge of mayonnaise on their cone of *friet*.

Each competitor charged along the top of their mound brandishing a gigantic pole that could be up to 13 metres (43 feet) long. They flung themselves off the wooden platform and simultaneously plunged their pole through the murky water into the mud at the bottom. The pole stuck, flexed, and then the competitor had around a second or so to shuffle up the poll in the manner of a baby grizzly bear. Forward momentum then took over, depositing them in a triumphant arc onto the sand. At least that was the idea. Sometimes they mismanaged the physics and sometimes they just fell in with a splash and a ripple of glee from among the deck chairs. It was a glorious way to spend an afternoon.

This first chapter is not about *fierljeppen*. But just as it took a bit of detective work to find that hidden rectangle of water and the elusive world championships, this chapter is about the hidden Netherlands that the rest of the world barely gets to see, let alone understand.

The walk that explains all this is across a province called Flevoland, just to the south of Friesland. Flevoland is almost entirely an artificial creation, claimed from the water just decades ago and planted with potatoes and tulips. It sits on the south-eastern edges of the large body of water that dominates the middle of maps of the Netherlands. For centuries this was the Zuiderzee, literally the 'Southern Sea', bordered by land to its west, south and east, and meeting the open sea in the north. That open edge was closed in 1932 by the building of the 32km Afsluitdijk, in effect an enormous dam. This created a large fresh water lake which the Dutch named the IJsselmeer, and it was from those waters that Flevoland was formed.* I started off in the new town of Emmeloord, smack bang in the middle of the reclaimed land, headed due west until I climbed the enormous dyke that marked the shore of the IJsselmeer, then headed a few more kilometres south to a place called Urk.

Urk is a very singular place. It had been an island until the grand construction projects outlined above meant that the billiard table farmland of Flevoland was built around three sides of it. As an island it had been synonymous with fishing, religion and isolation. Now, as a semi-island it remains synonymous with fishing, religion and isolation. For me Urk is the ultimate manifestation of the other side of the Netherlands, almost as much as a day out in Friesland watching athletic young men and women fling themselves out over a rectangle of water armed only with a terrifically long pole.

* * *

On a glum low-cloud day in 1976 a bus drove through the rain to the new town of Almere. A woman called Lia de Clerck was sitting at a window seat, and had watched the featureless landscape zip past with a look of silent anticipation on her face. She got off with her husband and two daughters and walked across what was

---

* Part of the newly-renamed IJsselmeer in the southwest was in turn separated by the building of further dykes and became the Markermeer. I recommend a map.

still a building site, with not a blade of grass to be seen. She was given a key, and television cameras followed her as she turned it in the lock of one of the newly built houses and went inside.

'Ik vind het grandioos,' she said, exploring the echoing interior of her new home. 'I think it's great.'

'Ja, fantastisch,' replied her husband, a half turn to the camera capturing his quiet delight.

Lia de Clerck was considered the first ever resident of the new town of Almere, in what later became the province of Flevoland. Although she said it needed a clean, their spanking new house of convenient rooms and orderly plasterwork was a world away from the cramped Amsterdam apartment they had just left. For Lia de Clerck this new beginning came with a promise, that the Netherlands could create land out of water, and transform lives with modernity.

Flevoland is pure essence of Netherlands. It is eerily flat; its soil is bounteously fertile; it is there because it was willed into being by humans. There are two Flevo-chunks, both reclaimed from the IJsselmeer in the 1950s and 1960s: Flevopolder, where Almere is located as a handy spill over for Amsterdam; and the Noordoostpolder, off to the northeast and where the walk in this chapter is located.

If this makes Flevoland sound unromantic then that is not entirely wrong. It is not a place renowned for its beauty, however much Lia de Clerck appreciated it, and I felt that I was a rare visitor to its tidy streets and pathways. I had modest expectations of the first half of this walk, and Emmeloord matched them perfectly. It proved to be pleasant in an anonymous, leafy way, a new town built for function rather than splendour, and there is nothing wrong with that.* It had its neat housing estates full

---

* It was named after an old abandoned village on the former island of Schokland, several kilometres to the south and now a rare raised chunk of earth in an otherwise unnervingly flat landscape.

of disorientating half turns and cul-de-sacs, and broad canal-side avenues where red, white and blue pennants blazed above immaculate front gardens and very square houses. There were parks and parades of ducks, playgrounds and little bridges. If you are born there you thoroughly enjoy the first 12 years of your life, then are desperate to leave. It seemed to lack a sense of identity, although to make up for this a sign on a mini-roundabout on its western edge proclaimed Emmeloord as the 'potato city', which is something that I feel I could get behind.

There is something very familiar about Emmeloord to anybody who has ever spent time in the Netherlands. The buildings, the waterways, the way everything has been sensibly planned by tall men with neat haircuts and dark suits. Just as most inhabitants of Delft live in anonymous, tidy suburbs outside the old *binnenstad* of higgledy-piggledy canal houses and ornate gables, so most Dutch people live on streets like those in Emmeloord. Lia de Clerck would doubtless have found one of the houses here as *grandioos* as her new home in Almere.

If Emmeloord felt familiar and a little unexciting, the next part of the walk was a surprise. It looked largely as I had expected: enormous flat fields, right angles and lots of straight lines. Roads just kept on going towards the horizon; as a friend of mine who had lived in Texas said, if your dog runs away you can still see it running a day later.

What surprised me was the way this created patterns and shapes, gave a patchwork rhythm to the walk. Fields were planted with different crops, so there might be potatoes in one field, the next might be ridged with fresh plough lines and the one after that planted with tulips of three different colours, red, yellow and white. The overall effect on a gloriously sunny spring day was like walking through a gigantic Mondrian painting, stretched starkly out under the sky, uncompromising and geometric yet compelling and striking.*

Step by step, details emerged. The roads were less relentlessly straight than they had at first appeared. They would push forward for hundreds of metres and then have a slight wiggle where they negotiated a watery ditch, before heading off for the horizon once again with renewed vigour. There were curious stranded parallelograms where sheep munched the grass and eyed passers-by with suspicion. Farmhouses were set back, guarded by dogs and surrounded by stands of trees. Outbuildings tended towards the ginormous, large enough to house the purposeful pieces of agricultural machinery that trundled along the roads, vast peacock tails of burnished steel sprouting from their rear ends.

In all my years in the Netherlands I had never joined the hordes that descended on the famous tulip fields of Keukenhof. But in Flevoland I found a couple of dazzling fields of cerise tulips to myself, up close. It was genuinely astonishing, a block of almost overwhelmingly vivid, living colour in the spring sunshine. The individual plants stood in long phalanxes, like regiments of brightly jacketed grenadiers off to wage war against Napoleon. They were intense, but also fading; the flower heads were wide open, and some petals had already fallen. This did not matter, because the farmer's crop is the bulbs rather than the flowers.†

---

* When making the videos that accompany this walk I unaccountably kept talking about Matisse, not Mondrian, wasting some excellent footage of potato fields.

† The bulbs are an enduring Dutch export to the rest of the world, and tulips have played a notable role in the economic life of the Netherlands. Between 1634 and 1637, at a time when the country was pioneering capitalism, there

Along the far side of the field was a row of gently swooshing wind turbines, and beyond that was the raised bank of a grassy dyke. This meant that after ten kilometres I had reached the shore of the IJsselmeer.

The path rose on a gradient gentle enough for a geriatric cyclist, crossed a cattle grid and reached the top of the dyke next to a picnic table of blue perforated steel, sunk into concrete. My path ran down to join a four-abreast cycle lane that stretched off into the distance, right and left, and then a stone rampart mottled with yellow lichen. A jumbled rocky breakwater protected the dyke from the inky blue IJsselmeer, now a giant, shallow lake. Further wind turbines turned offshore, and pairs of retired cyclists on bicycles with sensible geometry and electric assistance pootled by. And off there, to the south breaking the straight lines like a pimple, lay Urk.

Urk has long been defined by its isolation. Appie Baantjer, the creator of fictional TV detective Jurriaan 'Jurre' de Cock, was born on Urk in 1923. In an article with *Trouw*[*] newspaper in 1987 he spoke about his experiences growing up there.[1] He said he remembered old men sitting around on winter evenings talking about Old Testament matters such as providence and the devil, and how the elders kept track of every couple so they would be able to identify fathers of any child that dared to be born out of wedlock. At one point the elders banned the first film that was to be shown on the island. 'Faith and superstitions are very close on Urk,' he concluded.

That physical isolation was breached in the 1950s when the Flevoland project linked Urk to the mainland. An article in

---

was an intense speculative bubble in the trade for tulip bulbs. At one point a single tulip bulb could cost as much as a large Amsterdam mansion.

[*] *Trouw* was originally founded as a protestant newspaper during the Second World War, but now has a broader readership.

Time Magazine from 1959 gives a flavour of the profound social changes that accompanied the loss of island status.[2] The article said that Urk was among the 'grimmest' of the 'world's dourest Calvinist communities', which is how much of the Netherlands must have looked to a booming 1950s America of soda bars and bubble gum pink Cadillacs. It is said that religious adherence was so strict that paintings were turned to face the wall on Sundays, and the only walk taken on the sabbath was to the door of the church.

That stifling religious conformity had evidently been shaken by the building works that became Flevoland, connecting Urk to the rancid godless evils of the outside world. Weekend reports of 'public cuddling' between young lovers became commonplace. Pubs had started to shut early at 10pm on Saturdays thanks to a booze-addled riot by 500 youngsters. The town's elders had cracked down on misbehaviour with a new law that criminalised trudging, slouching, lounging, sauntering, flocking together or lying after dark on public roads. One old timer told the reporter, 'Our world is turned upside down nowadays in Urk, and all because of that rotten dike.' From Urk, the outside world often looked like something to avoid.

I have been in Urk in the dead of winter, and on that bleak day this world of overbearing religiosity and insularity permeated its dank atmosphere. Despite its physical links to the rest of the Netherlands it maintained a feeling of deep isolation. But when I walked there with a certain lightness in my heart after a good day of tramping across tulip and potato fields, the atmosphere felt very different.

For a start, after a grimly rainy spring this was a glorious day of hope and sunshine. Mothers and grandmothers were delighting in taking their children to the little beach that nestled under the northern corner of the town itself. I paid for a ticket and climbed the staircase to the top of the lighthouse where a Dutch flag gently flapped and visitors took selfies across the roofs of rows of fishing cottages.

This felt quite interchangeable with other small Dutch seaside towns. From the lighthouse I did notice multiple church towers, but maybe I subconsciously sought them out simply because it was Urk. It was when I climbed down and turned the corner into the port that Urk felt like Urk. It is heart and soul a fishing port. The harbour was stuffed with resolute fishing boats, and I could see the hulking shapes of industrial seafood units and warehouses off to the east. There were pleasure boats and there were tourism facilities, but they felt like they were there for the spare change, not for the big money. And when I say big money, I mean Big Money.

Urk's fishing fleet is a multi-multi-million euro business. Although technically the town now sits on a lake, and its fleet has to motor for 50 kilometres across the IJsselmeer before reaching the salty sea, its fleet is renowned across the Netherlands for its professionalism and effectiveness.

An investigation by the broadcaster NOS into a practice called pulse fishing gives a glimpse of life inside the Urkish fleet. The practice involves zapping fish with small electric currents, forcing them to rise off the sea bed and into a boat's nets. It has now been outlawed as both cruel and so highly efficient that it devastates fish stocks. The TV investigation followed an Urk fisherman with an impenetrable accent, a storeroom full of unused pulse fishing equipment and an air of disbelief that it had been banned. 'It defies all logic,' the man muttered thickly as his boat ploughed through the darkness. The TV report then cut to him in the crew quarters, reading the bible out to his men as the boat lurched from side to side: 'At the same hour came the disciples unto Jesus, saying, Who is the greatest in the kingdom of heaven?'

This curious mixture of industrialised fishing and deep religion is still going strong in Urk. When I popped into the Boni supermarket a mother and daughter were at the till, paying for a perfectly normal basket of shopping while wearing bonnets and dresses straight out of the seventeenth century. Heading out of town there were fish-processing facilities on the right, and the *Jezus redt!* (Jesus saves!) institution on the left, complete with church and dormitory blocks. Urk does things its own way.

Urk was in the headlines during the Covid pandemic because its own way of doing things sometimes clashed with what the government was telling its citizens to do. In January 2021 a Covid testing centre near the harbour was set on fire during a riot protesting against a government curfew. The rioters also threw fireworks and attacked police cars. What happened in Urk helped spark the nationwide Covid riots creeping towards Delft that I mentioned in the introduction. It was at this time that Urk began to symbolise for me the other side of the country that few outsiders are even aware of.

* * *

International views of the Netherlands tend to be blinded by one of the world's most pervasive national stereotypes. I call it *Brand Orange*, that perception that the Netherlands is extremely liberal, orderly, friendly and has an enormous sense of fun. Look at the enlightened approach to drugs, to the sex industry, to crime and punishment. From across the North Sea the Amsterdam of the 1960s and 1970s was a place of excitement and cutting edge broadmindedness, almost a reflection of its seventeenth-century incarnation when Amsterdam built its reputation for tolerance. Look also at the crowds following the national football team, with their exuberant orange costumes, their joyful bouncing around and the way they drink Heineken until they are in a party mood (never a smash-up-foreign-things mood). *Brand Orange* is why, after the elections of 2023, I had very well-informed people ask me how the super-liberal Netherlands could have ended up with the Islamophobic populist Geert Wilders propelled to the verge of power. My answer was that the Netherlands is not always the super-liberal place they imagined it to be. *Brand Orange* only represented one face of the country.

If we go back to the post-War period, when *Time* magazine was publishing its article about grim Calvinist communities, the Netherlands was quite a grey and hidebound place. The Netherlands had suffered during occupation by the Nazis, and had lost its empire soon afterwards. It was a soggy, deeply conservative backwater. Albert Camus wrote *La chute* [*The Fall*] after spending time in Amsterdam in the 1950s. He was profoundly unimpressed by the hard beds, the fog and the damp. He wrote that Amsterdam was a place where pipe smokers watched the same rain falling on the same canal for centuries upon end.

This was reflected in the state of the national football team. It managed to qualify for the World Cups of 1934 and 1938, but was rubbish, eliminated in the first round on both occasions. The Dutch then failed to turn up again until the mid-1970s. The football they played was crude and agricultural. The Netherlands was (quite literally) a team of cloggers, a dour, provincial team from a dour, provincial country.

Compare this with the reputation that the Dutch team has broadly enjoyed since the 1970s, exemplified by Johan Cruyff, the extravagantly talented Netherlands number 14. Suddenly the men in orange were cool, vivid, modern, exciting and counter-cultural all at once. They reinvented the global sport, they wore some of the most stylish shirts ever designed by human hand and they became the team that every neutral wanted to win.

Johan Cruyff may personify this dramatic change in the Dutch national brand, but he did not suddenly materialise in the 1970s complete with flowing mane of hair, ready to transform how the world thought about the Netherlands. The roots of *Brand Orange* lie further back. In the 1960s the Dutch baby boom generation was growing frustrated with the greyness of life and the stultifying weight of tradition. Like boomers elsewhere they had grown up into a more affluent society than their parents, were slightly bored with life and were utterly sick of hearing about the privations suffered by their elders. They were also exposed to music, fashion and attitudes from far beyond their little corner of Europe. They looked abroad and liked what they saw.

The boomer generation translated their frustrations and youthful idealism into 'happenings' and 'uprisings'. These were centred on the atmospheric old canal-side houses of old Amsterdam (other cities such as Rotterdam were more focused on the virtues of hard work). One impresario, Robert Jasper Grootveld, organised a series of anti-consumerist, anti-tobacco happenings in an old garage. These attracted a motley crew of anarchists, activists and narcissists, and the happenings morphed into a movement.* When John Lennon and Yoko Ono flew in to their comfortable room in the Amsterdam Hilton and stuck signs on the window notifying the world of 'HAIR PEACE' and 'BED PEACE' on the window, the transformation from dour Calvinism to 1960s alternative hippy epicentre was complete.

---

* One offshoot was a group that left white-painted bicycles out for public use, in effect creating a prototype bike sharing scheme.

This was the vibrant new world that Cruyff was erupting into.* Serendipity had brought the visionary Rinus Michels in as the head coach, professionalising the entire set up and giving Cruyff's magical talents the platform to perform. Under Michels, Amsterdamsche Football Club Ajax pioneered what became known as *Totaalvoetbal*, or Total Football. This was an extremely aggressive and ultra-modern system that turned traditional structures and formations on their head. Players' positions were fluid rather than fixed, switching around and bewitching opponents in a carousel of movement. Johan Cruyff was at the centre of this, the outrageously gifted conductor of the orchestra. Ajax duly won three European Cups in a row.† The Dutch national team then qualified for the 1974 World Cup, were the best team in the competition and lost a heart-breaking final against their more pedestrian rivals, West Germany.‡ Four years later they once again reached the final and lost to the hosts, Argentina. They were modern and cool, heroic and tragic.

This new Netherlands was a whirlwind of style and iconic orange shirts, and with Cruyff involved it was never short of attitude. He was a natural insurrectionist, at home directing freeform *Totaalvoetbal* or throwing proverbial grenades at the establishment. After the Dutch national team signed a contract with Adidas he signed one with their rivals Puma, defiantly wearing their boots and having two stripes on the sleeves of his 1974 kit rather than the Adidas three worn by his teammates.

---

* The first years of his career were spent in the earlier version of the Netherlands, where he played football for Ajax Amsterdam while working odd jobs for a printer and selling *Sport World* magazine on the street.

† Fans of their arch-rivals from Rotterdam, Feyenoord, will remind you that Ajax's victories were preceded by their own European Cup triumph in 1970.

‡ One player, Willem van Hanegem, was clear about how bitter feelings were: his father and two brothers were killed by a bomb during the Second World War, and he spoke openly about his hatred for Germans.

When in 1983, in the autumn of his playing days, he found out that Ajax were not willing to offer him a new contract, he did the unthinkable and signed for their great historical adversaries Feyenoord down in Rotterdam. Just because. He was contrary and mercurial, a genius with the ball at his feet and the cool personification of a transformation from potato-eating stolidity to *Brand Orange*.

There is very little sign of *Brand Orange* in the 1970s blocks of Emmeloord, the potato fields of Flevoland or those Urkish communities drawn tight by religion and fishing in the treacherous North Sea. This walk is a reminder that much of the Netherlands is at heart somewhere on the scale from moderately conventional to deeply conservative, cleaving to tradition and happy to be so.

I was pleased to be able to talk over these aspects of Dutch life with one of the country's great public figures, the journalist and historian Geert Mak.[*] I met him in his publisher's office on Amsterdam's Prinsengracht on a gloriously sunny September day in 2024, his fluffy, tousled white hair made of the same chuckling geniality as his personality. He spends his time between the Amsterdam that he has written about so compellingly and a house in faraway (for the Netherlands) Friesland.

'You have two kinds of the Netherlands,' he told me. 'There is a big, deep cultural divide somewhere near Utrecht. The western side is very Atlantic-orientated and outward looking, rather republican, rather modern. The eastern part of the Netherlands is feudalistic, rather conservative.'[†]

---

[*] When he introduced himself he seemed uncertain which one of these to emphasise. His recent work shows that he is far further towards the historian on the journalist/historian scale than I am.

[†] He noted that the far north was 'really Scandinavian'.

When I asked him how the electoral success of Geert Wilders' anti-immigration populism had changed his mental picture of the Netherlands he gave me a surprising answer. 'Part of the rebellion of the Wilders movement is that this [eastern] part is finding its political [voice]. It's a mentality which always existed, but it became stronger and stronger, and is stimulated by the fear, not really of immigrants, but the fear of falling, from the middle classes.'

This fear of falling is partly stoked by socio-economic uncertainty. 'The big majority has a rather good life, but I think one-fifth, one-sixth of the population has real financial problems.' These socio-economic problems were then exacerbated by disruption to communities and to the certainties of Dutch life, especially for the more conservatively minded. 'For a lot of people there is no balance between place and space any more. You need space, you can do what you want, but everyone's feeling a bit that they want to be at home, some steadiness.' The example that Geert Mak gave was Amsterdam, and he became very animated as he gave me the figures that showed this: 46% of the people who had lived in the city in 2013 were gone within a decade. 'Really this is a washing machine,' he said with a chuckle. 'This gives the background to the *onrust* among people, their longing for steadiness. It's not just the immigrants, we are all changing fast.'*

In common with much of the rest of the Western world, the Netherlands has become very secular (with the exception of Muslim immigrant communities). Despite this, religious faith is deeply and sincerely held in many corners of the country, with a true bible belt cutting through its eastern half.† After the

---

* *Onrust* means unrest or restlessness.

† A friend of mine whose wider family is from the bible belt says that she has

elections of 2023 I engaged in a fascinating email conversation with Jan Schippers. He is the director of the research institute that sits behind the SGP, a conservative Calvinist political party that maintains a steady if small presence in the Dutch parliament.* As a citizen of deeply secular Britain, I confessed that I found it peculiar that an overtly religious party continued to have a role in public life. Jan Schippers' replies were patient and thought-provoking, and although they were couched in the language of his faith they also meshed with those of Geert Mak.

'For many people, only what you can count, measure and weigh is relevant,' he wrote, but this sells us 'short as human beings'. He was worried about the atomisation of society, what Geert Mak might have called an imbalance in favour of space over place.

'In order to achieve your full potential as a human being, you also have to rely on others. Love is a verb and also means that you care about someone else. [...] At first glance, individualisation brings a lot of freedom. But freedom is not free, you cannot separate it from your responsibility with impunity.'

Material prosperity might have increased but spiritual well-being had not, and impacts within society ranged from a weakening of marriage to addiction, suicide, loneliness and mental health problems among young people.

Jan Schippers was clear-eyed about when the deep problems within Dutch society started to grip the country: the 1960s and 1970s, just as *Brand Orange* was taking form. But when I asked him about the SGP's relevance in such a changed and often secular country, he replied with confidence that ultimately their

---

been frowned upon for turning up to family gatherings in trousers rather than a skirt.

* The SGP is the *Staatkundig Gereformeerde Partij*, or Reformed Political Party.

policies came down to 'sober and common sense'. He noted that when people entered their preferences in one of those online quizzes that then tells you which party they should vote for, many found that the SGP was the best fit, purely on its policies. However he did worry that the SGP might lose vote share as the decades wear on and the Reformed Church faces relative demographic decline. He wrote that in the age of the smartphone and internet there was a greater range of media available to younger people, even in religious families ('in my parents' home we had a Christian newspaper and the radio, but no TV'), and this was slowly eroding the number of believers out there.

Did the prospect of the Netherlands losing its religion worry him? Not really: he shared a fascinating chart from the Social and Cultural Planning Office that placed party supporters according to whether they thought the Netherlands was going in the right direction and whether they felt happy about their own life.[3] The supporters of most parties had symmetrical views of the country and their own lives, in that their personal happiness level closely correlated with their confidence in the Netherlands. Supporters of the PVV of Geert Wilders, notably, sat on the far bottom left, denoting unhappiness about absolutely everything. SGP supporters, on the other hand, were massive outliers: far less happy about the direction of the country than anybody else, but extremely high (a close second place) for personal contentment. Their personal faith was a buffer against the godlessness of the modern Netherlands.

The country may be changing, but the SGP's small and steady vote share (it received 2.08% and three members of parliament in the 2023 election) suggests there remains a place for its particular faith-driven political platform. Meanwhile, the numbers voting for parties such as Geert Wilders' PVV suggest that there is a larger constituency of Dutch citizens with a gloomy outlook on the trajectories of both the country and their own lives.

One lightning rod for such dissatisfaction is the creeping internationalisation of the Netherlands, a catch-all category covering everything from disquiet over immigration to housing shortages and the amount of English that is being spoken in the country's cities. The Dutch are famously the world's most proficient non-native English speakers. Although this has been a boon for its outward-facing economy and has given its big cities a welcoming and international air, it has come at a cost. The Dutch language, that fantastical construction of violent consonants welded unwillingly to looping vowels, is under pressure. In big cities, substantial numbers of shop assistants have only basic Dutch, relying on English for detailed questions (to the befuddlement of older Dutch speakers). In 2024 the transport company Arriva announced that it was set to hire non-Dutch speakers for its buses in Limburg thanks to a shortage of drivers.[*] That same year one online recruitment platform reported that 8% of the vacancies on its Netherlands site did not require the applicant to have Dutch language skills.[†]

Meanwhile Dutch universities have leveraged the country's facility with language to ramp up the number of courses that are taught in English. By 2023 there were 123,000 foreign students in the Netherlands, 30,000 of whom were non-European. This has been a good earner for the universities, and they argue that it has helped establish the Netherlands as a global knowledge and innovation hub. Many locals have chaffed against the influx, complaining about the extra pressure this was putting on the

---

[*] The new bus drivers are from Croatia.

[†] The 'Indeed' recruitment platform reports that its sites in other European countries have rates between 3% and 6%.

housing market and the poor Dutch skills of students who had very few reasons to learn the local language.* Increasingly some of those foreign students have felt 'negative sentiments' towards them.[4] The backlash has now turned political. In 2024 the outgoing education minister Robberd Dijkgraaf submitted a bill to restrict universities' freedom to offer courses in English.[5] The new education minister, Eppo Bruins, told parliament that he aimed to reduce 'excessive internationalisation' in higher education, as this put 'enormous pressure on the system, on lecturers, and on the national budget'.

This is a dangerous and difficult game to play. Multinational companies have located themselves in the Netherlands because its easy approach to language and international outlook have made it an accommodating country for skilled but footloose employees. Technical universities such as those in Eindhoven and Delft feed highly qualified graduates directly into local industries. Disrupting this flow can be dangerous. ASML, an extremely high-end link in the global microchip industry, has threatened to leave the Netherlands if the government tinkers with its own supply of top international talent, whatever language they are comfortable in.[6] One report in 2024 put the Netherlands bottom of 89 countries for labour shortages. (It noted that the second year of decline in its business climate was also due to challenges in energy infrastructure and unpredictable governance.)

It is tough for politicians to balance such pressures from an international economy with an instinctive nativism easily exploited by populist insurrectionists. Language remains the most obvious challenge, although given the similarities between Dutch, German and English this should not feel insurmountable.

---

* Foreign students working as shop assistants helps explain the lower proficiency in Dutch.

A lexical study of the interrelatedness of European languages gave a score of 25 to Dutch/German and 37 to Dutch/English, denoting that each pair is relatively close.[7] (For comparison Russian/Ukrainian scored at 38 and Spanish/Italian at 41.) For English speakers there is also something of the uncanny valley about Dutch phrases, which can veer into the deeply amusing: *hondenfokker* for dog breeder; *slagroom* for whipped cream; *basterdsuiker* for brown sugar.

In the real world, however, Dutch is such a crunchy language to get your tongue around that the public broadcaster NOS has even announced that it will carry a news programme in simplified Dutch, aimed not just at new arrivals but also at Dutch natives with lower language skills. Although I signed up for a three-times-a-week course in my first month in the country, it continued to frustrate me throughout my years there.* In my defence this was partly the fault of the Dutch themselves. In Delft most attempts to practice speaking the language to shop assistants results in insistent answers in perfect English. The rare local who responded to my faltering Dutch without switching to English would launch gruffly into rapid-fire words that seemed aimed at proving a point rather than helping me practice.

Perhaps the high water mark of foreigners learning Dutch was in the mid-1850s. At the time Japan was rapidly westernising and shedding its former isolationism. It naturally looked to its own previous contacts with Dutch traders for inspiration, along with their Dutch-born governmental advisor Guido Verbeck. By the 1860s, however, Japanese students who had arrived in

---

* The largest group of students on the course was post-graduates from the Technical University of Delft, looking to stay in the Netherlands for work. Notably most had already spent a couple of years in the country and were only investing in learning Dutch once it was obvious they wanted to stay longer term.

Holland, expecting it to be something of a power centre for the whole of Europe, came to the realisation that this was far from true. Instead of a European lingua franca they had been learning something far more niche.*

A wander around the harbour in Urk makes it clear that compromises can be found that marry a firm line on culture and an accommodation with the modern world. Just look at those Urkish fishing boats that sail the seas with the most modern kit while the crew digests passages from the Old Testament between shifts. Up in Friesland, where we spent that enjoyable afternoon watching *fierljeppen*, there is nothing manufactured about regional identity or the enduring use of the Friesian language. The international students working a shift at a shoe shop in Den Haag may struggle with their Dutch, but the small towns like Pijnacker, a bare couple of kilometres outside Delft, were solidly Dutch speaking.

The strength of *Brand Orange* lies in its foundations in a country so distinctive and so wholeheartedly Dutch that it could not be mistaken for anything else. The same goes for the more traditional sense of Dutchness that permeates throughout the eastern half of the country. Those concerns about the erosion of Dutch speaking seem to me to be a signal of a deeper sense of unease that something is out of kilter in the Netherlands: the housing market, precarious family finances, the fairness of society or the washing machine *onrust* that Geert Mak spoke of. The Netherlands is not going to lose its robust sense of itself any time soon, however much English (or Arabic) is spoken on the street corners. But if outsiders want a better understanding of

---

* As recounted in Ed West's excellent *Wrong Side of History* substack, 'We hebben een serieus probleem', which I recommend for those interested in unpicking headlines such as 'Hitler dood. Wat nou?' https://www.edwest. co.uk/p/we-hebben-een-serieus-probleem.

why the country of drugs and sex and tulips is looking towards more populist politicians for solutions, get out of Amsterdam, go east and walk from Emmeloord to Urk.

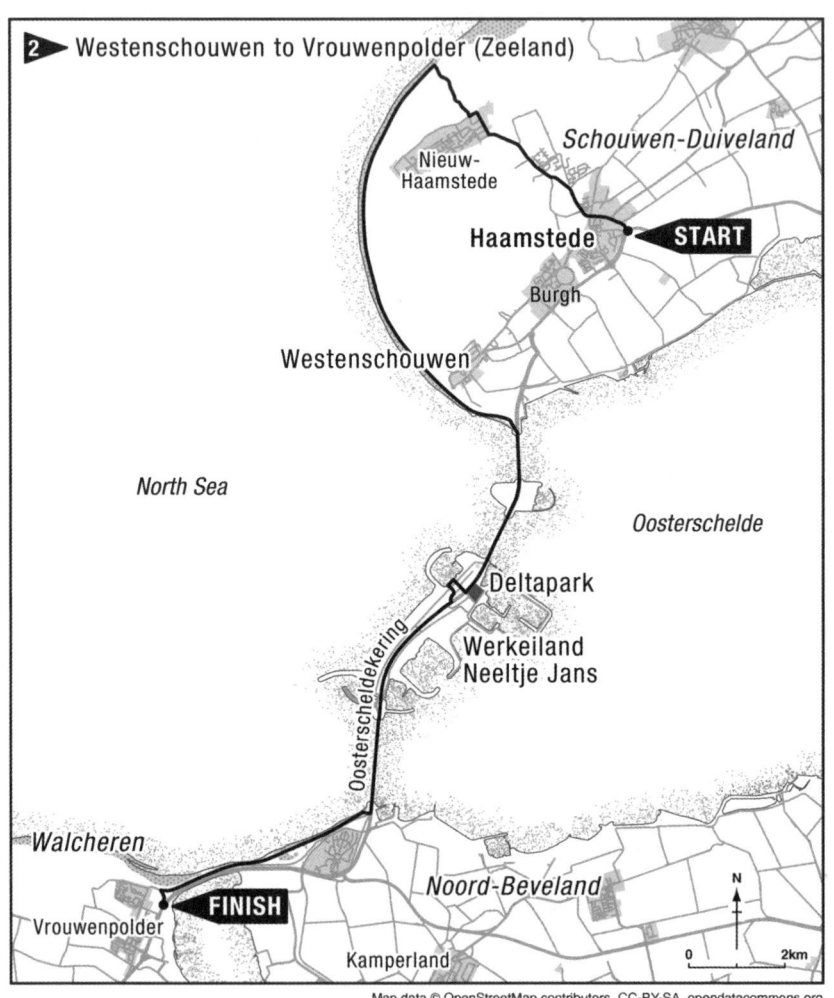

2 Westenschouwen to Vrouwenpolder (Zeeland)

Schouwen-Duiveland

Nieuw-Haamstede

Haamstede ◀ START

Burgh

Westenschouwen

North Sea

Oosterschelde

Oosterscheldekering

Deltapark

Werkeiland
Neeltje Jans

Walcheren

Noord-Beveland

Vrouwenpolder

FINISH

Kamperland

N

0   2km

2

WESTENSCHOUWEN TO VROUWENPOLDER (ZEELAND)

This second walk is in Zeeland, across the great and vulnerable estuary of the mighty rivers that cut across the country. It starts from the island of Schouwen-Duiveland, across the flood defences of the Oosterscheldekering to the island of Noord-Beveland, and on to what used to be Walcheren but is now the peninsula of Midden-Zeeland. The villages of Westenschouwen and Burgh-Haamstede both have good bus links and places to stay, so are perfect places to start the walk. Head roughly west or northwest on the roads and tracks that crisscross the area, before heading through the dunes to the long sweep of beach. Turn left and walk with the open sea on your right. You will eventually see the imposing Oosterscheldekering heading off into the estuary from the southern tip of Schouwen-Duiveland. Simply climb up and begin walking across it. There are a couple of artificial islands, the second one being large enough to poke around looking at beaches, mussel beds, wind turbines and the amusements of the Deltapark Neeltje Jans. After the last stretch of Oosterscheldekering you can clamber down from the structure and on to the bicycle path that heads off to the west. I finished the walk by soaking my feet in the surf and then taking a bus from the village of Vrouwenpolder, a few kilometres further on.

* * *

Ferry Bouman was not an untypical villain. He was bulky, taciturn and matched a hairless pot belly with a slick of greasy hair, swept back from his forehead. You could tell that he had reached his position in life with a few ruthless applications of violence. He struggled to synchronise a drug distribution business with the demands of a wife who was hungry for friendships beyond what was usual for a gangster's moll. As such he might have been at home cosying up to Tony Soprano in New Jersey. But instead, he was a very Dutch villain: although he maintained a gaudy mansion that had local policemen sniffing around simply on the grounds of bad taste, he preferred to live in a caravan on a holiday park.

Ferry Bouman's caravan was in truth a chalet rather than a caravan, a miniature house made of beige bricks, a peculiarly green-tiled roof and a barrel-load of whimsy. His brother-in-law lived next door with an impressive collection of defiantly twee dolls in shiny dresses on his windowsill. Outside there was a forlorn little artificial lake. The occasional white, blue and yellow Limburg flag, complete with angry-looking red lion, fluttered listlessly on the breeze. As well as his brother-in-law, Ferry Bouman had the help of an intellectually-challenged wannabe kick boxer named Jurgen van Kamp, who also lived in the park. In the Netflix series *Undercover*, the two detectives charged with infiltrating Ferry Bouman's criminal activities also set up base in their own static caravan just across from their target. The entire set up scored heavily on holiday park relatability, as well as violence and the inevitable sexual tension between the detectives Kim and Bob.

The Dutch holiday camp may be universal, but comes in many different flavours. At core it is a patch of land, often landscaped with more inclines and hillocks than typically found elsewhere in the Netherlands. Caravans and cabins are dotted around, maybe surrounded by trees and lawns, all connected by a complex network of winding tracks where bicycles zip back and forth. The solidly middle-class ones come with an assortment of Volvo SUVs and Mitsubishi Outlanders, each one cantilevered with a family collection of bicycles. The dodgier ones in Limburg come with criminals and their cronies along with undercover odd-couple detectives.

Just like Ferry Bouman in his miniature home, the Dutch take holidaying very seriously. As of 2024, Dutch people owned 618,000 camper vans and caravans, which is one for every 29.5 residents. The Netherlands also has 151 campsites per million inhabitants, compared to 120 in France, 38 in Germany and 28 in Italy. This figure is even more remarkable when you see just how many of those campsites scattered across the rest of Europe are also filled up with Dutch holidaymakers.

This mass enthusiasm for holidaying is exactly as the government intended it. Back in 1969 the Netherlands implemented the vacation pay law, which gave workers an allowance of 8% of their gross annual salary to go on holiday. The government's hope was that this would keep the population healthy and motivated, while also incentivising them to go and spend money. Zeeland, the archetypal Dutch holiday province, benefitted greatly from this burgeoning mass enthusiasm, the relentless Dutch urge to go on holiday by car, motorhome or bicycle. The small village of Westenschouwen, on the western edge of the island of Schouwen-Duiveland, was where my family had its first Dutch beach holiday, and this is where my walk started. It is dominated by a sprinkling of campsites and vacation homes, and time hangs lightly in the air among holidaymakers with little need to be anywhere or do anything other than relax and eat cheese sandwiches. Cycle paths bustled with middle-aged Dutch couples pootling this way and that, and family groupings that always involved some sort of trailer carrying toddlers, dogs and collapsible windshields. The sand-dusted path wound its way into a forest jam-packed with recreation facilities and pancake houses, across a run of dunes and on to the beach.

Zeeland's shimmering beaches are superb, stretching way off into the hazy distance and amplifying the feeling that real time had been suspended. Children splashed around in sun-warmed tidal pools, and dogs ran madly in and out of the surf. Older couples sat at beach bars, nursing glasses of Heineken and munching on deep-fried snacks, staring out across the North Sea from behind weatherproof glass screens. Those screens are more than just windbreaks. They are a symbol of the Dutch need to control nature and shave off its rougher edges. After all, the Netherlands would not exist beyond a few marshy swamps and flood-prone meadows if nature had not been tamed and bent to the will of the resourceful inhabitants. The province of Zeeland is ultimately the estuarine delta of the great rivers that empty out into the North Sea, a scattering of islands with impossibly long, glittering beaches and lush fields. It is marginal and transient land, where mighty rivers meet the sea, where those holidaymakers with their lobster skin sit on deck chairs on beaches that are at the mercy of nature, however tranquil they seem. Nobody goes for a swim into the estuarine waters off these islands. They are far too treacherous. The simple fact that this estuarine delta is now a holiday playground rather than a liminal zone of sandbars and scouring tides, of inundations and vanishing land, is testament to Dutch success in taming nature. After all, Zeeland was at the centre of a natural disaster that traumatised the country back in 1953, and did much to shape it in the decades that followed: 1953 was the year that water tried to destroy Zeeland.

* * *

It was the last day in January. A furious wind was blowing from the northwest. It was part of an extreme extratropical cyclone that had already resulted in the sinking of the *Princess Victoria*, a ferry trying to cross the Irish Sea, with the loss of 135 passengers and crew. As it worked its way down the eastern edge of Britain the storm pushed the waters of the North Sea southwards. The coasts of England on one side and Belgium and the Netherlands on the other created an enormous funnel, barely relieved by the narrows of the Straits of Dover at the bottom. This geography meant that those waters had nowhere to go. Worse, the storm coincided with an exceptionally high tide, raising the water level even further. Worse still, the great continental rivers that traversed the Netherlands were swollen from winter weather. As they reached the coast they met the storm surge.

At first the high water was a curiosity. Members of the Dutch public had climbed the dykes to see the spectacle. But the waters kept rising. Not long after 6pm national radio warned of 'dangerous high water'. Most simply went home to hunker down by the fire. During the long hours of the dark January night that sightseeing spectacle was to turn into a national disaster.

Those stormy north-westerly winds continued into the night, and all along the coast of the Netherlands the high water was biting hard into the dykes. Meanwhile the winter waters were flowing remorselessly down those great rivers from central Europe. The surge peaked at 3.35 metres above the average sea level, and some waves were recorded at nearly 5 metres. The pressure on the defences around the great Dutch estuaries was enormous. The dykes were overwhelmed, and once they started to give way a total collapse became inevitable. A wall of freezing water broke through, sweeping everything before it.

One 18-year-old, Piet van den Ouden from Oude-Tonge, saw water rushing through the letter box of his front door. After he and his family had fled upstairs he looked out and saw that the other side of the street had vanished. He watched as the house of his eldest brother collapsed, and then his father began to cry. The floodwaters came in the darkness, in the dead of the night, after people had switched off their radios and gone to bed. People were washed away, farm animals drowned and entire communities were destroyed.

When daylight came the land had become water. Surviving houses and barns sat like islands, gathered around what used to be villages and roads, now submerged. A child had been born in the attic of a house, surrounded by the ruins of seven that had collapsed. In the Netherlands alone 1,375 square kilometres of land had been flooded and nearly 50,000 buildings damaged; 1,836 people were killed, along with 30,000 livestock. The east coast of England was also badly hit, and lives were lost in Belgium and Scotland, and at sea (including on the *Princess Victoria*). In total nearly 2,500 people died.

If the physical damage from the flood was enormous, the psychological cost to the Dutch was perhaps worse. Of course the Netherlands had suffered floods before, but this was a terrible reminder that when nature attacked on several axes at once it was overwhelming. Those defences that the Netherlands had built up and steadily improved over centuries were as nothing.

I own a large-scale map that shows the Netherlands, Zeeland and those great rivers a handful of years before the 1953 flood. In places the water runs into countless interwoven channels as it forces its way to the sea. The islands that form the delta look tenuous, like they are used to being bullied and pushed around.

An alarmingly large swathe of the entire country is shaded dark, indicating that it is below sea level. My map is of a country on the edge, that had spent many hundreds of years in a daily existential struggle to survive.

Pliny the Elder visited this corner of Europe in the first century CE when it was a remote and hostile frontier for the Roman Empire. He famously described it as a 'pitiful land flooded twice a day', where it was difficult to say which part belonged to the land and which part to the sea. Locals lived a miserable existence 'on self-made heights, where they warm limbs stiffened by the northern winds on a fire of dried mud.' This understandably did not appeal much to the Romans, who made a mental note not even to bother creating a wasteland and calling it peace.

After those winter floods of 1953 the Dutch faced the same choice as ever, but with even more urgency. How could they secure this vulnerable, flat, watery land so they could turn their radios off, climb into their beds and hope not to get washed away in the night? After all, there would always be water in the Netherlands, and a flood was simply a case of that water being in the wrong place.

In ten months the dykes that had been destroyed in the great flood had been closed, but more was needed. Real life was not like the tale of Hans Brinker, the fictional Dutch boy who famously stuck a finger in a dyke to prevent a flood. The Dutch had to be proactive; if they waited and reacted, they would face systemic collapse. One contemporary *New York Times* report on the type of construction that could protect the Netherlands after the floods carried a map depicting two vast potential seawalls.[1] One capped the islandy northern reaches of the Netherlands, from the tip of Nord Holland across the Wadden Islands and nearly on to the German border, a total of something like 200 kilometres. The other was shorter but was designed to seal off the estuaries of Zeeland from the North Sea. Where the water from those great rivers was supposed to go does not seem clear. For all its grandiosity it seemed as doomed as the summer holiday dams that I would build with my brother across a determined little mountain stream.

Luckily the Dutch government had more insight into water management than me, my brother or whoever put together the *New York Times* graphic. It set up a 'Delta Commission' within 18 days of the 1953 disaster, with a mission to analyse what had gone wrong and what the country ought to do about it.

The result was the Delta Works, a project so impressive that the American Society of Civil Engineers has named it as one of their Seven Wonders of the Modern World. In effect it shortened the entire coastline of Zeeland and South Holland, spanning vulnerable gaps in the coast with a series of dams and dykes, artificial islands, barriers and sluices. The project's core was an extraordinary structure called the Oosterscheldekering.

The Oosterscheldekering's five sections are the centrepiece of this walk. I climbed on to the northern edge directly from the sands of Strand Burgh Haamstede. There was, inevitably, a beach café nestling safely behind its rampart of glass panels off on the left. To the right the run of stronghouses, each topped by a pair of white metal columns, stretched off like a giant's wall across the estuary. The violence of the water that forced its way through the barrier was not just visible, but audible. Cormorants dried their wings on buoys, whose ropes were pulled taut by the strength of the current. Squadrons of terns divebombed into the eddies, shrieking with delight. Forget about the Netherlands being a boring place to walk; this is a landscape full of theatre and drama.

They may have been conceived in 1953, but the Delta Works were not completed until 1997, at a total cost that stretched far into billions of guilders.* The Oosterscheldekering structure itself is uncompromising, abstract and hard edged, formed from concrete and white steel. Up close it is alive with movement and strength and purpose, each element calibrated differently to adapt to the dynamic force of the water. The escaping water between each set of two stronghouses churns with different patterns, different concerns and different noises. The Oosterscheldekering sits in nature, working with it. By walking across this you get a sense of the beauty of this resolute structure as well as its scale.

This may not be a beauty for everybody. When I grew up near Middlesbrough a standard school art project was to draw the industrial landscape of Teesside, the steelworks and chemical installations, the pipes and flare towers and hulking tanks that helped inspire local boy Ridley Scott when imagining the cinematic world that became *Blade Runner*. We gained an appreciation that beauty was not simply Constable's bucolic *The Hay Wain*. It could be something far more brutal and indigestible, belching fire and steam with its steel glimmering through the smog. If you are the same, the Oosterscheldekering could be for you.

The structure is more than just the steel, with its barriers and sluices. There are artificial islands flush with gargantuan wind turbines, sandy coves and mussel beds. I passed a chunky green and yellow tractor, a marina bobbing with dinghies and yachts, and countless bicycles. Even the less engaging parts of the artificial islands were captivating in their own way: the asphalt by the side of the road sometimes resembled a solidified lava flow, peppered with blown sand, and beyond that there were myriad patterns of lichen and minute flowers. On one island you will find that most Dutch of leisure facilities, an amusement park

---

* At the time a guilder was worth roughly half a US dollar or a third of a British pound.

themed around anti-flood infrastructure. The Deltapark Neeltje Jans boasts sea lions, water slides and a detailed explanation of hydraulic flood gates. This spoke to a truth about the Delta Works, that it has a public visibility that is part of its legitimacy. Such infrastructure does not sit apart from Dutch society, but is firmly embedded in it.

* * *

In October 2012 another deadly storm was gathering in ferocity, this time on the other side of the Atlantic. From the safety of his home in the Netherlands a man called Henk Ovink followed the progress of Hurricane Sandy on his iPad, watching as it cut a swathe of destruction across the Eastern Seaboard of the United States. The storm ravaged the New York and New Jersey area, smashing up buildings and entire sections of road, killing 233 people and causing $70 billion worth of damage. In the aftermath of the storm Barack Obama's White House was eager to understand what had gone wrong and how it should prepare for future events. There was only one man to call: Henk Ovink, soon known in White House circles as 'Henk the water guy'.*

I interviewed Henk Ovink for a radio feature soon after arriving in the Netherlands in 2017, when he was the country's Special Envoy for International Water Affairs. He was sharp minded and charismatic, and straight away I saw the country and how it worked in vivid technicolour. He introduced me to the idea of 'water democracy', the foundation upon which the

---

* 'Henk the water guy' was blunt in his assessment of the American system of each town being responsible for its own flood defences, building them with no thought of the impact on neighbours. He called this 'stupid infrastructure'. The US was obviously better at responding than preventing, and to combat this, he pushed the culturally Dutch solution of getting people round the table to talk, understand, work and innovate together.

Netherlands had been built. When I was researching this book, just like President Obama, I knew there was only one person I had to talk to. I got back in touch.*

'Water and the Netherlands are synonyms,' he told me, and this made the Netherlands special. Water dominated the country. It had the sea, its dynamic coast, the rivers that came down from Belgium, France, Germany and the Alps, then the water that was every present under foot.

'To live in such a place, it has so many water dynamics! Woah! You have to think not twice but ten times. You have to think about water every day, with every guilder or euro spent. Do you care for it? Do you pollute it? Is there too much water? Is there not enough?'

This brought us back to the concept of 'water democracy'. 'You need water, you can't drink sand eh? Water literally connects across health, energy, food, environment, infrastructure, climate. If you want to deal with those challenges, you have to include everyone, and that's where this collaborative model started to emerge.' This collaboration was not just cultural, but institutional. 'We had farmers, businesses, individuals, literally sitting around what we call the polder table where all these interests needed to be matched. What was the infrastructure you had to put in place for water management, safety, quality, waste?'

Water was at the heart of the Dutch system, because it dominated everything in their fragile land. The socio-political system that they developed to manage it was democratic, because they realised they had to give everybody a voice. It built a cultural dispensation to coalition government, multilateral negotiations and the *grote mond* (big mouth), where everybody had a voice.

---

* At the time of writing he is the Executive Director for the Global Commission on the Economics of Water, which has a connection to the organisation that I still do work for, the World Resources Institute.

This allowed them to reach compromises that balanced complex interests, and manufactured consent for the expensive communal efforts needed to build infrastructure such as dykes and pumps, canals and polders.

'This was an endeavour that no single farmer could do on their own,' says Stientje van Veldhoven, a former State Secretary for Infrastructure and Water Management in the Dutch government.*

'They had to collaborate with other farmers, so this collective management of the water and land was an important aspect of how our country and society developed. That's why Dutch culture is sometimes called "polder culture". You had to take decisions together, to agree amongst all of you, compromise. You depended upon each other. There was a need for continuous collaboration and consultation and agreement. The following year you'd have to deal with each other again. The *poldermodel* translated into this kind of collaborative culture and consultation culture in all fields of life, in Dutch society, and this flows from the way the country was actually built.'

Without the *poldermodel* the Netherlands might never have emerged from Pliny's 'pitiful land' of marshes and inundation. It might never have had the foundations to kick off its virtuous cycle of ever-more ambitious water management and economic dynamism. It might have never developed into a global power. It might never had given the world Vermeer and Cruyff. It would never have developed the Delta Works.

Although the Dutch absolutely love to have an argument, the collective nature of the polder system is to be seen throughout Dutch society. In the late 1980s and early 1990s the Dutch economy was arguably saved from crashing thanks to the coming

---

* At the time of writing Stientje van Veldhoven is Vice President and Head of the Europe Office at the World Resources Institute.

together of government, companies and labour unions to make mutual concessions. Another example is in the airline world, where the venerable national carrier KLM is partnered with Air France. They, like all legacy airlines, have been under extreme financial pressure from low-cost airlines. When Air France announced a package of cuts and cost savings an unfortunate manager was cornered by an angry mob and had his clothes ripped off. At KLM, by contrast, the staff and management met, discussed it all and made appropriate changes in the name of a more profitable airline. Industrial relations in the Netherlands tend to be far less antagonistic than in neighbouring countries: in 2017 only eight days were lost through industrial action for every 1,000 employers, compared to 123 in France.

Historically the Dutch system also led to a greater degree of religious and ideological tolerance, which helped it to pioneer the modern, liberal capitalist state. A British merchant and traveller called Peter Munday wrote of Amsterdam in 1640:

> The Citty is nott divided in to parishes as with us, butt every one goes to what church hee pleases, there being only 8 or 10 publick churches beside the English, French, Lutherans, Anabaptist, etts., and Jewish Sinagogues... A Tolleration of all sects [of] religion.[2]

Although many found this stimulating, religious refugees who fled to the Netherlands to escape religious prejudice elsewhere in Europe were often in turn offended by Dutch liberalism and tolerance, and shipped themselves off to the colonies of North America instead in a fit of puritan pique.

The good sense and rationality of this system, allied to the shortages of resources in a small country, has helped to shape a highly capable technocratic state. One visible example is the Netherlands' deeply impressive bicycle infrastructure, which did not just arise organically from a love of two-wheeled freedom:

it was the product of ultra-rational decisions made about how roads should function. A 1966 traffic law had dealt with dangerous junctions and road configurations simply by trying to outlaw them, but this led to a confusion of lots of different road categories. Traffic deaths actually peaked in 1972. This changed through the 1990 traffic code and a 1994 traffic law, which together cut regulations but emphasised good design as the way to make roads safer. Streets were put together in a way that prioritised bikes over cars. Massive amounts of data continued to be collected and crunched, with recommendations made (but not dictated). Road managing authorities are free to do what they want, but are found liable when something happens if there are more empirically robust options available. Everybody is treated like a responsible adult, and then incentives are applied and the expectation is that you make the right choice.

Naturally enough, the technocratic Dutch state is exemplified by the Ministry of Infrastructure and Water Management. Together with the largely autonomous Water Boards it is responsible for the maintenance of the Netherlands' defences against water ending up in completely the wrong place.* There is a large budget that runs over several years, with no political back-and-forth on such an important issue. 'It's totally non-political; what needs to be done gets done,' says Stientje van Veldhoven, who ran the Ministry for several years.

What needs to get done is not only a question of steel and concrete, but of working with the structures and strictures of nature. In 2007 the government kicked off the 'Room for the River' programme. If nature was a wild animal, the idea

---

* The water boards were set up in the thirteenth century to organise the collective maintenance of dykes across different communities and towns. They continue to play an important role, not least because of heavy cows and sinking land, as you will discover in the next chapter.

of barricading it in was useless; it was too powerful and would simply break out. Instead, you had to give it space enough to be wild, while still protecting what was important. The four great rivers—Rhine, Maas, Waal and IJssel—all had to be given space to flood safely across farmland and parks, and even car garages and playgrounds, without sending water through anybody's letterbox. 'The focus has been on creating space for big rivers to overflow into land that cannot be used for building houses, but that could be used for grazing cattle,' Stientje explained to me. 'The farmers know they may have to evacuate the cattle at short notice so the water can flow there rather than an urbanised area.'

Our conversation moved on to the changing nature of the threat, as Europe faced more extreme and unpredictable weather. 'In 2021, it was my last day in government,' she said. 'We had this really awful torrential rain just above where the Netherlands, Germany and Belgium meet, and so we had floods.' I remembered the horrifying TV footage of the catastrophe, with picturesque German villages of gables and timber beams having their hearts ripped out by the savagery of the flood waters. They were scary. Two hundred and forty-three people lost their lives. But what struck Stientje as unusual was where the flooding was focused.

'It was not the big rivers that actually created the problem, but a small river that had not been managed. Big floods from smaller rivers are something that we hadn't seen before. And there are also droughts. When I came into office in 2017 we had never faced a serious drought, but did soon after. So now we have to re-engineer our water system, which was built to get water out as quickly as possible, to now also be able to retain water.'

The Netherlands has spent the best part of a millennium facing the challenge of too much water, and some of it being— as in 1953—in completely the wrong place. But as Stientje van

Veldhoven suggests, the challenge is changing. Sea levels are rising and weather is set to become more and more extreme. The Dutch know a lot about technical solutions, whether as hard as the white steel and concrete of the Oosterscheldekering, or as soft as a deliberately floodable car park. They also have the time-honoured socio-political cheat code of the *poldermodel* to underpin it all. But will this be enough, as environmental pressures start to divide the Dutch into winners and losers?

* * *

The last stretch of my walk across the Oosterscheldekering saw another beach panorama open up as I neared the island of Noord-Beveland. I sat down on a rocky rampart and looked back at the remarkable 8 kilometres of metal and concrete that I had just trekked across, taking the time to examine it from a distance. Just as among the potato and tulip fields of Flevoland, Zeeland's canvas was composed of large, shimmering blank shapes that dissolved into each other as the sun moved lower into the southwest: the sky, now streaked by wispy clouds; the wide strip of sand stretching off to nowhere; the expanse of the sea itself. The uncompromising brutalist shapes of the Oosterscheldekering ran off like the flick of the artist's brush, drawing a border and imposing a transient Dutch order on those vast expanses.

A man down on the beach was fishing in the turbulent waters near the Oosterscheldekering, his wife a patient two steps behind him, enjoying the peace and possibly wondering when the local fishmonger was going to shut. A young boy ran with a puppy on the sand nearby, reminding me of my own son running with our puppy, Baffo, on our own first Zeeland trip. I wanted a cold beer and a shower, but my feet were sore and the water looked delicious. I walked across the sand, took my boots and socks off and stood ankle deep in the surf. The boy's father was 10 metres away, and trying to take a photograph of the Oosterscheldekering. He was obviously struggling, but however he framed it the enormous structure was always going to be overshadowed by nature.

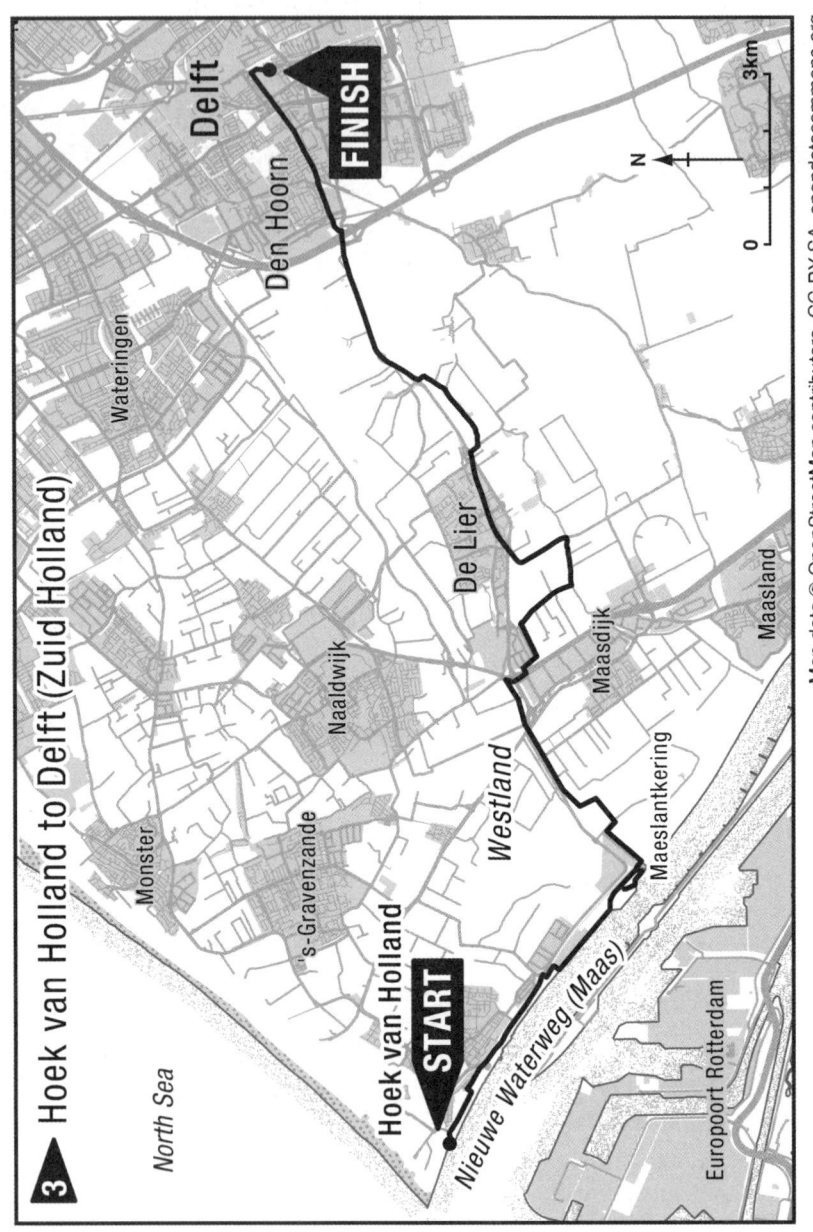

3 Hoek van Holland to Delft (Zuid Holland)

North Sea

Monster

Wateringen

's-Gravenzande

Naaldwijk

Den Hoorn

Delft

FINISH

De Lier

Westland

Maasdijk

Maasland

Hoek van Holland

START

Maeslantkering

Nieuwe Waterweg (Maas)

Europoort Rotterdam

N

0   3km

3

HOEK VAN HOLLAND TO DELFT
(ZUID HOLLAND)

You could begin this walk right where Hoek van Holland meets the North Sea, but I began at the rail station that lies a bit further inland. Either way, head east next to the raised cycle path that is built on a dyke, with houses (and a city farm) on your left and the river on your right. A roundabout offers the chance to track down to the edge of the river on the Slachthuisweg and the Maeslantkeringweg, surrounded by port infrastructure. This takes you to the remarkable two-armed anti-flood defences of the Maeslantkering, where you can get a guided tour. The artificial hillock behind it is a good vantage point for munching on a kaastengel cheese stick and contemplating the mighty Europoort Rotterdam. Just after, you need to tack inland along the Oranjekanaal, which takes you into the agricultural heart of Westland municipality, with its endless glasshouses and agro-industrial infrastructure. There are lots of alternative little routes and cycle paths that you can follow, just so long as you are heading roughly eastwards. My route took me past a couple of large road junctions and looping slightly south through an area heavy on chrysanthemum cultivation, before emerging back up in De Lier, a village with some useful shops. From there I headed northeast, where the glasshouses of Westland gave way to the pastures of Midden-Delfland municipality, eventually reaching Den Hoorn. I followed a canal called De Kickert right up to Delft itself, with the glorious old binnenstad ahead and the station 100 metres to the right.

* * *

It was a clear-sky day in early August, on the banks of one of the few canals that had not turned vivid green from zillions of pieces of tiny summer pond weed. The lady to our right had a seventeenth-century facial expression and an outrageous costume that combined Delft porcelain with pantomime dame. Booming, thumping techno filled the air and that familiar aroma of lightly-spiced frying meat products drifted around on the breeze. Delft's neatly balanced Hambrug was open, its drawbridge of asphalt and steel propped open in deference to waterborne traffic. Just beyond that was the Zuidkolk, a basin of open water that allowed the longest of long barges to negotiate a vicious 90 degree turn on the canal that linked Den Haag to Rotterdam.

And then they came, each one heralded by cheers from the canal bank: a floating, waving and very surreal flotilla of vessels, each decked out with extraordinary displays of prime, cultivated vegetation. One boat pulled three rafts, each designed to look like a car and festooned with colour-coded fruit and vegetables: the first yellow and orange, the second green and the third pink and purple. A traditional barge was surely ready to sink beneath a violent floricultural explosion of sunflowers and lilies and chrysanthemums. One barge was inspired by Piet Mondrian, a block party of right angles, red and yellow, white and black, all beneath a gyrating inflatable tube 10 metres tall. Another was a sickly pastiche of Willy Wonka candy pinks and sugared yellows, its fancy-dressed crew waving at the gathered crowds and feeling the insistent bass-heavy techno throb. There was a flower-power barge filled to the brim with hire-costume hippies. And there was one in inevitable orange. By turns my then-four-year-old son was confused, gob-smacked and delighted. None of us had ever seen anything like it.

The waterborne parade was nothing less than a gaudy and demonstrative celebration of agricultural bounty, the product of a marriage between the spectacular fecundity of the Dutch soil and the miraculous ingenuity of the Dutch farmer. Each float, each barge was sponsored or constructed by one of the agricultural concerns, farms and companies that were based in the area just south of Delft, known as Westland. The spectacular display was testament to their commercial might, a Roman triumph of dahlias and carrots rather than barbarian slaves and captured chariots. If one of the most remarkable figures about the Netherlands is that it is the world's second largest agricultural exporter, Westland is ground zero for that figure.*

Westland and its farms are the central character in this walk, but it all starts off at the evocatively named Hoek van Holland (Hook of Holland, or more literally the Corner of Holland). Walks that begin at the Hoek do so in the shadow of the British writer Patrick Leigh Fermor, who used the Hoek as the entry point to the great continent that lay before him. (Thanks to the vast Europoort it still has that function for many of the world's cargo containers.) Fermor began his epic walk across Europe there in 1933, finishing up in Istanbul on 1 January 1935. This walk is not quite so ambitious: it progresses along the Nieuwe

---

* Although it is the second largest exporter of agricultural products after the United States, some of those exports are in fact re-exports thanks to the Netherlands' position as a trade hub. In 2023 this accounted for around a third of the total figure (but still!). agrimatie.nl/SectorResultaat.aspx?subpubID=2232&sectorID=2243&themaID=2276&indicatorID=3425.

Waterweg of the Maas river as he did, but then turns directly inland across Westland to Delft.*

Just before you make that turn towards Delft you will pass an extraordinary structure called the Maeslantkering. It echoes the Oosterscheldekering of the last chapter, and was designed to protect Rotterdam, just upstream on the Nieuwe Maas. The Maeslantkering consists of two latticed white steel arms, each the size of the Eiffel Tower, that pivot across the water and into place when floods are threatened. Next to it is a small artificial hillock that would be unremarkable in any other country, but here provides determined cyclists the rare chance to test their strength in riding uphill, even if only for 300 metres.

When this walk turns away from the river and heads north it disappears into a warren of cycle paths and lanes that thread their way through the glasshouses and agro-industrial facilities of Westland. This is farmland as interpreted through a science fiction lens. As you near Den Hoorn and Delft, the glasshouses give way to strips of grassy pasture trodden on by cows and bounded by water. Then you follow a canal lined with fancy houses right through until Delft station, on the edge of its gorgeous old *binnenstad*. This was a fine place for us to live for the four years we were in the Netherlands, and it is a fine place to end this walk.

Even if I use the word 'miracle' a little bit too frequently when talking about the Netherlands, I will resolutely defend its use for Westland. The farms of this little municipality are a literal agricultural miracle, creating bounty from the minutely controlled climatic conditions within its endless glasshouses. What they do with sowing and growing and harvesting is also echoed in the way the country has hot-housed itself by applying resourcefulness to its geographical inheritance. The Dutch have

---

* You are then welcome to continue to Istanbul.

done so much with so little actual land that the country can feel like a computer programme such as 'SimCity', each tiny plot or parcel clicked on and assigned a specific use by a tall man in a dark suit.

However, this is not just a story about success. Intensively managed Dutch farms are at the sharp end of the country's environmental problems. There is a price to be paid for turning this unlikely corner of the Eurasian landmass into far more than the sum of its parts (not just in agriculture but the way the entire land area of the Netherlands is used). Trying to solve the environmental challenges associated with intensive agriculture is creating political turbulence, most visibly in the uprising by the nation's farmers. Their dramatic tractor-borne protests have sparked similar movements across Europe, and propelled their bolshy representatives into the corridors of government.

The question that lies behind this chapter is how this fits in with the Dutch need for all its people—all its sectors—to pull together in the *poldermodel*. Are the farmers demanding special treatment on the basis of weaponised tractors and a sentimental position at the heart of the Dutch story? If so there is the potential for the country's future environmental problems to create wave after wave of other beleaguered groups demanding special pleading. Or are the farmers simply demanding the recognition and accommodation that is their due? After all, within living memory something happened that seared into Dutch minds the necessity of always making sure the country could feed itself in a time of crisis.

* * *

The year 1944 was a bitter one for the Dutch. The massive military setbacks that Nazi Germany was suffering in all theatres of the Second World War only seemed to prompt it to respond with ever more brutality, for instance in the vicious urgency with which it targeted the continent's remaining Jewish populations.

The successful Allied invasion of Normandy had put the Nazis on the backfoot in western Europe, but their occupation of the Netherlands continued with the same degree of enervating thuggery as before.* The route that the Allies plotted to take them into the heart of Nazi Germany bypassed much of the Netherlands, with their spearhead aimed at the German borderlands to their south. There was one gallant attempt to strike through further north, outflanking German defences by seizing a route over the great rivers that cut through the heart of the Netherlands.† But when *Operation Market Garden* failed, the Allies renewed their focus to the south. The Nazis, resentful after seeing how many Dutch people had tried to help the Allies, struck back at the Dutch population with vengeance. The main result was the *Hongerwinter*. ‡

At a time when the whole of Europe faced shortages and privations, the *Hongerwinter* came from a direct and deliberate decision by German leaders to starve the Dutch. Up until September 1944 60% of produce from arable land had already disappeared off to Germany. Dutch farms faced shortages of labour and animal fodder, fertiliser and machinery. By 1944 the population was scrabbling for calories from a nauseatingly sweet mash of beets, rough bread and potatoes. Then, after the failure of *Operation Market Garden*, the Nazis imposed an embargo on all food imports into the Netherlands.

The results were catastrophic. Food shortages caused widespread malnutrition, especially in the western cities far away from farmland, exacerbated by freezing temperatures. During that

---

* See Chapter 7 for more on the Second World War and how it shaped the modern Netherlands.
† This is dealt with in more detail during the walk for Chapter 7, which is the centre of *Operation Market Garden* territory, between Nijmegen and Arnhem.
‡ *Hongerwinter* is simply 'hunger winter'.

winter of 1944 into 1945, tulip bulbs became a key part of the diet, along with anything else found to be even vaguely edible. People started to weaken, to fall ill and to die. The Dutch government in exile in London were aware of the crisis on the other side of the North Sea, and the Prime Minister Pieter S. Gerbrandy warned Winston Churchill that 'starvation in the cities—the term is not too strong—is imminent.' A deal was eventually struck with the Nazis that allowed the Allies to bring 3,000 tonnes of flour, margarine and cod liver oil on two ships from Sweden. But despite boosting morale this delivery was too small to avert the crisis.

By early February 1945 the populations of the large cities of western Holland were surviving on between 500 and 800 calories per day, with major disease outbreaks and a crippling shortage of coal for heating. Pets were eaten or abandoned to their fate, crazed and wretched. Drinking water was a problem: beyond the rivers there are not many sources of fresh drinking water in the Netherlands as canal water is not potable. When the canal network froze this prevented barges from transporting what little food there was. By spring many were struggling to get 400 calories a day, and thousands were tramping out of the cities to beg and forage. Those who had lost over 25% of their bodyweight were sometimes allowed extra rations of bread and beans, but there was simply not enough to go around. Sir Jack Drummond of the British Ministry of Food conducted post-War research and noted that 'People dropped from exhaustion in the streets and many died there. Often people were so fatigued that they were unable to return home before curfew; so they hid in barns or elsewhere to sleep, and there died.'

By the time the Netherlands was officially liberated on 5 May 1945 an estimated 20,000 people were dead from starvation, with many more dreadfully weakened, malnourished or gravely ill. One newspaper article covering a cycle race the following month lamented that the competitors were too weak to provide a proper racing spectacle thanks to malnutrition ('...the riders showed little fight'). The *Hongerwinter* left lasting physiological damage and scarred the national psyche deeply. The Dutch resolved never again to lose control of their food supplies.

The Netherlands has the ingredients to make food security achievable. You get a feeling for the power of location on this walk. On the stretch between Hoek van Holland and the Maeslantkering you cannot help but notice the extensive port infrastructure on the waterways to your right. Riverine ships laden with containers shuttle back and forth, and specialised vessels bristling with equipment and purpose bob along from one job to another. The location is not just about excellent transport links for exports and imports. Because the Netherlands is a delta it has fertile soil. Add to that the enterprise and ingenuity of the Dutch, which you see all around during the middle part of this walk, through the agro-industrial complex of Westland, and you have a compact agricultural superpower.

Well before the Second World War the Netherlands was taking advantage of industrialisation and urbanisation to develop and modernise its farming sector. In 1870 in Europe it was second only to Belgium in agricultural production per hectare, and third in production per farmer (behind Denmark and Britain).[1] Dutch agricultural cooperatives and its sophisticated infrastructure translated into productivity, and it was successful in servicing new markets, especially across the North Sea in Britain. The tough economic times of the late 1920s and 1930s hit many of its smaller scale farmers hard, prompting the government to step in. Its strategy was focused on food security and exports, and it found a role providing more systematic support and direction for Dutch farmers.

This governmental role included helping to marry agriculture to technology, making the most of what little land the Netherlands had. The use of agro-tech continues to be a defining feature of

Dutch agriculture to this day. In fact the broad willingness to innovate, invest in and exploit new technologies is manifested in the extraordinary mass of orange-tinged glasshouses that you will walk past in Westland.

The origins of these overgrown greenhouses lie in the specialisation of Westland's old country estates in high-value products like orchard fruit and grapes. The main challenge facing the farmers was the Dutch weather, and the answer to this came with the growing availability of cheap, mass-produced glass. Simply growing or starting plants under glass protected them from the worst the skies could chuck at them, allowing farmers to reach export markets outside regular seasons. Early potatoes, for instance, required forced germination indoors, but could be sold in Britain for a handsome profit.

Glasshouses proved an effective and lucrative technology, and even as far back as 1904 glasshouses covered 46 hectares of land. By 1966 they covered 6,000 hectares of the Netherlands, and now fully 80% of Westland's agricultural land is under glass. A satellite map of the region looks more like a fragmented bathroom mirror than rolling farmland. Rotterdam's wharfs could export knowledge-intensive niche products and bring in the coal to warm the glasshouses, however bitter the winds blowing in off the North Sea. Coal then gave way to cheap and plentiful gas after the gas field discoveries of the late 1960s. Because the glasshouses were used for high-value, often perishable crops such as flowers and tomatoes, this in turn seeded a close-knit infrastructure of production facilities, auction houses and logistics networks. Westland is now a densely packed ground zero for the Dutch agro-industrial complex. 'Horticulture in the Netherlands is fascinating. The greenhouses and their production levels, their control over conditions, their use of CO_2, also biological pest control.' Martin van Ittersum is Personal Professor in the Plant Production Systems Group at Wageningen University, the research brain at the heart of that agro-industrial complex. His enthusiasm for the miracle of Dutch agriculture was evident when I spoke to him on the phone. 'High agricultural productivity is an enormous achievement, even with the environmental costs of intensivity. The yield increases that we've seen after the Second World War, and the levels that we're achieving now, it's just phenomenal.' He points to the money that the Netherlands gained at the end of the War thanks to the American Marshall Plan as one of the key enablers of the sector's development. This was channelled into agricultural equipment, research and education, helping to fund capital-intensive forms of farming. Families also started to leave the land, looking for other opportunities as the general economy started to take off, and this allowed the farmers who remained to scale up.

Some examples of Dutch agro-tech are eye-catching, such as growing hydroponic tomatoes on a stone wool substrate woven from basalt and chalk fibres rather than soil, fed with minutely calibrated nutrients dissolved into water. * There are also quixotic attempts to grow difficult and high-value crops such as vanilla, that are usually resistant to the muddy charms of a Dutch polder in deep January. The clothing manufacturer G-Star RAW has worked with Wageningen University to grow cotton under glass, with claimed results of 95% lower water usage and a productivity increase of something between five and 23 times. The sector and its associated research arms are happy to test new solutions,

---

* Hydroponic crops are grown using water-based nutrient solutions rather than soil. This can lead to much higher yields and far greater efficiency. For instance a kilogram of tomatoes might need 15 litres of water if grown hydroponically, rather than over 60 in normal conditions, while also occupying a fraction of the land. For an example see 'This Dutch tomato farm might just solve the global food crisis', *Agritech Future*, 9 May 2022. https://www.agritechfuture. com/smart-farming/this-dutch-tomato-farm-might-just-solve-the-global-food-crisis/.

discovering for instance that while a single hectare can yield a tonne of soya protein to feed livestock, it could instead yield 150 tonnes of insect protein. Others are testing out vertical farming and cell-cultured meat.

One of my favourite examples of clever agro-tech is the *tulpenselectierobot*, which rumbles across tulip fields at 1 kilometre an hour, using Artificial Intelligence to identify sick plants and terminate them with extreme prejudice. The Selector180 costs €185,000 and looks like a cross between a zippy urban microcar and one of those remote-control bomb-disposal vehicles that worked the streets of Belfast in 1985.

The irony of these remarkable attempts to make land more efficient and productive is that Dutch intensivity can instead come at an alarming environmental cost. Pesticides are blamed for destroying ecosystems and contributing to Parkinson's and other neurological diseases. The country's famous tulips are determined consumers of pesticide, but the lily industry, which has grown 28% in a decade, uses far more (12% of total Dutch use). In 2023 one lily grower overturned a verdict that prevented him from using pesticides, allowing him instead to use four different types. In Sevenum in Limburg residents went to court to prevent lilies being grown in a field bordering their gardens.* The farmyards that you walk past will often be home to tanks of chemicals as much as conventional tractors.

Agriculture has also been blamed for falling biodiversity. The halving of butterfly numbers between 1992 and 2023 has been blamed on farming practices such as the application of too much

---

* The Dutch flower industry has a large carbon footprint. The Flemish sustainability organisation *De Transformisten* says emissions total around 2.4 megatonnes of CO_2. The local council in the town of Zutphen decided to ban floral gifts to certain deserving citizens after a motion from the pro-animal PvdD movement was passed. This was not universally accepted as wise.

manure for wildflowers. The underlying eco-crisis of intensive agriculture is believed to be contributing to the destruction of some of the oak forest ecosystems in the Hoge Veluwe National Park. Chemical imbalances can have horrible impacts on birds: European sparrow hawk eggs can fail before the chicks hatch, thanks to depleted levels of amino acids in the mothers.

Meanwhile the mechanics of repurposing marshes and swamps into modern farms, towns and light industrial estates has also had an impact. After all, keeping Dutch feet dry is not just about ringing the land with dykes and pumping the water out to create dry-ish polders. The pumping has to continue, because the polders need to be dry enough to allow heavy dairy cows to graze without turning the land into a muddy morass. That pumping then causes the polders to sink between the hoofs of iconic black and white Friesian cows.

'The country has fallen four metres in the last thousand years,' says Jan Bonjer, who holds the grand title of Dijkgraaf ('Dyke Count') for the Hollandse Delta water board to the south of Rotterdam. He describes the position as being like a mayor for one of the water boards. They continue to have extensive responsibility for the management of Dutch water systems. 'We pump ourselves downwards, so parts of the Netherlands are like a bath tub,' he told me when we spoke on the phone.

'There's also an issue with soil salinity, because when the sea level rises and the land sinks, the sea and the salty water intrudes more into the Netherlands. The big problem with salinity is that we don't see that process. It's like a sniper: it's happening now and it's rather urgent, but you can't see it.'

While it is hard actually to see that the Netherlands is being turned into a giant, sinking bathtub, some animal welfare concerns are harder to miss. The countryside is dotted with vast industrialised factory farms that have led to the Netherlands housing a remarkably dense animal population.* I only ever really noticed their presence when reading regular newspaper reports of fires in factory farm units, incinerating the thousands of miserable animals inside.† They also contribute to the most high-profile and contentious issue facing the Dutch agricultural sector: nitrogen.

What the Dutch call the *stikstofcrisis* has been growing for decades. (The Dutch word for nitrogen is literally derived from *stik*, meaning 'suffocation', and *stof*, meaning 'stuff', which is suggestive of what it can do to wildlife.‡) Nitrogen is part of farming, present in fertilisers that farmers apply to crops to make them grow better, and in the manure produced from the back end of all those cows, pigs and chickens. The trouble starts when there is excess nitrogen, which can lead to pollutants such as ammonia and ozone. Ammonia creates dead zones in waterways where there is insufficient oxygen for organisms to live. This takes out a chunk of the food chain, creating further knock-on effects. For instance if water snails die off, birds will miss out on the calcium from their shells, leading to brittle bones that snap easily. Impacts such as this then throw the entire ecosystem out of balance, which might then lead to more weeds or pests, which in turn requires greater use of chemicals such as pesticides or herbicides.

As far back as the late 1970s the Dutch recognised that their intensive farming system, and in particular the dairy herds that insisted on expelling large quantities of nitrogen-rich manure

---

* In 2020 there were 3.8 million cows, 11.9 million pigs and 90.2 million chickens living in the Netherlands, along with 17.44 million people.

† The Dutch Association of Insurers reports that 62,000 animals were killed in such fires in 2024, including 54,000 chickens in one single incident. See https://www.verzekeraars.nl/publicaties/actueel/aantal-stalbranden-blijft-hoog-meer-dierlijke-slachtoffers-in-2024.

‡ In Chapter 5 I mention a Dutch use for nitrogen that literally involves suffocation.

from their bums, was causing serious environmental problems. Measures were put in place to cut the excessive quantity of manure being spread on fields (around 600kg per hectare). In the two decades from 1990 dairy farmers cut nitrogen emissions by two-thirds, as awareness of the problems associated with nitrogen grew. For instance in 2019 there was a Council of State ruling that nitrogen emissions were harming nature reserves across the Netherlands, although at first there was not much systematic probing of all the links in the causal chain. In 2020 that changed and the *stikstofcrisis* blew up.

The spark for this manure-rich explosion was a study called 'Niet Alles Kan Overall' ('Not Everything Is Possible') that advised drastic measures and pinpointed dairy farms as the key sector that had to reform.[2] The recommendation was for a halving of nitrogen emissions in a decade. This was not taken gladly. The dairy sector had already been cutting nitrogen emissions, and at the same time farmers were rapidly expanding with the encouragement of government. This meant farmers had bought more land and invested in high-tech equipment, taking on a lot of debt to do so. Although the dairy sector only accounts for 1% of the economy, anyone who has seen a Dutch businessman wolf down a lunch consisting of a cheese and butter sandwich and a tall glass of milk knows that dairy lies at the heart of national identity. The farmers were outraged, and details of government proposals that included voluntary buyouts of farmers only poured petrol on to the fire.

The farmers had already been organising before the 'Niet Alles Kan Overall' report, and in October 2019 they first deployed their secret weapons: tractors. A protest was organised, officially involving 75 tractors arriving on the Malieveld, a large open space near the seat of national government in Den Haag. In the event 2,200 turned up, causing more than 1,000 kilometres of traffic jams in the process. This was shock and awe in rubber boots and clogs.

Populist politicians started turning up to farmers' protests, spotting an opportunity (but doubtlessly also genuinely outraged to the bottom of their cheese toasties). Weird conspiracy theories about nitrogen floated around, sometimes mixing with theories about Covid once lockdowns and vaccines became part of everyday life. One fringe group that emerged was the hard line Farmers' Defence Force, which boasted an insignia of crossed forks on their quasi-military badges. Another more mainstream grouping was the *BoerBurgerBeweging* (BBB, Farmer-Citizen Movement), which at one point in 2023 polled at 22% and did well enough in the national elections later that year to help form the government. The BBB provided the government with its new Minister of Agriculture, Fisheries, Food Security and Nature. Femke Wiersma is young, glamorous and had taken part in a 2010 reality TV series called 'Farmer Wants a Wife', subsequently marrying a dairy farmer from Abcoude near Utrecht.

The farmers' uprising has been a genuine political earthquake in the Netherlands. In its most basic form it turned taciturn farmers into political activists, led to widespread and ongoing disruption across the country and gave the sector a direct role in national government. Internationally it led to copycat tractor protests across Europe, giving farmers a voice and a weighty weapon of steel and sharp edges that allowed them to have their voices heard. The uprising also connected environmental concerns directly to agricultural policy. Many centre-right politicians responded by seeing farmers' interests as a lightning rod for their own unease about the demands of climate action.[*]

---

[*] This was particularly evident during campaigning ahead of the July 2024 European Union parliamentary elections, where noisy farming lobbies linked with other groups sceptical about the costs of climate action. This encompassed

For me, what was most striking about the farmers' uprising was that a small but noisy interest group within the Dutch economy demanded that its voice be heard above all others. This looked to me like special pleading, and that is something that does not sit comfortably with the sense of all pulling together and societal fairness that underpins the Dutch *poldermodel*. Farmers already enjoy outsized status compared to ordinary citizens within the decision-making apparatus of some water boards. But do they really deserve to be treated as an exception in facing down the environmental problems their farms have in part created?

Although in my ten walks across the Netherlands I was spending plenty of time tramping across farmland and past mighty agro-industrial concerns, I was never going to be in a situation where I could buttonhole a passing farmer and ask him his views on life, the universe and everything. But in between my walks I did get the chance to talk to one of the Netherlands' most interesting farmers, on a glorious April day in the deep green countryside near 's-Hertogenbosch.

* * *

Klaas Jan van Calker is an amiable dairy farmer with a disarmingly English accent, the face of a thinker and an absent-minded quiff of fair hair. His rubber clogs and forearms are built for work, and he divides his time between a part-share in a dairy farm, and conducting research into how it can all be done better. When I met him he offered me a sandwich and a look around his rather lovely garden. A couple of contented looking sheep were munching away behind moveable electric fences in the garden, keeping his lawn trim.

'Do they have names?' I asked, naïvely.

---

issues such as inflation and the cost of living, food security and the wisdom of rapidly rolling back the carbon economy.

'No. My daughter gives them names, but I don't give them names.'

'Ah. That's part of being a farmer.'

Klaas Jan chuckled. 'I think so.'

This set the theme of my visit: I was sympathetic and well-meaning, and had identified with the countryside since I was a child. I was also handy with a chainsaw and had chickens back home; he was a farmer. We were different. Farmers sit outside modern urbanised society, consumed by a way of life that is often barely viable with pressures the rest of us struggle to understand. My job was to try to bridge the gap in understanding between the two, especially when it came to the sensitive issue of bovine emissions.

'What you don't put in the cow doesn't come out of the cow.' Klaas Jan waved his arm to suggest a hot stream of liquid poo squirting out of the business end of a cow.

'We have a dairy farm that has 160 dairy cows, and we are also a research farm for Wageningen University. So we actually monitor our emissions for ammonia and methane. How can we reduce these emissions by 30%? Okay can we add water to the manure? Can we have better ventilation in the barn? Can we experiment with feed additives? If you increase the longevity of dairy cows, then you need less young stock, so less inputs for the same amount you produce, and that reduces the emissions.'

'Are these measures that will find their way onto other Dutch farms within 5 years?'

'Some of these measures are already rolled out widely, because there are concerns about the environmental impact of the dairy industry in the Netherlands. So all the farms are really keen to reduce their impact. Many are reducing the nitrogen in the diet of the dairy cows. If a cow is grazing outside you will have less ammonia emissions, so that will also have a positive impact. So that's where the dairy industry has been paying premiums for farmers who graze [outdoors].'

Klaas Jan painted a convincing picture of a sector that knew its challenges and was determined to face them, however angry some of those men and women in tractors. The farm itself, a short cycle ride away, backed up his fine words. In one large barn we were greeted by glassy muzzles poking through metal bars. Long prehensile tongues looped out to probe what was going on, cows' eyes rolling around to weigh us up. Half the roof above us was covered in solar panels. A calf enclosure boasted a blue ball, hanging down from a rafter for the animals to nudge and play with. The cows in effect organised their own milking, their own feeding, directed by technology, as if guided by an all-seeing omnipotent dairy god. Everything was automated and electrified and optimised, first for productivity, and second for environmental impact.

'We are a small country, not a lot of land, so the land is quite costly. So the dairy sector is always trying to innovate, to increase productivity. If you can maintain a certain level of production, but drastically improve the environmental impact, then we are making the good steps.' This was a change from 20 or 30 years ago, when the emphasis was on squeezing the land.

'Up to the 90s the focus was how can we increase productivity: more inputs, more commercial fertilisers, if we need pesticides we'll use pesticides. What we do now is much more learn from nature, work with nature. How can we cut down commercial fertiliser? How can we bring in legumes? How can we capture nitrogen and phosphorus? How can we, with a different crop rotation or different way of growing potatoes, reduce pesticide use because we have biodiversity to protect against the pests?'

'What's the future for Dutch farms? Will there be as many in the future?'

'That's really a political choice.' It was one of those rare moments when Jan Klaas van Calker did not sound like he and his colleagues could find all the answers themselves. It begged an obvious line of questioning.

'Has it surprised you how political the farmers have become in the last few years?'

He hesitated.

'Yes, and I think that's a bit unfortunate on both sides. There's a lot of polarisation in the discussion. I think society really supports farmers, and many farmers are interested in the transition, but it becomes so political that the long-term perspective has not been considered.'

'Do Dutch farmers feel that they are a special sector of workers, that they represent something that others do not understand?'

'Yes, I do think that since 2019 with a lot of farmer protests, the perception is that there is a significant gap between the countryside and what's being discussed in the big cities in the Randstad.'

'Do you know any of the farmers who've taken part in the big protests, going to the Malieveld?'

'Yeah yeah. I think many farmers do support the protests, obviously without the violence, just to show that their voices are heard, and that really all they want is a long-term perspective.'

'But a long-term perspective is what politicians are not very good at.'

'No, and that's a challenge.'

We spoke about other things: milk prices and ammonia emissions and how much energy is stored in a length of coppiced willow, ready to rejuvenate in a mud bank. 'So much power in it, right?' This was a reminder of farming as a vocation, as a parallel society with a special communication channel to the natural world. 'It's a way of living, the combination of strategic thinking about the future of the farm as well as the physical work. The unpredictability of the weather, working with animals.'

'You said your son wants to be a farmer,' I said. 'What does he like best when he sees you working?'

'If I gave him the option to stop school and just be continuously on the farm then he'd do that, because he loves to work with the tractors and machines. If you're fifteen then that's really nice! But he's getting a bit older and he's working with the cows and the calves, and he has the talent for it.' Klaas Jan paused, then added what did not really need to be said. 'Farms are family farms,' he said. 'Our farm has been in my in-laws' family for five or six generations. You want to give it over to the next generation.'

I drove away from that dairy farm just outside 's-Hertogenbosch and its 160 computer-controlled cows with a sense that people like Klaas Jan van Calker would find a way to keep their businesses—and way of life—going. The BBB might make its noise and the tractors might periodically occupy the Malieveld, but this nation's farmers were used to thinking their way around a problem and coming up with a clever, viable solution. They have to.

* * *

The Netherlands has never been short of clever farmers like Klaas Jan van Calker, clever researchers like Martin van Ittersum, clever politicians like Stientje van Veldhoven or clever technocrats working hard behind the scenes to make the country function. Together and over centuries, these people have created an extraordinary country where agriculture is super-efficient and a large number of people live good lives on a small and unlikely chunk of land. This walk through the agricultural concerns and greenhouses of Westland shows how much can be packed into a remarkably small space. I saw several examples of a farmhouse utterly boxed in by the encroachment of glasshouses on every side, leaving barely enough space for a garden and some children's toys. The trouble the Netherlands now faces is that it is increasingly evident that squeezing so much out of this unlikely chunk of land comes at a cost, just as it is clear that the wider environment is also changing.

Zoom out a little and consider the bigger picture of Dutch environmental fragility. In the last chapter we saw how the combination of a flat delta, several continental-scale rivers and the North Sea could lead to watery disaster. At the same time we also saw how the Netherlands had evolved as something of a flood-resolving mechanism for this chunk of Europe, providing the Dutch with a land where the water is kept in the right place and their feet are dry. So far, so good, but unfortunately there is more to the dynamic than that.

When Queen Beatrix opened the Oosterscheldekering in 1986 she declared that 'The flood barrier is closed. The Delta Works are completed. Zeeland is safe.' This was a ringing endorsement of the Dutch ability to arm wrestle nature, gripping hard, tensing its sinews and pumping its muscles. After the floods of 1953 and all those billions of guilders spent it was also exactly what the Dutch wanted to hear. If another confluence of unlikely factors came together as they did on that deadly night in 1953, Dutch feet would remain dry. What has changed since then is the impact of climate change: the more extreme oscillations in weather patterns and the creeping rise in sea levels. Forget the high waters of 1953; what lies ahead could be far, far worse.

'When the first influences of climate change came to our knowledge there was a big dissatisfaction,' Jan Bonjer told me. 'Because we thought we had arranged everything with the Delta Works, and now we have to start work again.' The Delta Works has always loomed large in his own life. His father was involved in the rescue operation after the great floods as a reserve officer in the Dutch air force. They used amphibious military vehicles that could both drive and float, left over from the Second World War, to reach stranded farms and villages. For years afterwards Jan and his father spent weekends in Zeeland watching the great anti-flood infrastructure projects being built. Now, although he says the Delta Works lulled the Dutch into complacency, he thinks they are preparing for the climate change challenge. 'They're waking up?' I asked him. 'They are waking up very much!' he replied. If Jan Bonjer is right that is very good news, because there are heart-stopping and credible projections of rising sea levels and large rivers engorged with the waters from extreme weather in the heart of Europe.

A challenge of a very different type might be the modes of thought that the Dutch have developed over the centuries to deal with the threat of inundation. Their remarkable system has triumphed again and again, and the evidence is not just on the battlegrounds of the North Sea and the banks of those great rivers, but in most citizens' transactions with an efficient fuss-free Dutch state. It works, they are doing well, and it is a shame that others were not so adept.

This often translated into a combination of complacency and easy arrogance. This was very evident in those first confusing days of the Covid pandemic. The travails and apparent failures of other governments grappling with Covid were greeted with sympathetic condescension, especially when people knew that I was British and my wife was Italian. Meanwhile they—the Dutch—were confident. Another crisis? *Hey, we're Dutch. We're good at that.*

But they were not. At least not so different from the rest of us. However admirable the ability of the Dutch to anticipate future challenges and meet them adeptly, they struggled just as much as others in pinning down this moving target. There was volatility, an essential unpredictability from one week to the next, one month to the next. Governments scrambled to formulate policies that were then found to be useless or half-baked. Few could even agree, even with themselves, over the severity of the crisis that we all faced. I asked Jan Bonjer what he thought the country had learned about risk during Covid. 'Yeah, that's a very good example,' he said. 'We had to deal with uncertainty. We thought we had the wealth and technological abilities to rule nature, and that's not the case.'

Understanding how risks are changing is critical for the Dutch. This is not just about flooded farmland and water pouring in through letterboxes, creeping levels of salt in the soil or gradual changes in average seasonally adjusted tides. This is about systemic effects that wheedle their way into distant corners of the economic fabric, that multiply and spin out of control, that are just beyond the horizon until they are smashing into you like a runaway juggernaut. Take the potential impact on property, for instance, a tricky and controversial issue chewed over endlessly by policy makers, journalists and middle-class dinner parties.

Delft is one of the Netherlands' property market hotspots, from its jumble of *binnenstad* canal houses to its indomitable 1930s brick homes. As you cross from open farmland into the Delft sprawl towards the end of the walk you will see some admirable housing stock. As you walk through neighbouring Den Hoorn with a canal on your right and the Hoornsekade on your left, you will pass gorgeous hundred-year-old cottages, pre-War villas with precise lines on their rooflines and modern McMansions. One imposing modernist dream is modelled on a ship bursting through foam-flecked waves of shrubbery. The canal, called de Kickert, runs straight ahead to Delft and is lined with pleasure boats tied up in the expectation of jolly weekends mucking about on the water. On the final stretch on Buitenwatersloot an enormous plastic swan bobs around on the canal. It is a lovely place to live, sitting neatly between Rotterdam and Den Haag, and friends of ours commuted from as far away as Utrecht and Amsterdam. We bought and sold two houses during our time there, and the market was obviously frothy with demand handsomely outstripping supply.

All of this is under threat thanks to climate change. For some of the Netherlands' housing stock the threat is real and physical. Older houses, like those in Delft, Gouda and Amsterdam, were built on wooden piles that were driven deep down into the wet ground many centuries ago. With an increase in periodic droughts some of those piles are being exposed to the air, causing them to dry out and crack. Gouda has a particular problem, built on peat marsh that is sinking at an increasingly speedy rate. Evidence of the looming problem is easy to spot in the city centre: the water level sits perilously high, just a centimetre or so from the tops of the canals, and cellars often need to be pumped out. Measures are being taken to manage the change in water levels with dams and pumps, but some fear that management is not enough. One city alderman, Michel Klijmij-van der Laan, has said that an entirely new set of solutions to save the city will be needed within a couple of decades.[3] Meanwhile a professor at Erasmus University, Jan Rotmans, has warned that the entire *Groene Hart* (Green Heart) area surrounding Gouda could be swamped, conjuring up images of floating cities by the end of the century.[4]

Full-blown floods or the need to expand flood prevention infrastructure such as higher and deeper dykes will also affect housing. Some studies suggest that dyke reinforcements may require as much as 90 metres more horizontal space. Given how many houses are within a *fierljeppen* vault of the sands, this would require the demolition of a swathe of housing all the way up the Dutch coastline. Think of the start of this walk, where the path tracks along the top of a dyke, separating the river from people's homes, with the North Sea just a skip away beyond the Hoek. The *Maeslantkering* might be ingenious, but solid earthen dykes like this one do the heavy lifting in keeping swathes of the Netherlands dry. Building them up would affect thousands of homes. Alternating droughts and floods are making the earth shift, causing foundation problems for houses of all types. Chief economists from several major Dutch banks have suggested that one million homes could have foundation issues by 2050.[5] Average repair costs would be around €54,000.* This might matter proportionately less to the owner of a €1 million mansion in Delft and rather more to the owners of a more humble rowhouse in an industrial suburb of Rotterdam. The longer it takes such costs or other impacts on house prices to reflect the climate risks, the greater the burden on younger generations who would not have benefited from previous stratospheric house price increases. Climate change is as much an equity issue in the Netherlands as in Niger.

Even more worryingly, Dutch family finances can be dominated by housing and mortgage costs. This means there is an enormous systemic risk from climate impacts on the property sector. The European Environment Agency's 2023 Climate Risk Assessment suggested that rapid rises in sea level could trigger tipping points in house prices, as perceptions of flood risk shift rapidly.[6] Reactive rather than proactive policies and a failure to communicate about those flood risks would exacerbate this effect, which would then spiral into reductions in the Dutch tax base, increased public expenditure and a further lack of confidence in government and the financial system. The plughole awaits.

The report from the chief economists of major banks warns that 'the majority of households believe they are privately insured against floods or would receive government compensation in case of floods, whereas in reality they aren't.' In the aftermath of the July 2021 floods in Germany, Belgium and the Netherlands that killed over 200 people the Dutch government rejected a plan for national insurance against major flooding. The scale of a major flood on the biggest rivers would simply be so great that premiums would be astronomic and pay-outs would bankrupt

---

* Individual costs would range widely up to €100,000, although most affected homes would face repair costs of €10,000.

insurers. (This is before we feed in the risks that are immediately obvious in the rollicking 2020s, starting with global pandemics, taking in war, global economic breakdowns and cyber sabotage, before ending up with dystopian AI-fuelled robot uprisings.)

This gap in the understanding of climate risk impacts means costs are not reflected in house prices. The report says that 85% of homebuyers are not aware of potential foundation problems (they are only mentioned in 2% of sales adverts). The most dramatic floods do make it into the media, but awareness of risks gradually dissipates as the news cycle moves on. The report suggests that climate risks would be communicated more effectively by giving property 'climate labels', similar to current energy efficiency labelling for fridges and houses. There is resistance: after all, who wants to be the one that finally has to factor in a large visible cost that was hidden when a property was bought?

Reading about these challenges brought me back once again to how the Covid pandemic played out in the Netherlands. The Dutch government seemed to struggle to communicate effectively about the measures they were taking, and struggled to get some citizens to act. I asked Stientje van Veldhoven, who had run the Ministry of Infrastructure and Water at the time, what she had learned from the experience.

'I think that the polder culture and consensus culture did make it more difficult to be very top down, to contain the disease in its earliest stages,' she answered.

'People are used to being heard and being involved and being listened to. Not just being overruled by a centralised government that says, this is how we're going to do it. And you also saw some intense protests when in the end it was done. I think we came late to the acceptance that there were really no other alternatives, as we tried to avoid these very disruptive measures, hoping that with less disruptive measures we'd be able to contain. And in the end we were not.'

Thankfully the Covid pandemic did not after all end with the near-destruction of the human race, even if at the time we could not be sure what form it would take. Writing this a small handful of years after it first appeared it is also striking how quickly much of the world has returned to normal. No doubt most governments in most countries have scribbled down a list of lessons that they learned from their own response to the pandemic, and those of others. From the Dutch perspective there has been much to learn about how the system that has so effectively grown to deal with the challenges the Netherlands has faced over many hundreds of years may not be the system that they need in the twenty-first century.

The last steps on the walk from Hoek van Holland ended at Delft station, where I half expected to bump into an old friend or see a familiar face. Neither happened, but everything did seem so familiar. Ahead was the *binnenstad* where my family had lived so happily during our four years in Delft. I remembered the good times and the summer when the sun was so hot it almost turned my visiting nieces and nephew from Scotland into frazzled bits of bacon. I remembered eating *friets* at the market place, and coming home with a broken rib after playing football against giraffe-like Dutch youths from the Technical University. I remembered when the snows had hit and the whole town trooped dutifully off to the nearby lake with their ice skates. Damned risky, I thought, especially as the lake was barely half frozen. But the Dutch seemed to have a different understanding of risk. And then Covid hit, and we ended up with the horrors of home schooling and a larder full of couscous. We were stranded in a small country a long way from family in Genoa and Northumberland, and worried about how the country was dealing with this strange, unpredictable, chaotic crisis. That is when I thought the Covid crisis would be a critical part of any future book that I wrote about the Netherlands, and also when we decided it was time to leave.

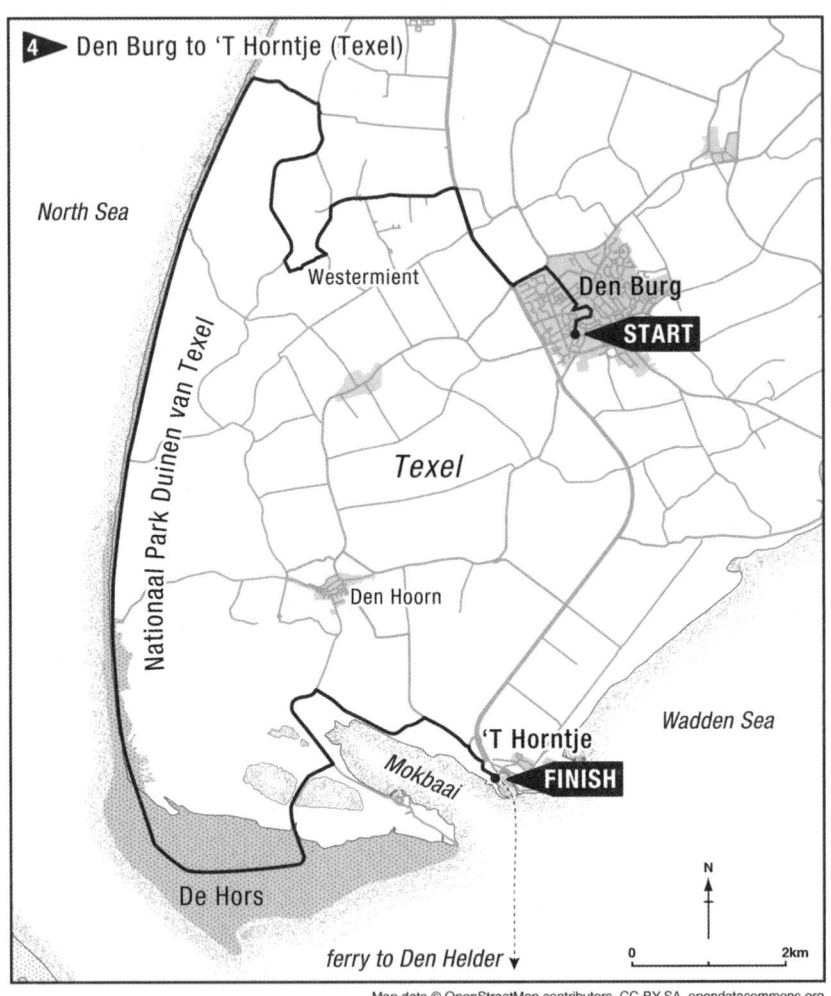

4 ► Den Burg to 'T Horntje (Texel)

North Sea

Nationaal Park Duinen van Texel

Westermient

Den Burg

START

Texel

Den Hoorn

'T Horntje

FINISH

Wadden Sea

Mokbaai

De Hors

ferry to Den Helder ▾

N

0   2km

Map data © OpenStreetMap contributors, CC-BY-SA, opendatacommons.org

4

DEN BURG TO 'T HORNTJE
(TEXEL)

I designed this walk on Texel to be easy to do in a daytrip from the mainland, as that is where I was staying. It is easy to adapt it if you are staying on the island itself. From the ferry terminal I took a bus to Den Burg, wandered around there for a bit and struck off to the northwest on Pontweg. I turned due west on Gerritslanderdijkje to the edge of the forests that lie between Texel's farmland and its dunes. At that point I improvised, picking paths simply because they looked nice, and knowing that if I continued roughly west I would eventually hit the dunes, the beach and the North Sea. Once there I turned left with the sea on my right, and walked. The southern tip of Texel is a wind-blown sandy expanse called De Hors. I followed the edge of the dunes until spotting the path that picked its way north through the bird and nature reserve. Back on the road I looped around the Mokbaai inlet until I reached the ferry terminal at 'T Horntje, which has regular sailings back to Den Helder.

* * *

When I met Tilly Kaisiepo we talked about gardening. I was living in a tight little canal house in the centre of Delft, so my gardening was reduced to fiddling with a handful of pots in the back yard. Tilly's home was an apartment block a short bike ride away, but she also had the Moe'stuin, the community garden in Delft's Poptahof. 'We have *kool*, we have courgettes. Here we have a *mooie* courgette.'* It was August and each of the wood-edged raised beds was overflowing with life: long, trailing tomatoes bobbling with green fruit, broad beans growing like vines and a single sunflower that had grown in a strange thick spiral like a snake. 'This garden is like my mother's garden in Papua,' she told me.

Tilly Kaisiepo's memories were of half a world away and almost a lifetime ago. In 1962 she was 11 years old. Papua, her old home, was being handed over to Indonesia, and she and her family boarded a plane for the Netherlands. 'We came on one of the last flights. KLM was bringing the Dutch people back to Holland, so everybody who has to leave the land, they flew KLM from Dutch New Guinea.'

As an 11-year-old she had expected to return to her tropical home. She never did. Her father was Marcus Kaisiepo, the chairman of the New Guinea Council that had been set up by the Netherlands to foreshadow a future parliament. When the Dutch East Indies became independent Indonesia in 1949, the Netherlands kept hold of Dutch New Guinea, the western half of the island of New Guinea. The Papuans are Melanesian and had little in common with the people from the great Southeast Asian archipelago stretching off to the west, the people of Java, Sumatra, Kalimantan and Sulawesi. But by the 1950s the Indonesian president, Sukarno, was agitating to take control of this remaining Dutch colonial territory. The tide of history was

---

* *Kool* is cabbage; *mooie* courgette means 'lovely courgette'.

firmly against the Netherlands, and it bowed to the inevitable. The territory was first handed over to the United Nations, then Indonesia. Any voices that protested against rule from Jakarta were silenced, and Marcus Kaisiepo would never be allowed to return.* A purse now hung proudly around Tilly Kaisiepo's neck, in the Papuan colours of a white star on a red background, plus blue and white stripes. It was one of the last physical reminders of a long-vanished dream of a politically or culturally independent homeland.

'You went straight into a Dutch school. What was the reaction of the other children?'

'They were told that we were coming. So they were okay with it, but they only looked at me and...' For a moment Tilly did not look like she knew what to say. 'For me it was a shock. We were a colony, Dutch New Guinea. So in my country you don't interact with white people, Hollanders. The Dutch people, they were the boss, and the Papuans, we were the...' Again, she lost the words she was looking for.

'We thought it was temporary, so we said goodbye [to West Papua], then we left. Not knowing back then that I'd still be standing here now, in Holland. I'm a mother, I'm a grandmother, and I'm still here.' She grinned, looking as vibrant as the flowers that surrounded us in her denim jacket and blue-and-white

---

* It may be worth consulting a map at this stage. New Guinea is an enormous, rugged island sitting to the north of Australia. Its eastern half is now Papua New Guinea, which gained independence from Australia in 1975. The other half, as noted, was part of the Dutch East Indies, but was considered different enough from the archipelago stretching off to the west that the Dutch held on to it after the formation of Indonesia. Once Jakarta wrested control of the territory its sense of independence was systematically crushed, and some estimates suggest that 100,000 or more Papuans have been killed in government-sponsored violence. There is no credible prospect of West Papua becoming the independent country of Tilly Kaisiepo's dreams.

dress. 'My people are struggling for independence. I'm a warrior. But I'm also a good oma [grandmother].'

Now Tilly Kaisiepo uses the Moe'stuin to build a community among others who, like her, were uprooted from their old homes. 'You've got Syrians, you've got Iraqis, Afghans, Somalis, Surinamese.' She tells newcomers looking for community not to talk about places they have all left behind. 'Leave your problems at home. Just come in the garden and plant, because that's good for your health.' Although the garden now has a waiting list she arranged for a table near its front gate, so even those not able to get their hands mucky could have a coffee surrounded by garlic flowers and roses.

'Would you like to see Papua again?'

'Only if it's independent.' Tilly's answer was determined and quick. 'I paid for a piece of land in the cemetery here in Delft, to be next to my father and my mother. If my country is not independent I will be buried here.'

There are plenty of others like Tilly, proud left-overs from when this tiny European country ruled one of the world's biggest empires. Strangely, if it was not for the Surinamese food takeaways and the Indonesian restaurants selling their elaborate *rijsttafel* of sambal and rendang and countless other dishes, a stroll around the Netherlands might not identify the country as a former colonial heavyweight. A quick glimpse at the skin tones of the national football team helps, but otherwise empire tends not hang heavily in the minds of modern Dutch people. If anything it is remembered as a source of vaguely-processed national pride. One poll on European attitudes to colonialism in 2019 showed the Dutch to be the proudest about their colonial history. Fully half said they were proud, compared to 32% of British people, 26% of French and 23% of Belgians.[1] Only 6% were ashamed, and 26% of

Dutch respondents said they wished their overseas empire still existed.*

'I think for Dutch politics, it's forgotten,' Tilly said, talking specifically about the West Papua issue. On one memorable occasion she had headed down to the Malieveld in Den Haag with a Papuan flag, hoping to engage strangers in conversation and thereby keep the memory of her homeland alive. Unfortunately she ran into a protest in favour of the Dutch Zwarte Piet tradition, involving Saint Nicholas' Christmastime helpers wearing blackface and curly wigs. The protesters took her presence and dark complexion to be an anti-Zwarte Piet counter-demonstration, and she was soon surrounded by absurdly dressed angry Dutch people with blacked-up faces. They told her to fuck off to her own country, and her attempts to explain the grievous injustice the Papuan people had suffered were ignored. (The police whisked her away, but her skirmish briefly focused some media attention on the West Papuan cause.) Few stand-offs could explain how so many Dutch have gone from proudly imperial to dimly parochial in the course of Tilly Kaisiepo's defiant lifetime.

'They want to wipe out this history that they have ever been in New Guinea. They want to erase it from the Dutch history. But I'm Papuan, it's my country. You took it away from us, and you gave it to Indonesia for all *your* right reasons, but not for us.' Her voice then became softer, less demonstrative, more plaintive. 'My Papuan people are still suffering every day. But if I tell my story, it's too much for the Dutch people. You cannot get away with giving people my country and letting Indonesia kill and exploit it and take away all their riches.' She smiled again, knowing and almost accepting the course her life had taken, and that history had taken.

---

* The 6% of Dutch being ashamed is in comparison to 14% of French, 19% of British and 23% of Belgians.

This fourth chapter, this fourth walk, is all about the Netherlands' global empire, the end of that empire, and the circumstances that led the lovely Tilly Kaisiepo to be talking to me about gardening and geopolitics in Delft's Poptahof. It is an enormous subject and, like a floundering East Indiaman jammed on a tropical reef, it is easy to be swamped.* For that reason this walk is set somewhere quite beautiful, but largely symbolic.

* * *

Texel is the largest of the Wadden islands, strung along the northern edge of the Netherlands from the tip of Nord Holland at Den Helder to the German border. It is 24 kilometres long, and most of it is lush green fields used for grazing by muscular Texel sheep. A thick barricade of heather-clad sand dunes cushions its North Sea coast, meeting the sea at a gently curving and seemingly endless white beach.

Many of the fleets heading off to the Netherlands' colonial possessions gathered here before striking out into the open sea, heading south past Zeeland and through the English Channel into the Atlantic. Most would then make sail for Brazil, tacking back across the ocean to round Africa at the Cape, before the long, hot journey across the Indian Ocean towards Java and the spice islands. Others would find their way to the Caribbean, to the northern coast of South America, to the mouth of the Hudson River, or even Japan or a southern continent that Europeans imagined existed somewhere beyond the edges of their maps.†

---

* An East Indiaman was a large ship used for voyages to and from the Indies, laden with passengers and cargo.

† One reason for this belief was the theory that every land mass in the northern hemisphere was balanced by one in the southern.

The walk on Texel gives you plenty of time to contemplate the juxtaposition of this little European country with the empire that it ruled, out over those waters. It starts on the trim streets of the island's biggest settlement, Den Burg, across onion fields into forests where it is easy to get lost or be run over by rogue cyclists. If you are lucky you will be spat out on to the dunes, and if you are even luckier the heather will be in flower with clouds scudding along in the sunshine.* The path beneath your feet will become fluffier, there will be an uphill, and then the beach, heading off into both hazy horizons. Ahead is the open sea, where the Dutch found their global destiny. The sands are decorated with frilly blue jellyfish and excited flocks of seagulls, razor clams and cuttlebones, along with the odd nude bather. After the vast open sands of De Hors, at the southern tip of Texel you skirt the Mokbaai nature reserve and end the walk at 'T Horntje, where ferries arrive from the mainland. These are the waters where the fleets gathered, dreaming of spices and gold, stiffened by the knowledge that most of those who sailed would never again see the land of their birth.

We had planned one holiday on Texel during the time we lived in the Netherlands, but cancelled thanks to a weather forecast that suggested we would be either stuck in a tent besieged by rain or end up watching it being blown somewhere towards Dogger Bank. We had, however, been to Texel's near-neighbour in the Wadden Sea, Terschelling, and it was glorious. We hired bicycles straight off the ferry, and spent a week scooting around between meadows and beaches, ice cream shops and pancake houses. Our only dog at the time, little Baffo, rode uneasily in a trailer behind my wife's bicycle, howling incessantly. My young son Luca sat

---

* The heather comes out in late summer and early autumn. Sunshine comes out when it wants to. When I did the walk I had flowering heather, sunshine, scudding clouds and rain, all pretty much at the same time.

in front of me on a tandem, belting out show tunes from the musical *Oliver*. It was quite a week.

While Texel itself can feel overrun by tourists, further up the coast the Wadden Islands are like a different world. That is how some islanders obviously like it. On Ameland, which is the next island along from Terschelling, the locals have become very touchy about a variation of the Sinterklaas Christmas celebrations, known as Sunneklaas. It involves men parading in masks around the villages of Hollum, Ballum and Nes, while women and children are safely locked up indoors. Outside scrutiny about its supposedly crass and misogynistic overtones has been firmly rebuffed. In December 2023 journalists reporting on Sunneklaas were attacked and their cars rammed. In November 2024 a local YouTuber was quoted as advising islanders to unite 'with pitchforks and torches' against journalists planning on a festive visit to their shores. 'Fuck off,' he apparently said. 'Finish them off. Shoot them down before they even get off the boat.' Rumours that the good locals of Ameland were planning to imprison outsiders in an enormous wicker man and then set fire to it are entirely fictitious.

Texel is far too plugged in to the Dutch mainstream to carry such a whiff of the far flung and barmy. The start of this walk, on the genteel streets and lanes of Den Burg, carries all the menace of a comfortable Saturday evening in front of the television. It has cobbles and gables, prim gardens and helpful ladies in shops full of knick-knacks. Nevertheless, standing on Texel's northern beaches it does feel like you are standing on the edge of something, in this case the giant Eurasian landmass. The shipping that you can see pootling this way and that offshore underlines that it is also highly connected. You are on the sea lane halfway between Iberia and Scandinavia, and just across from you is England. Behind you, the Netherlands is at the confluence of those great river systems that open up routes right into the heart of continental Europe. The Dutch had a geographical inheritance that was ideal for trade; it was a natural place to land goods on the way to somewhere else and make a bit of money on the deal.

At first it was the more southerly Dutch-speaking towns such as Antwerp and Bruges that established themselves as centres for wool and luxury goods such as spices. More northerly towns such as Middelburg and Amsterdam dealt with lower value goods including timber, herring and salt. This southern ascendency ended following the outbreak of the decades-long Dutch Revolt against Spanish rule in the late 1560s.* Among those who fled north to escape the fighting and Catholic persecution were large numbers of wealthy, experienced and well-connected protestant merchants, many of whom brought their expertise to Amsterdam. The city's population began to grow rapidly, from around 30,000 inhabitants at the start of the Revolt to 110,000 by 1628.

Meanwhile the trade routes that connected Europe to the rest of the world were being transformed. Multiple routes had linked Eurasia overland, connecting China and the far reaches of Asia across mountain ranges and deserts, forests and steppes to Persia, Arabia and ultimately Constantinople. From there, Genoese and Venetian merchants dispersed goods to markets and ports across Europe. The entire chain could take months or even years, especially for the spices that came from tiny islands in the hidden corners of the massive archipelago that stretched off beyond the coasts of Southeast Asia.

These spices were enormously valuable in the West, as preservatives and medicines, and to bring flavour to bland or spoiling food. Despite the prices they were paying, European

---

* It continued until 1648.

merchants could only plug into the spice trade once they had reached the shores of the Mediterranean. The only way this could change was if they could find a maritime route directly to the markets near where the spices were grown.

In 1488 the Portuguese achieved this after rounding Africa and turning into the Indian Ocean. This opened up new trade routes that circumvented the long overland routes. The Portuguese guarded their knowledge closely, but competition to learn the secrets was fierce. In the 1590s a Dutchman called Jan Huyghen van Linschoten published three books detailing what he had learned from years spent among the Portuguese in Goa and the Azores, at last giving his countrymen the keys that unlocked the East.

The first Dutch expedition to what they called the Indies set off in 1595. The *Eerste Schipvaart* was in itself unsuccessful, commanded by impetuous and suspicious leaders who left a trail of beheadings, cannonades and eventual mutiny across the Indian Ocean.* Fewer than 100 out of the original complement of nearly 250 crew made it home alive. The cargo of pepper, nutmeg and mace that they carried back to Amsterdam was barely enough to cover costs, but was enough to whet appetites. The *Tweede Schipvaart*, which set off in 1598, was better planned, better led and a great success.†

This naturally led to more expeditions, each funded by different competing consortiums. Then Dutch commercial common sense took over and they decided to replace the free-for-all by working together. Their idea was to form a joint stock corporation that could combine their money and talents in a monopoly enterprise. The *Verenigde Oost-indische Compagnie* was formed in 1602 and dispatched its first (very

---

* *Eerste Schipvaart* means First Fleet.
† *Tweede Schipvaart* means Second Fleet.

successful) fleet that same year.* The VOC was hard-headed, ruthless and effective. It was prepared to use violence to take over the scattering of tiny islands (now in modern Indonesia) that actually produced the spices, such as Ambon, Tidore and Ternate for cloves and the Banda islands for nutmeg. They cornered markets, crushed competitors and reaped massive profits.

The men that formed up a VOC crew in this period were as ruthless and aggressive as any in the seventeenth century. Many were the men known as the *grauw*, from the gutter and the jail. Others were willing to take on enormous risks because of the potential rewards on offer. Life on board was in turns brutal, boring and grim. It would take roughly 200 days for the voyage, during which the drinking water turned to slime, the food crawled with maggots and the men became a mess of sores, grudges and missing teeth. The risk of shipwrecks was a terrifying reality. When the *Batavia* ran aground on a chain of small islands off Western Australia most of the 341 on board survived, only for their ordeal to degenerate into a horror of mass murder, infanticide, sex slavery and starvation. For those who survived the journey, life in the tropics was little better: gruelling, disease-ridden and very often deadly. Over the VOC's lifetime the chances of an individual making it back to the Netherlands was less than one in three.

The man who shaped this scattering of profits, blood and spice into an empire was Jan Pieterszoon Coen, an impressive, austere and single-minded figure. He cautioned his men not to spare his enemies, believed that God had to be in favour of whatever they were up to, and was prepared to use the utmost

---

* The *Verenigde Oost-indische Compagnie* or VOC means United East India Company, but is commonly called the Dutch East India Company.

violence to secure trade monopolies for the VOC.* When he attacked Lonthor in the Banda Islands he massacred thousands with the help of Japanese mercenaries, replacing them with slave labour. He turned Batavia into the capital of the Dutch East Indies after wrestling the English for control of the town, and rebuilt it in Dutch fashion with canals and gabled houses with leaded windows.† His legacy was the vision of the East Indies as the cornerstone of a Dutch commercial empire, fighting off Javanese attacks and European rivals to establish an enduring presence that was to last more than 300 years.‡

On the other side of the globe a western Dutch empire was also coalescing, driven by the *Geoctrooieerde Westindische Compagnie*.§ Dutch territories ranged from Manhattan, the Hudson valley and parts of the eastern seaboard of the modern United States, down across the Caribbean to Surinam and even chunks of what is now northern Brazil.¶ The Dutch engaged enthusiastically in the Atlantic slave economy, with posts in West Africa and modern Angola, and sugar plantations were established in their holdings in the Americas.

---

* The most famous Jan Coen quote is '*Dispereert niet, ontziet uw vijanden niet, want God is met ons*' ('Despair not, spare your enemies not, for God is with us').
† Batavia became Jakarta, the capital of modern Indonesia.
‡ The Dutch East Indies was by no means a complete territory during those three centuries. It remained centred on Java, with other territories such as Sumatra, Bali and Borneo gradually (and bloodily) brought under Dutch control.
§ The *Geoctrooieerde Westindische Compagnie* or GWC was the Chartered West India Company.
¶ The southern bit of Manhattan was called New Amsterdam. Famously under the Treaty of Breda in 1667 the Dutch exchanged Manhattan with the English for the miniscule spice island of Run. The Dutch influence is still visible in modern New York, for instance in names such as Harlem (Nieuwe Haarlem) and Flushing Meadows (named after the Dutch port of Vlissingen).

At their most productive, these twin imperial projects brought riches back to the Dutch Republic that buttressed its position as a first rate maritime, trading and cultural power. This was the Dutch Golden Age, the time of Rembrandt and Vermeer, of flourishing towns and social progress.* Wind filled the sails of ships that buccaneered across the seas and of windmills that pumped the land dry. But it was not to last.

In Dutch history 1672 is considered the *Rampjaar*, or 'year of disaster'. The Netherlands found itself fighting the French on land and the English in the North Sea. The country itself was politically divided (and extremely complicated). In essence the House of Orange had lost control of the running of the Dutch Republic in 1650.† In their place a very capable man with a fine moustache and ebullient hair called Johan de Witt had taken political control, through his holding of the office of Grand Pensionary of Holland. De Witt may have had a fine mind, but after a series of maritime face-offs against the English he was blamed for neglecting the army and the Republic's land defences. When the French army broke through from the east a panicked mob in Den Haag lynched De Witt and his brother Cornelius, famously finding time to eat their livers. The Dutch, once again under the House of Orange, were able to hold the French at bay after flooding a defensive barrier known as the Waterline. The Dutch had also defeated an Anglo-French fleet off the English

---

* Of course it was not social progress for all, and especially not for the victims of the imperial projects, as we will see later on. The term 'Dutch Golden Age' is now contested in some quarters.

† The workings of the Dutch Republic can be difficult to pin down as it was a decentralised federation of seven provinces that threw off Spanish rule and declared independence as the United Provinces in 1581. It was often dominated by the wealthiest province, Holland, with the Princes of Orange in the influential office of *stadtholder*.

county of Suffolk, the siege of Groningen had been lifted and the Dutch Republic survived to see 1673 arrive.

Despite this last-ditch survival the *Rampjaar* was disastrous enough to signal the end of the half-century Dutch Golden Age. Its economy had taken a kicking, and Jan Vermeer's wife was to complain that among other impacts this destroyed the country's previously buoyant art market. The ripples of this internal turmoil spread out around the globe. The GWC was already struggling, relying on the slave trade for its survival but weighed down by debt and straining under the challenge of protecting its territories from European competitors. The VOC was also troubled. Cultivators had found ways to grow spices in territories far away from the Spice Islands. This sounded the death knell for the market that had enticed the Atlantic powers into the Indian Ocean in the first place. The venerable old VOC, that motor of Dutch economic dynamism, was toiling under towering overheads and losses, Chinese middlemen taking an increasingly large slice of the commercial pie. The global economy was shifting, and with it Dutch imperial potency.

For the many who were on the receiving end of this potency that was no bad thing. Dutch territories in the Caribbean and the north coast of South America were focused on sugar plantations, and in human terms that translated into misery, slavery and death. The territory of Berbice, which is now part of Guyana, had been Dutch from 1627, and consisted of long, rectangular plantations that had been hacked out of the rainforest along the Bernice and Canje rivers. Each was named after parts of the Netherlands, women or states of mind that bore little relation to those who grew, cut and processed the sugar cane: Zeelandia and Amsterdam, Cornelia and Juliana, Mon Repos and Solitude, Goed Fortuin and Providence. Most of the enslaved people who toiled there were African, along with a scattering of indigenous people. In 1763 70 enslaved people on the Magdalenenberg plantation rose up against their tormentors, sparking off a rebellion 3,000-strong. Many of the white Europeans fled, but 60 were trapped inside a burning plantation house. The leader of the rebellion, a redoubtable man called Cuffy, offered to end the violence, saying that it was an uprising against a small number of particularly cruel plantation owners. He said they did not seek war, but if no peace was agreed they would 'fight on until there is no Christian left in Berbice.' The Dutch stalled for time, and the rebellion lost momentum. Cuffy himself committed suicide after his leadership was challenged. It all ended when 600 Dutch soldiers arrived in Berbice and re-imposed control. One thousand eight hundred rebels were killed, some burned alive or broken horribly on the wheel. So ended the first organised slave revolt on the American continent. Berbice as a sugary outpost of hell never recovered, and it was gradually abandoned amid severe financial problems and a downturn in the sugar trade.

Jump forward into the nineteenth century and two close events played roles in the evolution of the Dutch imperium. First, a rebellion by a Javanese aristocrat in 1825 morphed into the bloody Java War. Victory five years later cemented more formal Dutch colonial rule in Java and underpinned a more systematic approach to both security and economic exploitation. This is a useful reminder that the Dutch East Indies was not a fully formed entity for most of its existence, but a patchwork of control, clients and conflict. Second, in 1830 Belgium seceded. Their union had been part of the post-Napoleonic settlement, founded in 1815 after the French defeat at the Battle of Waterloo. A newly-oversized Netherlands (that included what is now its southern neighbour) was intended by the victors in the struggle against Napoleon to be a North Sea buffer state against expansionist ambitions by France or any other aggressive continental power.

Both of these events imposed a high economic cost on the Dutch. The Java War had been extremely destructive, and the protracted and lengthy conflict with secessionist Belgium deprived the Netherlands of its advanced economy. Belgium was one of the first parts of Europe to industrialise, and boasted a sophisticated textile trade, along with raw materials that included coal. Deprived of the resources to enter its own industrial revolution, and with its own economy ailing, the Dutch were prompted to pivot economically to the colonies, especially the Dutch East Indies.

The chosen method was the introduction of the cultivation system (*cultuurstelsel*), which forced farmers to grow cash crops on a fifth of their land.* The colonial administration then made its money by selling on the coffee, tobacco, quinine, sugar and indigo. On the one hand this exploitative system resulted in misery and the deaths of thousands in famines and epidemics, but on the other hand the Dutch found it extremely lucrative, at times accounting for more than half of their tax revenues. Soon, the fifth of land that farmers had to give over to cash crops was doubled to two-fifths.† The extractive Dutch approach extended to land taxes, pawnshops and monopolies on salt and opium.

The cultivation system was the backdrop for one of the Netherlands' most celebrated and hard-hitting works of literature, published in 1860. In *Max Havelaar, or the coffee auctions of the Dutch Trading Company*, the reader learns about the injustices of a system that paid 'the Javanese just enough to keep him from starving, which would lessen the producing power of the

---

* If they had no land they had to do 66 days of unpaid work for the Dutch authorities.

† And the 66 days of unpaid work became 200 days.

nation.'* This periodically led to famines, when 'mothers offered to sell their children for food, mothers ate their own children.' Meanwhile the Dutch colonials lived a life 'replete with luxury: a billiard-room, a library, a covered iron and glass conservatory, and a cockatoo on a silver perch.'† At the end of the book the author interrupts the story to say that he only wrote the book so people would read his speech on why the system of colonial rule was wrong. It was in effect an anti-colonial pamphlet more than a book.

The moral outrage that followed the publication of *Max Havelaar* back in the Netherlands contributed to the cultivation system being abandoned.‡ In its stead, the plantation system involved private companies setting up cash crop plantations. It was undoubtedly far less inhumane, but discontent and rebellion continued to both bubble and rage in the Dutch East Indies. Dutch expansion across the archipelago had led to bloody conflicts that stretched into the twentieth century. Subjugating Bali took half a century. The Aceh War (Aceh is on the northern tip of Sumatra) lasted four decades up until 1914 and cost 100,000 lives. On top of these endless military challenges, the cash crop export system took a hit in the Great Depression. Exports from the Dutch East Indies fell from 1.5 billion guilders in 1929 to below half a billion by 1935.

Pressure for reform, even independence, was growing within the outposts of empire. In the Dutch East Indies a hardcore intellectual and political resistance was forming, the post-

---

* The book was by Multatuli, a pseudonym for Edward Douwes Dekker, who had served as the Assistant Resident of the Dutch government in Java.

† According to the marvellously named Batavus Droogstoppel, a rich coffee trader.

‡ The Stichting Max Havelaar launched the world's first fair trade certification label in 1988.

independence leader Sukarno prominent within it. The most famous agitator in the western hemisphere was Anton de Kom, who was born in Paramaribo, Surinam to a father who had been born in slavery. He gained an education, and while working in the Netherlands in the 1920s became active in left wing circles. His return to Surinam was brief, before being banished back to the Netherlands as a danger to public order. That is where he wrote and published his most famous work, *Wij slaven van Surinam* (*We slaves of Surinam*), which was added to the Dutch literary canon. He continued to agitate through the years of Nazi occupation, before being arrested in 1944. Not long before the end of the War he died of tuberculosis.

Earlier attempts to make Dutch rule more sympathetic in Southeast Asia were abandoned in the face of economic contraction and social unrest.[*] Governor-General Bonifacius Cornelius De Jonge instigated a crack-down and declared that 'We Dutch have been here for 300 years. We will stay here for 300 more. After that, we can talk.' Right-wing groups such as the *Vaderlandsche Club* (Fatherland Club) bloomed. Behind the segregated schools and the neat lawns in front of whitewashed buildings the Dutch East Indies seethed with tension and the threat of insurrection. But an even greater calamity was about to visit the archipelago.

In 1941 the mother country, the Netherlands, was already suffering under Nazi occupation in a Europe swiftly spiralling down into a bitter and ghastly war of annihilation.[†] Members of the more pro-Nazi right-wing groups were promptly deported from the Indies to Surinam, but the real threat to the colony was to come from an Asian power. Imperial Japan fought its horrific

---

[*] The more sympathetic system was known as the 'ethical policy'.
[†] This is the subject of Chapter 7.

Pacific war with the explicit aim of capturing natural resources such as oil and rubber, primarily from the Dutch East Indies.

The full invasion began in January 1942. The Dutch sabotaged their own oil installations, and the imperial military force (the KNIL) fought alongside Allied troops. Horrible atrocities were committed by the Japanese, such as the beheading of over 300 Australian and Dutch soldiers after fighting on Ambon. The campaign was soon over: the fall of the great British bastion at Singapore sealed the fate of the Dutch East Indies, and defeatism took over. Some Dutch soldiers, who had seen their country fall to the Germans and who were mainly prepared for smaller scale colonial engagements, simply gave up. They got drunk and sang that everything was turning to shit. After all those centuries as the imperial Netherlands, the country had been humbled.

The sight of Asian soldiers defeating the Europeans spurred many locals to support the new overlords, but they were soon to find that Japanese rule was even worse. Women of all races were forced to work in military brothels, and executions of civilians were commonplace. The biggest killers were food requisitions, economic collapse and simple neglect. The Japanese controlled the rice supply, and local populations were their lowest priority. Nearly two and a half million died from hunger, along with a further 400,000 forced into labour. A United Nations study found that 4 million died in total from a population of 68 million.

Meanwhile Dutch civilians were interred in *jappenkampen* (Japanese camps), which ranged from repurposed schools and mental asylums to simple warehouses. They faced brutality, rampant tropical diseases and starvation. Some were reduced to eating snakes and candle wax. Joty ter Kulve, who had enjoyed an 'El Dorado' childhood in a whitewashed colonial bungalow in the village of Linggajati, was 14 years old when what she called 'yellow guys on motorcycles' arrived.[2] She was sent to a camp with her sister and mother (her father had died before the War) and was surprised on the journey when the local people hurled abuse at them. In the camp there were only a couple of water taps for 1,500 people. Rats crawled over sleeping bodies in the open dormitory and they were stalked by cholera. Across all the camps 13,000 internees died. Soldiers were taken away to prisoner of war camps, and 18,000 were put to work on the infamous Burma railway.*

The commander of the Japanese invasion forces, Hitoshi Imamura, had behaved slightly less murderously than many of his peers, but was one of many who faced charges after the War. In 1947 he was sentenced to a decade in prison by Australia for war crimes that included imprisoning Allied soldiers in bamboo pig cages and throwing them into the sea for sharks to eat. He was racked with remorse, and considered his ten-year sentence too light. When he was released he built a replica of his cell from Sugamo prison in his garden and lived there until his death in 1968.

* * *

The Second World War was a traumatic and humbling experience for the Dutch, whether at home in the Netherlands or across the seas in their great Southeast Asian imperial possessions. But even in the darkest days the country was trying to frame a post-War imperial future. Queen Wilhelmina, who had fled to England when the Nazis invaded, gave a landmark speech in December 1942 that showed the way the Dutch government was thinking. In the speech the Queen spoke of partnership and self-reliance, of a commonwealth between the Netherlands, Indonesia, Surinam

---

* The death rate among Dutch POWs was 17%.

and Curaçao.* The *San Francisco Chronicle* was one of many newspapers to welcome this, noting that the continued move away from the 'earlier period of pure exploitation' towards 'native' political responsibility was being done in 'very sound fashion'.[3]

However, as liberation drew closer the mood changed. Standing on the coast of Texel with a small country behind you and the enormity of the world in front of you, it is easy to imagine how the war-ravaged Netherlands must have felt about reclaiming their status through empire. A popular phrase from the time was '*Indië verloren, ramspoed geboren*', which translates as 'Losing the Indies brings disaster'. The Netherlands was a grey, ruined country in a ruined continent, and harnessing the productive power of the Dutch East Indies seemed an obvious route to recovery. After all, despite their waning economic fortunes the Indies had contributed 15% of Dutch pre-War income.[4] Even now, in more prosperous times as you walk across Texel, you get the feeling of being somewhere compact and provincial. Den Burg itself has a toytown feel about it with pretty houses that look like they have been shrunk to fit. Being a colonial power gave the home country a status that belied the Netherlands' size and wartime humiliations. When the Second World War ended the Dutch were resolved that the empire would continue, even if reform would follow.†

Other European countries were making the same calculation, but in each case they faced growing indigenous movements determined that the future was theirs to seize whatever the colonial powers wished. In the Indies the main protagonist was a long-time revolutionary, a former guest of Dutch detention

---

* The Queen's reference to 'Indonesia' rather than the 'Dutch East Indies' was itself an indication that the colonial relationship was being re-examined.

† How this fitted in with discussions about the Netherlands' place in the world is the subject of the eighth chapter of this book.

facilities, and—to many Dutch—a collaborator with the Japanese. Sukarno's life's work was winning independence for the giant archipelago. By the end of the War he had galvanised mass support for the project and built an armed force capable of taking on the Dutch overlords.* When liberation from the Nazis in Europe and the Imperial Japanese in the Dutch East Indies came, the nationalists under Sukarno were ready.†

The ensuing struggle lasted from 1945 until 1949, resulting in Indonesian independence and the end of those three centuries of Dutch rule across the archipelago. Just as with other decolonisation struggles it was a grubby, nasty business, full of confusion and blood, dead civilians and unanswered questions. It was also ruinously expensive, costing an estimated 3 million guilders a day at a time when the Netherlands was only just staggering back on to its feet.[5]

Many Dutch conscripts turned out to have little appetite for more war: 120,000 men were conscripted to fight on the other side of the world; 6,000 refused to go, and were hunted down like criminals until as late as 1958. One notable reluctant conscript was Poncke Princen, who eventually defected to the Indonesian side during his service in the East. The Indonesians awarded him the Guerrilla Star, but struggled with his innate rebelliousness that saw him continuously in and out of prison.

It is now well documented that war crimes were committed by both sides during the independence struggle. On the Dutch side the most notorious leader was Captain Raymond 'The Turk'

---

* He had mobilised this armed force of 37,000 soldiers with the assent of the Japanese.

† The Dutch East Indies were largely bypassed by fighting as the Allies gradually worked their way up the western Pacific, island by island, in their efforts to defeat Japan. The Japanese garrisons in the Indies then surrendered when Japan itself surrendered.

Westerling, who was born in Constantinople of Dutch and Greek parents. He led a unit in Sulawesi that terrorised villages and conducted summary executions, later admitting to killing 563 by his own hands. Others copied his methods out of a combination of racism, expediency and the sheer frustration of battling an incoming tide. An engaging 2020 film, *De Oost* (*The East*), is based upon the Westerling story, following a conscript who falls into the officer's ghastly orbit before rebelling and ending up one of society's long-haired outcasts back in the Netherlands.*

The end of the struggle was certainly bitter for the Netherlands. Countless men had been killed, the great Dutch East Indies had been lost so soon after recovering it from the Japanese and prestige had been ground into the mud. The country that had stood so proudly at the head of a global empire was reduced to a small, soggy corner of western Europe.

At the talks that determined Indonesian independence the prime minister, Willem Drees, made a speech in November 1949 that was heavy with history. He spoke of how the first voyage had set off from Texel in 1595, taking 446 days to sail the same distance that a plane could now cover in two days. He emphasised that the Dutch had gone not as conquerors, but in search of trade and profit, and he was clear-headed about the inevitability of Indonesian rule, even if this had been rather accelerated by war and revolution. Financial interests dominated to the end, and the Dutch demanded 4.5 billion guilders from Indonesia for the transfer of sovereignty.† Tellingly the speech was delivered in

---

* The plot turns on the conscript's background as son of a Nazi collaborator. See Chapter 7 for more on how the children of collaborators suffered after the War.

† At independence (admittedly archipelagic) Indonesia had less than 5,000 kilometres of railway, compared to over 25,000 kilometres in India.

Dutch, repeated in English and then time ran out before they could give the *Indonesisch* version.

Although it was never going to turn its back on the Golden Age of empire, the Netherlands had resolved to turn its back on the Dutch East Indies and those last dismal, grubby years of struggle. The nastiness of the late 1940s, when they had battled Sukarno's guerrillas in the paddy fields, the unlucky villages and the deadening jungles, were lost in the shadow of the Second World War. This is why the conscript lead character in the film *De Oost* ends up as a bedraggled and disturbed cast-off on the dank streets of his homeland, part of the flotsam of a conflict many tried to forget. It is also why there was a conspiracy of silence and forgetting about some of the excesses perpetrated by the KNIL in those years of fighting.

The most prominent whistle blower to break that silence was Joop Hueting, who spoke on Dutch television in 1969 about atrocities that he had been involved in. He told familiar tales of combating an enemy that disappeared into communities and landscapes, of kampongs riddled with bullets and horrible tortures, and prisoners shot because they did not have the men to guard them. His smart suit and a haircut that framed his prominent ears made him look like a well-respected town notary, even if his eyes visibly glistened with the weight of his testimony. Afterwards the broadcaster received nearly 900 letters from veterans giving their own perspective on events, many disparaging the blunt version that Joop Hueting recounted.[6]

More specific war crimes also went uninvestigated, including those of Raymond Westerling. He was interviewed on camera in 1969, but Dutch broadcasters declined to use the film until 2012. Only in 2015 did a court in Den Haag find the Netherlands responsible for the war crimes perpetrated in Sulawesi. Westerling kept himself busy during his later life, alternately running a second-hand bookshop, trying to make it as an opera singer and then working as a swimming pool lifeguard in Doorwerth, Gelderland. He died in 1987. A few years later, the deserter Poncke Princen eventually paid the Netherlands a visit, and it finally set off an introspective media storm about how the Dutch should remember the conflict. In 2022 Prime Minister Mark Rutte apologised for Dutch crimes in Indonesia. The government agreed that conscientious objectors (*Indonesië-weigeraars* or Indonesia-refusers) who knew about the excessive violence being used could have their reputations restored.

Sometimes there is a place for forgetting: the abrupt turning away from the grubby end of empire in the 1950s and 1960s did allow the Dutch to reimagine their country as something less than a global empire, and thereby seize the opportunities of post-War Europe.* Although there has since been more scrutiny of those messy final years—indeed the entire three centuries of Global Netherlands—the holiday makers that you see cycling along the byways of Texel do not look especially burdened with post-colonial guilt. The Dutch are not alone in this, even if they have rosier views of their imperial past than other European nations. In 2006 the Prime Minister, Jan Peter Balkenende, called on his fellow politicians to show more of the 'VOC mentality' during the annual budget debate. Those unfortunate souls who were shipped off to fight in the Indies are also now largely forgotten, occasional events like the release of *De Oost* notwithstanding. In our four years living in Delft I never saw a single person pay the slightest attention the town's small monument to the Dutch soldiers killed during the independence war. The monument lists 16 men who lost their lives for this failure, below a military helmet over a crossed sword and jungle greenery, and the words 'Voor orde en vrede' ('For Order and Peace'). The contrast with

---

* See Chapter 10.

the dutiful attention paid to the victims of the Second World War is stark.

While the *binnenstads* of these flat lands are jam packed with physical monuments to the mighty Golden Age, the most striking manifestation of the later empire are people. Many thousands had their lives transformed by the Dutch retreat from imperium to small, dune-rimmed European country, Tilly Kaisiepo among them. They (and over 200,000 Dutch settlers who returned to Dutch shores in the 1950s) were the empire's driftwood. Of all these, the Moluccans have perhaps the most tragic story. Their home had been the constellation of tropical specks between Sulawesi and West Papua that were once the fabled spice islands. After independence many resented the Javanese domination of the new Indonesia, and felt themselves to be different: a disproportionate number of Moluccans had served alongside the Dutch in the KNIL, and many were Christian rather than Muslim. In 1950 a rebel movement declared the independence of the Republic of South Maluku. The rebels promptly suffered defeat against the Indonesian military and withdrew to the mountains on the island of Seram, struggling on until 1963. Three years later, after the capture and execution of their leader, the remaining rebels and their families sought sanctuary in the Netherlands. However the Dutch viewed them as temporary residents and housed them in a scattering of camps. You can see a bucolic looking green and white Molukse Barak full of steel framed bunk beds in the Netherlands Open Air Museum near Arnhem.* Isolation and frustration led some to commit terrorist acts, including attacks on a train and a school. Only in the 1980s did the government make a concerted effort to integrate the Moluccan community,

---

* The building had previously housed members of the far-right NSB and Nazi collaborators.

raising educational standards and tackling high unemployment rates.[*] The Republic of South Maluku still exists in its Dutch exile, and around 3,000 gather for a memorial ceremony every year in the city of Apeldoorn.

For all that Tilly Kaisiepo has spent her life in the shadow of the tragedy of West Papua, I felt that she was one of the lucky ones. She has her flat in Delft's Poptahof, the Moe'stuin garden, her grandchildren and a sense of purpose, however frustrated. She has positivity, a beaming smile and a Dutch life, and that purse in the colours of the West Papuan flag hanging around her neck.

* * *

A wide, sandy path led past a bicycle parking lot through a gap in the dunes to the open expanse of the beach itself. There was a beach bar, facing the waves like a fortress with its protected decking, fire bowls and familiar menu of crunchy bar snacks. A row of dinky little coloured huts stretched off on either side, before thinning out and ceding control to the blown sand. Groynes ploughed headlong into the water, battling with the forces of nature but only ever aiming to slow, not stop, long-shore drift. I could see an echo of the tentative patterns of Dutch colonisation on the wild beaches of Texel, edging its civilising mission into expanses of territory, corralling and controlling, in the hope of holding back space and nature.

A clutch of naked 60-year-olds dipped into the surf, defiant but alert to the power of the currents that worked along these coastal borderlands. Clouds of gulls squawked warily as I walked past them, those closest to me rising into the air before settling

---

* The most famous son of the Moluccan community is the footballer Giovanni van Bronckhorst.

where they felt safe. A fishing boat chugged determinedly a couple of hundred metres offshore. Up in the dunes my map marked a concrete bunker that would have made an interesting diversion if I had had the time. It looked like a modernist concrete art gallery, an immense chunk of Nazi determination to defend what they had stolen.

During the early 1940s this coast was once again a frontier, with the unsinkable British aircraft carrier lurking just out of sight over the horizon. An invasion here was improbable, but it lay on the routes that legions of Allied bombers took from their bases in eastern England to lay waste to the cities of the Third Reich. Many of those Lancasters, B17s and Halifaxes never made it past the anti-aircraft flak batteries of Texel, and the quiet cemetery in Den Burgh is now filled with row after row of graves for those young airmen.

One of the most peculiar stories from those dark years was the Texel uprising. The Nazi garrison on the island included many Georgians, who had fought in the Red Army before being captured and given the choice of starvation or a new beginning in German field-grey uniforms. As the War reached its bitter end deep inside continental Europe, the Georgians staged an uprising, knowing that inaction would only result in deportation back to a vengeful Stalin. They coordinated their rebellion, murdering their former German comrades in their beds, then holding off the inevitable reprisals. Some were sheltered by Dutch civilians, who once again paid a high price for their resistance to the Nazis. More than a hundred local residents died, along with nearly 600 Georgians and over 800 Germans. The Georgians that survived were repatriated to the Soviet Union, but despite their years in German uniform they were ultimately considered by the authorities to have led a heroic insurgency against the Nazis. Texel itself was one of the last parts of Europe to be liberated.

My route took me around the southern edge of Texel, an ethereally pale, shifting lunar landscape facing the straights where those VOC fleets gathered before heading off to the ends of the earth. I tacked inland past the dunes and lakes of a protected nature reserve. I saw spoonbills overhead and oyster catchers digging around in shallow waters. A scattering of day trippers were gathered at the ferry terminal, waiting for the next Den Helder sailing in the September sunshine. I bought an ice cream, peeled off my boots and socks, and looked at the sun flecking off the dark waters where the Dutch empire began.

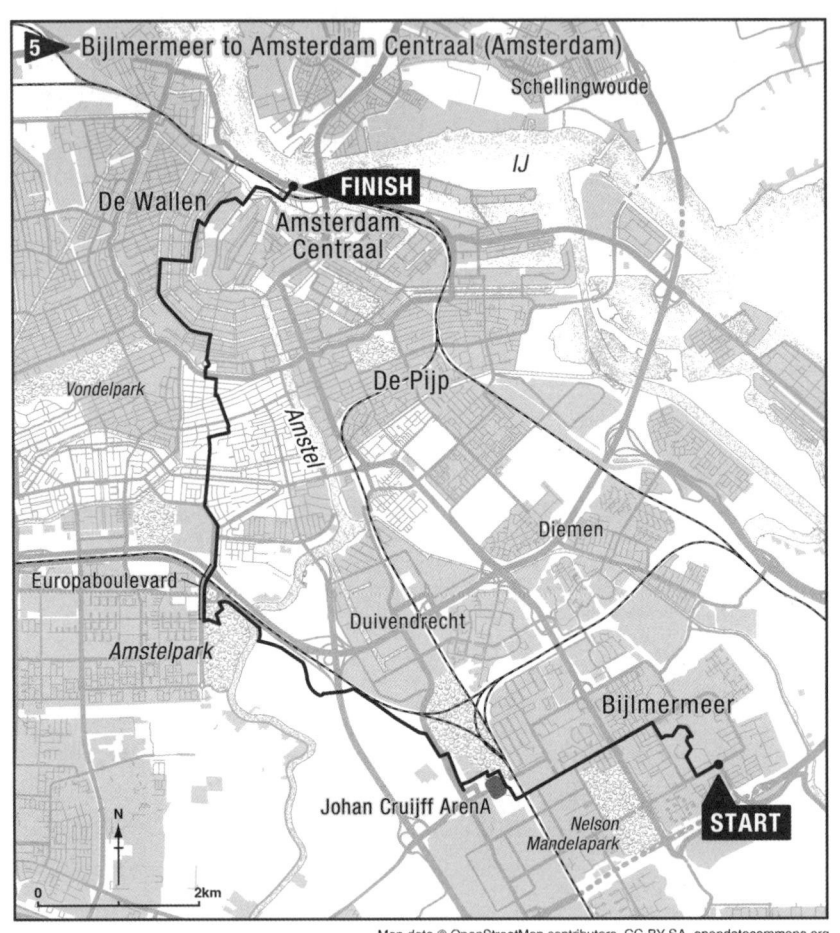

Schellingwoude

De Wallen

FINISH

Amsterdam
Centraal

IJ

Vondelpark

De-Pijp

Amstel

Diemen

Europaboulevard

Duivendrecht

Amstelpark

Bijlmermeer

N

Johan Cruijff ArenA

*Nelson
Mandelapark*

START

0   2km

5

BIJLMERMEER TO AMSTERDAM CENTRAAL
(AMSTERDAM)

This walk begins in the Bijlmermeer estate in the southeast suburbs of Amsterdam, easily reachable by Metro (Kraaiennest station on Line 53). Make note of the way the giant monumental tower blocks jig and jag around the trees and ornamental lake, visit the Papa Sem bridge, then head for the northwest corner of the estate. Turn left on the Bijlmerdreef road until you hit the rail tracks, then follow directions for the imposing Johan Cruijff ArenA. Loop around to the north, turn west then north along the edge of the Holterbergweg. Just before a motorway flyover turn left on to a lane called the Buitensingel, heading west. You will need to peel off on to a bridge over the motorway, continuing in the same general direction through a deceptively rural landscape. You will cross the Amstel river next to the motorway, and be able to pop into the pretty Amstelpark. On the other side of the park is the Europaboulevard, which you will follow due north into the centre. I took a few side streets through the De Pijp suburb and the Sarphatipark, but assuming you continue north you will eventually meet the old centre of Amsterdam near the

Rijksmuseum. From there I picked my way along interesting looking canals before entering the Wallen and heading for the crowds milling around Amsterdam's central station.

* * *

It was dusk on 4 October 1992. El Al flight 1862 was on a short, routine stopover at Schiphol airport, on an overnight cargo run from New York to Tel Aviv. The Boeing 747's engines roared, it picked up speed as it blasted along the runway, then lifted off to the north before making a sweeping eastward turn, as graceful and steady as a giant turtle. Flight 1862 looped around the northern edge of the city of Amsterdam, and was over the town of Muiderberg when disaster struck.

The mechanical failure that led to ruin was in a single fuse pin on the number three engine pylon. This connects the inner starboard engine to the wing. It sheared off, transferring a sudden extra load on to the other fuse pins, which stressed and failed instantaneously. But instead of falling away from the wing as it was designed to do in an emergency, the engine thrust forwards for a split second before falling back and smashing off the number four engine, further out on the 747's gigantic wing. Both engines tumbled down into the waters of the Gooimeer. The leading edge of the wing had become a ragged mess of burst hydraulic lines and destroyed leading flaps. The plane immediately yawed to the right and the fire alarm went off.

There was a massive overload of information in the cockpit, as the crew struggled to work out what was going on and what they needed to do. Captain Yitzhak Fuchs fought to keep control of the plane as it flew over densely packed suburbs and small towns, completely unaware that they had entirely lost both engines on his starboard wing. The first officer, Arnon Ohad, immediately contacted air traffic control and told them there was an emergency. The controller gave them a heading to Schiphol's runway 27, and scrambled the emergency services. Flight 1862 was too high and going too fast to land, so the controller routed Captain Fuchs on a gigantic loop over Amsterdam to allow them to lose height before he lined up correctly for touchdown.

As the plane continued its rightward turn it also began to lose speed, but that in turn caused the damaged right wing to produce even less lift. This made it dip further into a roll. Then the roll became a sharp bank as aerodynamics overpowered the pilots, forcing it into a brutal downward spiral. Arnon Ohad called out one final message into his microphone. 'Going down, 1862, going down, going down.'[1] The controllers in the tower at Schiphol could see the explosion over the east of the city of Amsterdam, the smoke and the flames in an area they knew to be full of houses and people. 'It's useless Henk, he's crashed,' said one controller to a colleague. 'One big cloud of smoke over the city.'

I remembered seeing the horrific footage of the El Al flight 1862 crash site on the TV news. The 747 had come down in the middle of several blocks of high-rise flats. I remember pools of fire burning in the night, the deathly gap where the plane had wiped out an unimaginable chunk of the buildings, the lights still on in tenth-floor apartments just inches away from the impact site. One eyewitness, Saul Rootenberg, who lived on the tenth floor of the neighbouring Gooioord building, remembered the entire building starting to shake just before the impact. 'We saw the plane flying lower and lower and dived to the ground when we saw it coming towards us. The whole sky turned red.'[2]

It is the location that makes the tragedy of flight 1862 so important for this chapter. When the emergency services arrived at the crash site they found far fewer casualties than might be expected after an ill-fated flying monster, brimming with aviation fuel, had crashed into residential apartment blocks. Many residents were outside, enjoying the unseasonably warm evening. But many other survivors had apparently fled rather than wait for treatment. Even working out who had lived—and died— inside the apartment blocks was to prove unsettlingly difficult, and the death toll of 47 people may easily be an underestimate.* The crash had taken out sections of the Klein-Kruitburg and Groeneveen apartment blocks in a place called Bijlmermeer. It was a nether region more than an Amsterdam suburb.

Bijlmermeer had originally been conceived as something of a modernist utopia. The blocks were distinctive, floor upon floor of concrete shaped into a broken honeycomb of gigantic walls that would tower over parks and pedestrian-only zones. It was carefully planned to be self-contained and self-sustaining, but when it opened to residents in the 1970s any self-sufficiency was forced upon it by isolation. It lay stubbornly out of reach of the metro line, and a single unpaved road was its only link to the city. The communal gardens were still bare mud, and there were few shops or services. Those who had signed up for apartments in the honeycombed garden paradise quickly realised their mistake, and simply cancelled their reservations. In doing so they cancelled Bijlmermeer's future. It became a ghetto, a dumping ground for those on the margins of traditional Dutch society, along with new arrivals from Surinam and immigrants from across the developing world. † Many had ended up there

---

* Many residents in Bijlmermeer complained of mysterious illnesses for years afterwards. This was variously blamed on: a chemical used in nerve gas testing, which was in the plane's cargo; depleted uranium used as ballast in the plane's tail; or simply the clouds of toxic dust and chemicals thrown up by the explosion from the plane and the building.

† After Surinam gained independence in 1975, those born there were given five years to secure Dutch nationality, but several hundred did not do this and spent the next decades undocumented, without official rights to work, travel

after landlords had bluntly refused them rentals in more established communities.

By the time Flight 1862 slammed into the housing estate, Bijlmermeer was falling apart both socially and literally. The *Leeuwarder Courant* had described it as 'a place without God or commandment. A grimy corner of the colourful Netherlands, a wild garden of a multiracial society in the making.'[3] Squatters and drug dealers moved in to unused, dank apartments, and many of the residents were undocumented. Bijlmermeer was a forsaken place, off the radar of the modern Dutch state.

The walk in this chapter starts off at the crash site. It connects the collapse of the country's centuries-old empire with the enduring issues of post-War rebuilding, emigration, and Amsterdam's fractious relationship with the outside world. Amsterdam has been the focal point of the Netherlands' projection into the wider world, but as Bijlmermeer suggests, the city has struggled in more recent times as the outside world has come to it.

After Bijlmermeer the walk heads across Amsterdam suburbia to the riot of geometric shapes that is Ajax Amsterdam's stadium. Then a confusing bit of semi-bucolic polder and a park that boasts a miniature train, to the Europaboulevard. The second half of the walk begins there, through smart and leafy streets where some of the luckiest Dutch citizens live, either enjoying sky-rocketing house prices as owners or long-term sub-market rate rents as tenants. This highlights a different challenge now faced by Amsterdam, the absolute pinnacle of the Netherland's housing crisis. The walk ends in central Amsterdam, home to seventeenth-century glories, mass tourism and sleazy sex shops. Arguably, this coming together

---

abroad or obtain health cover. The Dutch government moved to resolve the situation in 2024.

of red light grubbiness, over-tourism and a housing crisis is the real legacy of the post-War liberal utopianism that Amsterdam still takes pride in embodying. The price of this is not paid equally by everybody.

* * *

The Bijlmermeer of today may not be perfect, but it has little of the benighted desperation that it suffered from in those early years. Lawns and trees are established in the parks, there are solar arrays on the roofs, and communities have taken root. Old men gather in the sun, arguing noisily like a colony of seabirds before nodding in contented agreement. Pushchairs are pushed and toddlers toddle. An occasional dreadlocked cyclist teeters by on something that is now more thumping sound system than bicycle. There is even the gold standard of Dutch respectability, an Albert Heijn supermarket, tucked in near the Kraaiennest Metro stop.

The site of the crash, where the Groeneveen apartment block had once stood, is now marked by a simple concrete bridge that is named after an astonishingly brave man. Pa Sem was one of 19 children, born as Willem Jacob Symor in Surinam on a former wood plantation. By 1992 he had made it to the Netherlands, and like many of his compatriots he was scrabbling to make a living in Bijlmermeer. In Pa Sem's case he mixed his daily struggles with a quietly determined effort to make the world a better place for his neighbours. He took advantage of some empty space in the Groeneveen block to run *Het Groentje*, a communal space that was available for social events like children's parties.* Immediately after the crash he fled the building. A girl ran up to him and screamed that her brother, a ten-year-old

---

* Pa Sem later returned to Paramaribo in Surinam and died in 2008.

Fig. 1: The *Markt* in Delft, the beautiful town that my family called home for four happy years.

Fig. 2: Front row seats at the Fierljeppen world championships in Friesland.

Fig. 3: The journalist and historian Geert Mak.

Fig. 4: Walking across a marvel of Dutch water engineering, the Oosterscheldekering.

Fig. 5: 'A Roman triumph of dahlias and carrots': the waterborne parade of Westland's agricultural might.

Fig. 6: Dancing cows as spectator sport: cows on a polder near Delft after being allowed out of their winter barn.

Fig. 7: Tilly Kaisiepo, keeping her memories of West Papua alive at her Moe'stuin garden in Delft.

Fig. 8: A fading memorial to Pa Sem, who demonstrated staggering bravery after El Al flight 1862 crashed into Amsterdam's Bijlmermeer estate.

Fig. 9: A single mundane example of the dozens of Dutch–Belgian borders that cut across streets, gardens and houses in Baarle-Nassau.

Fig. 10: Nijmegen's railway bridge across the Waal, one of the large rivers that flow through the middle of this flat country.

Fig. 11: Skating and sledging on a frozen canal on our old street, Vlamingstraat, in Delft.

Fig. 12: The Dutch doing things their own way: a boatload of
blacked-up Zwarte Piets accompanies Sinterklaas
through Delft.

Fig. 13: An unsettling *Berenkuil* sculpture in Maastricht's
Aldenhof Park.

Fig. 14: 'Crashed flying saucers that bristle with heavy-calibre guns': Fort Ében-Émael, just across the border in Belgium.

Fig. 15: Madurodam, a miniaturised version of the Netherlands, complete with soaring cathedrals, humdrum housing estates and sewage treatment plants.

called Reinaldo, was still inside. He returned to save the boy from the inferno, a blazing cave where flames roared up the walls and ceilings rained fiery hell down from above. A burning pipe fell on Reinaldo's head, which Pa Sem grabbed. It melted to his hand, and although he was able to get the boy through the door and safety, he only managed to squeeze through the door by twisting the pipe over his head, his clothes now also on fire. Reinaldo survived, but Pa Sem suffered third degree burns and was unconscious for weeks afterwards. A photo of him in *De Telegraaf* later that year has him in a beautifully patterned shirt, his head, face and hands covered in the deep and painful scars that he would carry for the rest of his life. The article is titled 'Pa Sem's wonderbaarlijke wederopstanding', or 'Pa Sem's miraculous resurrection'.[4] Think of the Pa Sembrug, a monument to a hero, as the start of your walk.

Bijlmermeer is just one of a patchwork of building projects and new developments in Amsterdam's south eastern corner. It is a land of prim and angular suburban housing solutions, from the dense pre-War apartment blocks of Zeeburg to the Minecraft landscape of Betondorp. Each grouping is tucked between a scattering of sports clubs and cemeteries, motorway flyovers and light industrial estates. It is prime Dutch suburbia, each chunk zoned and designed for optimal Dutch suburban life, the opening up of virgin territory to house a swelling population.

This is where you will also find the Johan Cruyff Arena,* the spanking new stadium where Ajax Amsterdam now play their football. Inside it has its impressive stands surrounded by the inevitable hospitality suites and enhanced revenue streams, the very model of a modern sporting arena. Outside it manages to sidestep the kind of strip-mall anonymity that is the fate of other stadia. Instead, pictures of the football icon the place is

---

* Officially the Johan Cruijff ArenA.

named after are complemented by a weird and seemingly random assortment of geometric concrete struts and supports. I liked it.

Not long after the stadium my walk ran alongside a couple of *volkstuinen*. These are self-contained clusters of cute little summerhouses, each with their own little garden and vegetable plot, lined up in rows on miniature canals like a suburban Dutch Hobbiton.* They are designed as an escape for town-dwellers, who can feed their own compost heaps and eat cheese toasties as they watch their carrots grow. They change hands (occasionally) for fairly nominal amounts of money. We tried to snare a *volkstuin* property when we lived in Delft, but the waiting lists proved too long. This was probably a blessing in disguise, as we were wary of upsetting the social order by neglecting to cut the grass neatly enough or failing to polish our windows.

My walk then took me past some cows, across the Amstel, near the miniature train in the Amstelpark, and on to the Europaboulevard. Throughout the walk there was a constant flow of cyclists in every direction, some in office suits and some in overalls, others on the way to lectures or hockey clubs. Toddlers busied themselves chasing the Amstelpark's ducks and pigeons, while their mothers chased the toddlers. Businessmen sat on benches pondering life and spreadsheets as they munched home-packed cheese sandwiches. The Europaboulevard itself seemed like a standard enough suburban multi-lane street. It was lined with trees and parked cars, offices and apartment blocks, and had a sense of purpose, like an artery of medium importance in a person's body. If some of the city's planners get their way the Europaboulevard will develop an even stronger sense of purpose in future years: this is the supposed location of a spanking new

---

* They are not just a Dutch thing. I have seen similar on the outskirts of cities across Europe, such as Warsaw and Vienna.

super sex megastore, plonked here in an attempt to excise some of the seediness that is plaguing this remarkable world city.

The last stretch of the walk, plunging right into the historical heart of Amsterdam, is a reminder of how magnificent the city can be. Physically it is like nothing else on earth, instantly recognisable with its canals and the whiff of a Golden Age when the Netherlands bestrode the world. But the whiff of grubbiness is never far away. You will catch it in your nose on a street corner, a mixture of cannabis and over-used cooking oil, stale Heineken and street corner rubbish that seems to be taking ever longer to collect. You will see the neon signs, the shops selling thousands of different types of tat, the posters advertising behind-the-scenes tours of lap dancing venues. There are the morose sex workers displaying their wares in windows, the stag parties enjoying a breakfast beer and the hen parties giggling away as they wave giant inflatable penises in the air. More prosaically you will just see lots and lots and lots of people: squidgy-thighed cruise tourists, streetwise kids on their fat-bikes, drug ravaged cadavers with hollow faces and pretty young women from across the globe festooned with tattoos like Scout badges. Golden Age Amsterdam built its glories by facing outwards, but now the outside world is all over Amsterdam, and the city is trying to calibrate a suitable response.

The racier parts of Amsterdam's centre were not always quite so seamy. The sex industry could look back on its own golden age in the last decades of the twentieth century, when the excitement of sexual liberation and red-blooded fun seemed to crowd out concerns about misery and seediness. The man who represented this red-lit golden age had a shock of tousled ice-blonde hair, a determined and forceful expression and a heavy jaw. It was a face built for survival in a tough business, and the man's name was Jan Otten. For decades he had been the face of Amsterdam's sex industry, and became known as the 'King of the Wallen', the world-renowned red light district. He was most associated with a strip club called 'Casa Rosso', which sported a logo of a kitsch pink elephant wearing a black tie. Back in the 1980s he had been a bouncer at Casa Rosso, but by 1997 he owned it. (I do not know the details of how this success came about, but I presume they would make for a remarkable MBA thesis.) Other venues followed: Bananenbar, Hospitalbar, Erotisch Museum, Sexy Loo, Theater 97 and Sex Palace Peepshow. His empire survived scandal and a deadly fire, the Covid pandemic and investigators linking him to unsavoury characters from the underworld. Even as an 82-year-old he still worked in the ticket office of Casa Rosso, charging €65 for an entrance ticket that included a complimentary drink.

When Jan Otten died his white coffin was paraded in front of sex workers twirling bright red umbrellas as a sign of respect. Ice cream was handed out, and old timers wondered whether the red-light district as they knew it would survive his demise, the internet and an increasingly concerted effort to clean up the city.

That is why Europaboulevard, at the centre of an unremarkable grid of streets and toy block apartments, is designated as the site of a mega brothel. Instead of the 100 red light windows of De Wallen it would house several floors of professionally administered lubricated fun. Plans for the mega brothel periodically bounce around the Dutch media, pondering the best measures for projected traffic movements and parking. Some arrangements would be unique to customers of sex centres: in Utrecht, the red-light district used to be a row of small boats, and the road that passed by had a small roundabout at each end to allow punters to drive back and forth, making a window-shopping assessment of the services on offer. The authorities say the shift from De Wallen would help reduce links to criminality and trafficking.

Their plan to pressurise existing sites to close includes enforced property buy-outs and changes to the law. Sex workers are not entirely convinced by the plans. Some call the proposed mega brothel an 'erotic prison', and worry about practical concerns such as changes to their commutes.

On the one hand this is obviously the work of the Dutch technocratic state, the tall men in dark suits who strive heroically to spatially align every square metre of the Netherlands with the optimal setting. But it is also a recognition that something has gone wrong with the way the city now works. More fundamentally, something has gone wrong with the excess of tolerance that has led to an engorged sex industry and druggy overspills in a city that all too frequently has attracted the wrong type of tourist. Amsterdam does not deserve this.

Back in the first chapter on Flevoland, Emmeloord and Urk I wrote about how the 1960s and 1970s wrenched Amsterdam into modernity. By the 1980s the course was set and the city ploughed on with an unapologetic progressivism. The roots of the permissiveness lie in the fundamental Dutch tradition of *verdraagzaamheid*, or tolerance towards different attitudes and beliefs.

Verdraagzaamheid has many roots, but the hundreds of years of broad consensus-based policymaking, the *poldermodel*, is at the centre of it. All sections of society tolerated each other in the name of communal action to keep feet dry. People were pragmatic and largely respectful of local compromises. This was buttressed by Calvinism, which encouraged a remarkably literate people to interpret the Bible in their own way and stand up for their opinion. Diversity was good, and new arrivals from Flanders, England and the Iberian Peninsula were seen as an additional source of strength. Added to this was a pragmatism that above all respected the art of the deal, recognising that it was better to do business with somebody you did not necessarily respect than lose the deal itself.* Communities tolerated each other, rubbed along and made compromises that were beneficial and eventually as easy to swallow as a *Hollandse Nieuwe* herring speckled with chopped onion.†

In the post-War period of strong economic growth, a welfare state was established that sought to move the country decisively away from the privations of the Nazi occupation. Fuelled by a radical 1960s-tinged progressivism and an excess of *verdraagzaamheid*, this welfare state mutated from supportive to overly generous. There were lots of ways of life and who was anybody else to say no if it did not directly harm anybody else, and there was money to fund it?

The government responded to Amsterdam's militant and increasingly organised squatter (*kraker*) movement by buying the buildings they had moved into, renovating them and giving them to the new residents at very low rents. Disability and unemployment payments were increased in the name of solidarity with and compassion for those unable or unwilling to work. The Beeldende Kunstenaars Regeling (Artist Subsidy Scheme) from 1949 even encouraged artists by buying their work if nobody else did. Artists submitted works and if they were not in the lucky 80% that were accepted, they could try again one more time. The fortunate artists would receive a fifth of the cash straight away, and the rest paid over several months. Because the BKR had no fixed amount in the national budget it was difficult to regulate eligibility, and costs were essentially impossible to control. The

---

* A more modern example of this was when the basketball star Michael Jordan was asked about endorsing a Democratic Party candidate. His response was very Dutch: 'Republicans buy sneakers too'.

† A salted North Sea herring that is lowered into the mouth and slid down the throat. It is a delicacy.

whole ludicrous scheme lasted until 1987, by which time more than half a million works of art had been collected.*

This generosity started to cause serious financial problems. Because Dutch tolerance implied that it was perfectly reasonable to choose any life that did not explicitly hurt others, some chose a self-indulgent path that leaned heavily on generous welfare but without the imposition of having to work. This started to impact the country's ability to function as a modern society. By the mid-1980s, Prime Minister Ruud Lubbers, leader of the centrist Christian Democrat Party, noted that the Netherlands was losing its balance, with 'too many people outside the system of production'.[5] The assumption that all of Dutch society was fundamentally thrifty and hard-working, underpinned by Calvinist virtues, no longer held.

The situation was exacerbated by liberal drug policies and *gedoogbeleid*, where certain laws are not enforced. Amsterdam's reputation as a place where you could head off to the nearest cafe and smoke a joint started to attract tourists who cared little for Rembrandt or exploring the history of the VOC. Hard drugs such as heroin and cocaine were even more of a concern, and the authorities tried to concentrate dealing on one particular street, the Zeedijk. By 1985, however, it became clear that this policy was not effective. Although there was a crackdown on dealing on the Zeedijk, the hard drugs problem just filtered out to other areas. One of those areas was the new housing estates of Bijlmermeer,

---

* Many of the collected art works were given to collections and institutions, although some were eventually simply returned to the artists themselves. Forty-eight thousand were sold to the Stichting Beeldende Kunst for a symbolic one guilder, which planned to gradually put them back on the open market. For more details go to https://bulletin.rkd.nl/en/2021-2/monument-artist-subsidy-scheme-history-controversial-artist-scheme-1949-1987/.

where many addicts were new citizens of Surinamese origin, alienated and struggling to adapt.[*]

The culture of tolerance and liberalism started to leach into other areas of Dutch life, with results both good and bad. In 1977 the first of a series of communes called Centraal Wonen (CW) was established, following a challenge from Lies van den Donk-Dooremaal, a teacher and mother of four. She wanted architects to come up with ideas to help women combine professional and home lives. The Centraal Wonen answer was to combine communal facilities such as kitchens and bathrooms with private quarters. Each of the 70 CWs still flourishing around the Netherlands is subdivided into clusters, for instance for those who like to party, or those burdened with work commitments.

In 2002 the Netherlands became the first country to legalise euthanasia, after a woman was prosecuted after giving her severely disabled mother 200mg of morphine. By 2023 there were more than 9,000 reported cases of euthanasia, and although the majority were for incurable cancer, 138 were for psychiatric reasons. Two-thirds of euthanasia cases concerned people over 70, and 40 involved people aged below 30.[6] This latter group provided a stream of feature photo stories for foreign newspapers. In April 2024 Jolanda Fun told *The Times* that most of the time she just felt really shitty, and sent out funeral invitations that said, 'After a hard fought life, she chose the peace she so longed for'.[7] She died on her 34th birthday. Within a month journalists were interviewing another photogenic young woman awaiting euthanasia, 29-year-old Zoraya ter Beek.[8] Half a year later they had the story of Romy, a 22-year-old woman who changed her mind about dying just as the doctor was about to put a syringe in her arm.

---

[*] Surinam became independent in 1975 and around half the population took Dutch citizenship.

Defining and refining the euthanasia law in the Netherlands is an ongoing process. In early 2024 several campaigners from the 'Last Will Cooperative' appeared in court charged with encouraging people to take a 'suicide powder'. Prosecutors alleged that they were part of a criminal enterprise, as manufacturing the powder is a complicated business. One defendant, named as Jos S, told the court, 'I've never been involved in setting up a criminal network. It feels like I have been caught up in a bad play.'*

One piece of Dutch ingenuity aimed at the euthanasia sector is a 'suicide capsule' that looks like the streamlined hi-tech cockpit of a solar-powered airplane. There is a large, curved window so that when somebody climbs inside they can see what is going on outside. They then press a button, the capsule fills with nitrogen, and the person slips off into a dreamless sleep as though in an airliner that has depressurised at high altitude. (Remember that the Dutch word for nitrogen, *stikstof*, comes from the words for 'suffocation' and 'stuff'.) The capsule was first used in Switzerland in late 2024, and a watching Dutch journalist was temporarily put into custody.

When the Dutch willingness to explore permissiveness combines with its technocratic instincts the results can be very positive. The Dutch prison system is often held up as a model for its effectiveness, its humanity and its good sense. In the ten years up to 2015 the country's prison population was cut by nearly half. Many criminals found themselves being supervised in the community rather than in jail. This brought large financial savings (community supervision costs around a tenth compared to imprisonment) and reoffending rates are often lower. The liberal regime within prisons is constantly being recalibrated, for

---

* Two of the six who appeared in court were convicted of participating in a criminal organisation with the aim of assisting suicide, after collaborating with a further defendant who was convicted in 2023. Four were acquitted.

instance in 2024 the junior justice minister Ingrid Coenradie announced that there would be a crackdown on what prisoners were allowed to wear. Certain brands would be banned and there would be a cap on how much items of clothing could cost. (She ruled out the introduction of prison uniforms, saying that prisoners were better behaved when they were allowed to express themselves more freely.) There is a similar openness to solutions for elderly care. One scheme provides free rent to university students who commit to spending 30 hours a month socialising with their older neighbours and teaching them skills such as using email.

Beyond attracting the wrong sort of tourist, part of the challenge facing Amsterdam is simply that its small centre is overwhelmed by tourists of all descriptions. In 2023 Amsterdam had 10.1 visitor arrivals per resident, comfortably at the top of a list of 20 cities drawn up by the *Economist* (Paris was second with 8.0).[9] In 2024 a group of well-known Amsterdammers wrote an open letter to *Het Parool* naming the sheer amount of rubbish associated with the tourist influx as their ongoing greatest annoyance. 'We live in Amsterdam on a garbage dump', they wrote, complaining about the plague of rats and seagulls that feasted on the trash. (Earlier that year a group of scientists had taken a very liberal Amsterdam line and urged residents simply to live alongside rats in harmony rather than condemn them.)

Calibrating policies to deal with the over-tourism challenge is difficult, not least because it brings in an enormous amount of money: the same *Economist* table that said Amsterdam received many more visits per resident also noted that it received much more tourist spending per resident ($11,200 in 2023, compared to $9,200 for Paris in second place). The challenge for Amsterdam is to encourage the right type of free-spending cultured tourist while deterring those whose to-do list is more focused on red-light tours than Rembrandt's *Night Watch*. Surcharges on tickets to the Rijksmuseum, for instance, would penalise the type of tourist the city would prefer to have, and few hen parties would be inconvenienced. One possible avenue would be to tax recognisable elements of the party industry: sex, drugs, alcohol and giant inflatable penises, with rebates available for citizens.* There is an 'Amsterdam Rules' website, which is aimed at guiding visitors towards more wholesome stays.[10] If you click answers suggesting that you would prefer cocaine to *poffertjes*, or pub crawls rather than something connected to Van Gogh, it raps you over the knuckles and issues a stern warning. Other micro-measures struggle to get traction: a plan to halve the number of river cruises was strongly opposed by luxury hotels, and a limit on the numbers queueing for French fries at a TikTok famous *friet stall* was overturned.

Restrictions on short term lets through platforms like Airbnb, and plans to ban the building of new hotels, hint at another concern. Very simply, the centre of Amsterdam has been hollowed out into something of a theme park for seventeenth-century glories and twenty-first-century grubbiness. Its Golden Age heritage risks being reduced to set dressing for bar crawls, trinket shops and high-speed tourism. Meanwhile Amsterdam is unsustainable as a city where modest incomes can support families. The most authentic expression of its famed bohemian edge is in fact just outside the city centre, in the dense streets of apartments that you will have passed after leaving the Europaboulevard. These streets are where Amsterdam feels at its most vibrant, a place where those who can afford it live in spruce little apartments, meet for *borreltjes* with their best friends

---

* This is from a suggestion by the economist Tyler Cowen, although he did not mention the inflatable plastic penises.

and discuss their rash of new tattoos. It is the type of place that makes me feel deeply uncool.

Ironically, the residue of the hyper-progressive politics that continues to hang in the Amsterdam air may be exacerbating the trials of the entire Dutch housing market. The Netherlands has the highest proportion of rent-controlled homes in Europe, a progressive measure aimed at keeping rental prices affordable for a presumed class of worthy strivers with moderate incomes. In 2024 the Affordable Rent Act moved a further 300,000 rental properties into the regulated market, meaning that 96% of the country's 3 million rental homes are now subject to price controls. Two and a half million homes have their rent capped at €880 a month if the household earns less than €52,671. The other half million has rent capped at €1,158 a month. Short-term leases have also been banned in favour of open-ended leases that in effect put the renter in full control of a property once they are in and the door is shut firmly behind them.

The impact of such policies is not what the high-minded architects of rent controls had in mind. With the threat of open-ended leases hanging over their heads, many landlords have targeted foreign tenants rather than local ones, presuming that their stays will be time-limited, affording them some sense of control over their properties. Klaas Knot, the Dutch central bank president, told the International Monetary Fund in late 2024 that the number of available private sector rental properties had fallen 38% from the same time the year before. Klaas Knot said there was a particular shortage of mid-range properties in new construction projects, the properties that he said were necessary for mobility among renters. Speaking of the Affordable Rent Act legislation, he noted that it was 'better to turn back halfway than to go astray completely'.[11]

One underlying problem is that the Netherlands has consistently failed to build enough new properties to keep up with demand in an expanding population. While it ought to have been adding 100,000 a year, on average over the last decade it has built around two-thirds of this target. In 2024 the country was short of 401,000 homes, compared to 390,000 in 2023.[12] The results have been predictable, with landlords fleeing the market and enormous shortages of properties for those who have not already got their foot in the (rented) door. In December 2024 it was reported that 450 candidates were chasing the average mid-price rental property in Amsterdam.[13] Those cool young families chatting to neighbours on the streets of De Pijp or heading to the Sarphatipark with a picnic are unquestionably the lucky ones.

The sales market is now running red hot, with demand far outstripping supply. Those not already on the housing ladder have nowhere to turn. On 2024 figures, buyers without an existing property to leverage would need an income of over €95,000 (twice the median Dutch income) in order to afford the average home. Tax breaks for homeowners add to the benefits enjoyed by the fortunate. As I write this in September 2024 Dutch residential prices have just hit a new high, averaging €466,000 per property (up more than 11% year on year). It is hard to reach any other conclusion than that the system has been built around the material situation and interests of an older and more fortunate generation with cast iron claims to progressive moral rectitude.

* * *

Despite the grubbiness and the incessant crowds, Amsterdam as an arrangement of bricks and bridges, space and water, is still quite glorious. This was the beating heart of the Great Small Nation that had triumphed imperially and artistically in the seventeenth century, where tall, thin houses towered over canals filled with carved houseboats. You could see the best of

Rembrandt and Van Gogh, break an ankle on an authentically steep staircase and feel English shame as you gaze at the carving from the stern of the *Royal Charles*, captured by the Dutch in their 1667 raid on the Medway.

The combination of teetering brick houses that frame busy lanes and canals is like nowhere else on earth. Mini versions can be found in places like Delft, Gouda and Haarlem, and grand takes on a similar theme exist in Bruges. But Amsterdam is unmistakable, eerily familiar and quite distinctive, laced through with a bohemian edge that owes much to recent history. As lovely as the buildings are, it is the houseboats that you see as you walk along Amsterdam's grand canals that give the city its edge. They have a bohemian quality to them, and you will catch glimpses of the details that make up their owners' lives: the wheelhouse with a windchime and a captain's chair perfect for reading a newspaper; the cat and dog bowls, carefully lined up in order of the beasts' size; the child's windmill toy catching the breeze where it stands in a plant pot

All the measures to curtail the excesses of over-tourism and rethink the fundamentals of Amsterdam's sex industry give me the sense that it is fast reaching a new phase of its life as one of the world's great cities. At its heart this includes a generational shift among younger and less secure Amsterdammers who have not benefited so grandly from its recent boom. This extends to the progressive attitudes that underpinned its most recent flush of growth. 'Youth Health Monitor' research in the city suggests decreasing tolerance of different sexualities among the young.[14] In 2023 fewer than half of high school students in Amsterdam considered it normal for two people of the same gender to be in love, with the figure as low as 32% for boys. Maybe the authorities will succeed in reading the room and reclaim the city from the excesses rooted in over-enthusiastic permissiveness.

The announcement that Amsterdam's authorities have launched a scheme cracking down on the number of plant pots placed outside apartments does not suggest they have yet calibrated their response quite right.

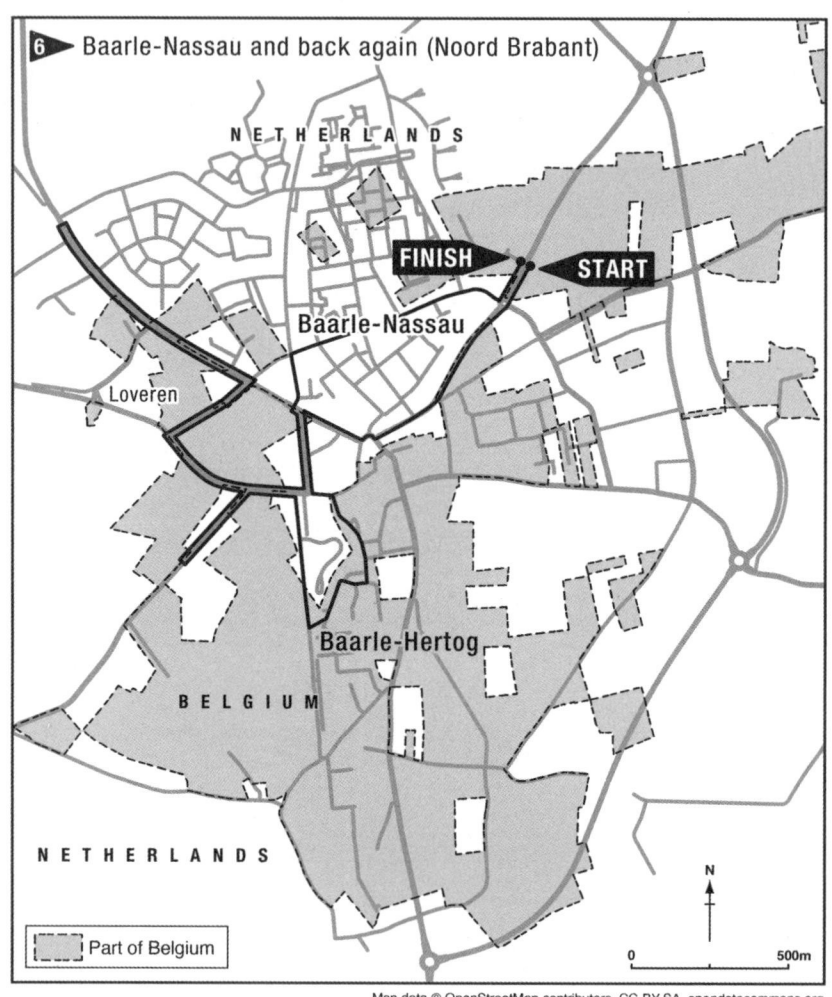

6 ► Baarle-Nassau and back again (Noord Brabant)

N E T H E R L A N D S

FINISH   START

Baarle-Nassau

Loveren

Baarle-Hertog

B E L G I U M

N E T H E R L A N D S

N

Part of Belgium

0   500m

6

BAARLE-NASSAU AND BACK AGAIN
(NOORD BRABANT AND BITS OF BELGIUM)

There is no defined route for this walk, which ends up being a meander through the confused borderlands of Baarle-Nassau and Baarle-Hertog. My own track involved parking to the north of the town(s), heading in and heading down whichever road, street or path took my fancy. I crossed multiple Netherlands/Belgium borders on the way, passed flags on civic buildings from both countries, and tried to make sense of it all.

* * *

Vlaardingen is not a place to catch the eye. It sits just to the west of Rotterdam, at the confluence of the Nieuwe Maas and the Oude Maas. Its river front is a mess of storage tanks, tangled pipes and wharfs that reach out over grey waters. We once bought a wood-burning stove from a shop on its outskirts, and in the incessant rain that afternoon it looked bleak and forlorn. Through its long and notable history Vlaardingen has had some difficult times; in 1163 it was hit hard by the Saint Thomas flood, and in 1574 it was burned down by 'water beggars' to prevent its capture by Spanish soldiers.* But now this small and slightly unprepossessing city is best known for an ongoing series of baffling attacks against an unfortunate plumber called Ron van Uffelen.†

The attacks started in 2023, targeting vehicles, commercial premises and even the home of the man now known nationally as 'the plumber from Vlaardingen'. They were mainly firebomb attacks, often using powerful fireworks. They became so frequent that van Uffelen's family was forced into hiding. In March 2024 the mayor, Bert Wijbenga, banned him from the municipality after an explosion burned down a neighbouring home. Photos of the scene showed dark brick houses and herringbone streets lit up by the flashing blue of fire brigade vehicles, orange flames billowing out from above a corner door.

That same month Kelly van Uffelen, the plumber's wife, gave an exclusive interview to the *AD* newspaper under the headline, 'For the first time the wife of an endangered plumber tells her story: "Our lives have changed forever".'[1] She said that a dozen attacks with bombs and heavy fireworks had prevented her and her sons from returning home. She was unable to sleep as she listened for suspicious sounds. Ron, she said, was forced to stay in hotels. He described the entire situation with unflinching accuracy as 'pretty shitty'.

The police continued their investigations, but were finding it hard to unpick why Ron van Uffelen was being targeted or who was to blame. They had suspects, but generally those believed to have planted explosive devices were youngsters who had simply been given a couple of hundred euros to do a job.

---

* The 'Water Beggars' were seaborne rebels against Spanish rule during the Dutch Revolt (1568–1648).
† Ron van Uffelen died in 2024 as I was writing this book.

The plumber from Vlaardingen was the highest profile firebomb victim in the Netherlands, but he was by no means alone. In 2023 there were over a thousand such attacks across the country, a threefold increase from the year before. The mayor of Rotterdam, Ahmed Aboutaleb, said his city was buckling under the literal explosion of violence. The attacks were often in residential areas, placed outside front doors and windows. Many were blamed on gangland feuds or business rivalries, and the immediate perpetrators were usually sub-contracted to do the deed, clueless youths as young as 13 clutching a handful of banknotes and a box of matches.

At one end of the scale we have this wave of firebomb attacks, and at the other end we have murder, assassination, narco-terrorism and threats to state security. The threat is real. This was brought uncomfortably home in July 2021, when a man with intense eyes and a determined jawline was gunned down outside a TV station on Amsterdam's Lange Leidsedwarsstraat. A woman living nearby heard shots and found the man on the ground, his face awash with blood. She held his hand until help arrived. He died nine days later and Dutch society was rocked.

That man was Peter de Vries, a crime reporter with a national profile and a price on his head. Between 1995 and 2012 he presented a TV show on high profile cases, and had continued to be the scourge of crooks and villains right up until the day he was shot.

Details from the de Vries murder trial transfixed the nation. The gunman was a failed rapper from Rotterdam who struggled with gambling debts and had very identifiable tattoos on his neck. The getaway driver was Polish. They had been instructed to eat the SIM cards from their phones and use submachine guns on the police, but did neither. The gunman had, however, confirmed to his colleagues that the attack was successful. 'That bullet went straight through his head,' his message said. 'Everything shot. Nice. That blood. Everyone screamed. He didn't move any more.' Peter de Vries was referred to as KK, meaning *krijg de kanker*, or 'get cancer', a peculiarly Dutch insult.* Two other men had filmed the attack on their phones and posted the videos on social media.

Six men were convicted of various types of involvement in the murder in 2024, but big questions remained. De Vries had been a confident to Nabil Bakkali, the key witness in the 'Marengo' trial against 'cocaine mafia kingpin' Ridouan Taghi and his gang. Taghi is suspected of organising the killing from his prison cell. (He has since been sentenced to life in jail for other killings.) Others have been caught up in related violence. A lawyer and judge who represented Nabil Bakkali, Derk Wiersum, was killed in 2019. In 2018 Bakkali's brother Reduan was also murdered.

It was alleged that the conspiracies of the 'Mocro Maffia' of Moroccan-origin gangsters went even further. The court heard that the gang was suspected of plotting to kidnap the prime minister, Mark Rutte, and target the royal family. Rutte, who was known for arriving at the prime minister's office alone on his bicycle, was placed under 24-hour protection by an armed police unit. Princess Amalia, the heir to the Dutch throne, was advised by the security service to live secretly in Madrid for a year. Her mother, Queen Maxima, said Amalia could hardly leave her house: 'It makes me a bit emotional. It has huge consequences for her life. It's not nice to see your child live like that.'

This chapter is about the Netherlands being a surprisingly unruly place. In truth, there is something uncompromising in the Dutch character that makes them truculent and unruly on an individual basis, whether rebelling against Spanish rule

---

* The Dutch specialise in insults and swear words connected to serious illness.

in the sixteenth century, against rules about torturing eels in the nineteenth, or against Covid-19 measures in the twenty-first. Sometimes it is group unruliness, as when Dutch teens dip under the Belgian border and bring drunken chaos to the Flemish coastal town of Knokke every summer. And, as the tales of the Mocro Maffia and the plumber from Vlaardingen suggest, unruliness is also manifesting itself in the modern Dutch state as serious crime. Vlaardingen itself could happily stand in as a film noir setting for any gritty TV crime drama, but is not the focus of this walk. Instead, the walk that accompanies this chapter is through a small political curiosity nestled deep in the bucolic farmland in the province of Noord-Brabant, a part of the Netherlands that has gained its own notorious yet unlikely connections to organised crime.

* * *

Baarle-Nassau is an oddity in brick. It is relentlessly low rise, and has none of the shabby, post-industrial charisma of Vlaardingen. I could help you place it by telling you that it lies a small handful of kilometres north of the Belgian border, but while that is correct in one way, it is also utterly misleading. Baarle-Nassau is just north of the *main* Belgian border, but then there are other borders, and other borders, and other borders. Baarle-Nassau is remarkable for the simple reason that it is a town where the borders almost outnumber the bricks. It is as though Jackson Pollock got hold of a map of the town and dripped borders on to it instead of paint. Barle-Nassau is deeply unruly when it comes to borders.

The town itself contains 22 exclaves of the neighbouring Belgian town of Baarle-Hertog, two of which contain Dutch counter-enclaves from Baarle-Nassau. In turn Baarle-Hertog, which is part of the province of Antwerp, contains more Dutch counter-exclaves. Confused?

What this means is that a walk involving Baarle-Nassau will probably involve crossing and criss-crossing more international borders than you have ever crossed in one day in your entire life. One house might be in the Netherlands but its neighbour might be in Belgium. Buildings on different sides of a street might be in different countries. A row of squat brick homes might have front doors that are Dutch and gardens that are Belgian. One disembodied chunk of Belgium is simply a four-sided shape chopped out of an otherwise Dutch field near the hamlet of Boschhoven, measuring not much more than a rough 30 metres by 90.

The reason for all this is the jumble of treaties, exchanges and sales that took place over several centuries between the Lords of Breda and the Dukes of Brabant. This was not an enormous problem in a Europe where maps often looked like pointillist paintings infected with chicken pox. But as territories congealed into nation states and Belgium declared independence from the Netherlands in 1830, it was clear that there was an issue to be resolved. The Treaty of Maastricht in 1843 (not the European Union one) codified the borders where they stood. I understand that one piece of territory was not assigned to either country until 1995, although frankly I do not understand why.

A few decades ago the rougher edges of the intermingled communities nursed an ongoing rivalry, and school closing times were altered to prevent dust-ups between Belgian and Dutch kids. Such friction is now over, and the tangle has become a rarely noticed backdrop to everyday life in both Baarles. Hardly anybody seems to notice the lines of white crosses that cut across seemingly random pieces of pavement at strange angles with a 'B' on one side and an 'NL' on the other. Paradoxically, the border overload seems to completely devalue the fuss of crossing them:

John Lennon might have found Baarle-Nassau the ideal place to imagine a world with no countries.

Some complexities do remain, especially on matters controlled by one or other town hall. The infrastructure that underpins a modern, functioning town means there are plenty of lengthy, detailed meetings about sewage pipes and road resurfacing. It can be difficult to organise building permits for a kitchen extension when a domestic wall cuts across an international boundary. Providing services such as education and healthcare can be fiddly.

Where there are complexities there are also opportunities. One bank that straddled the border was reportedly able to move paperwork from one side of a room to another so that it could avoid the prying eyes of tax inspectors from either country. Shops have been able to do something similar by shuffling around their stock. Residents have exploited loopholes by knocking through a new front door into a different territory, effectively changing their national address and allowing them to benefit from more relaxed regulations on tax or the sale of fireworks. Lockdown sceptics were able to avoid more stringent Covid restrictions simply by keeping to bits of town in the country that was more relaxed at any given time.

This walk in Baarle-country is different from the other nine in this book. In the others the walk leads with a sense of purpose, through or past or over or into things that explain something. You see the bits of the puzzle that fit what the chapter is about, step by step. Given that this walk focuses on criminality and organised crime, I could hardly sketch out a walk that might see intrepid readers wander past narco-terrorist hotspots, drug factories or gangland torture chambers. I would hate to think that even a small fraction of readers was tortured to death because I directed them down the wrong country lane. Instead, this walk is a confusing bit of fun, a *borderfest* unlike anywhere else on earth, and one that fits the theme of being unruly. And, importantly, it is in Noord-Brabant.

This southern Dutch province has cropped up unnervingly often whenever the police have discovered some narcotics facility or broken up a drugs gang. Those narco-terrorist hotspots, drug factories and gangland torture chambers that I mentioned above have all been discovered deep in the Noord-Brabant countryside, among the cows, the hedgerows and the farmhouses. Baarle-Nassau may feel like an amusing diversion in the age of the nation state, but the Noord-Brabant countryside that surrounds it is a key part of the serious crime wave that many Dutch feel is sweeping their country.

Geography is the simplest explanation for this. Noord-Brabant sits close to the ports of Rotterdam and Antwerp, where illegal drug shipments turn up with alarming regularity. Just as the farmers growing their flowers and tomatoes in Westland benefit from the geography, infrastructure and transport links of this northwest corner of Europe, so do the drug gangs. Noord-Brabant is a perfect distribution point that links narcotics arriving in major European ports with the rest of the continent. Because it is on the Dutch side of the border with Belgium, some laws about drugs are more relaxed and sentences are lower than if they were a few kilometres further south. It is rural, with a string of smaller cities such as Breda and Tilburg, surrounded by swathes of deep, remote farmland, where time seems to stand still and everybody keeps to their own business.

In 2024 an example of this came to light in a field just outside Baarle-Nassau itself. It was an unremarkable plot where the farmer had grown onions. Except that the fertiliser used on the field was apparently a mixture of manure and the waste products of crystal meth production. Take also the sleepy town of Halsteren, for instance. It seems utterly unremarkable, with the usual scattering of high street names alongside independent shops: there is Albert Heijn for groceries and Kruidvat for things that sit on bathroom shelves, fresh meat at Frank and Marleen van der Zande's *slagerij*, or some apples and potatoes at *Monique's groenten & fruit*. Just outside the town there are the remnants of a star-shaped fortress, boasting a curious new bridge which plays cleverly with the idea of the Netherlands having so much territory below sea level. On the Mozesbrug (Moses bridge) visitors cross a waterway below the level of the water, as though the water had been biblically parted to allow dry-footed passage. For sleepy old Halsteren this bridge is the equivalent of Disneyland.

Erik de Jonge, a local forest ranger, was not taken in by the sheer ordinariness of the Halsteren countryside. Back in March 2021 he was following up on reports of a drug lab in a farm building when he smelled something on the breeze from the direction of a copse. He investigated, and spotted some twigs that had been sawn and seemed obviously out of place. He brushed the twigs away and uncovered a carpet on the ground, which in turn hid a nailed-down piece of wood. Below that was a pit, and from the pit came what Erik de Jonge described as a great whiff of chemicals.

What the forest ranger had discovered was the biggest drugs-related dump ever found in the Netherlands, used to dispose of the corrosive chemicals that are used to purify narcotics. The chemical contamination at the dump poisoned the soil fully 8 metres down into the earth. Four hundred neighbouring trees had to be cut down as part of an extensive clean-up operation that involved giant earth movers excavating a hole big enough to swallow a modest football stadium.

The chemical dump that Erik de Jonge found is an indicator of how the narcotics trade centred on the Netherlands is changing. Until recently the focus for policemen digging around for smuggled drugs in Rotterdam's port was for tangible items like solid blocks of cocaine, hidden behind shipments of bananas from Latin America. Technology, however, has changed everything.

Now the cocaine is more likely to have been dissolved into a liquid and impregnated into other materials such as the packaging in which the bananas have been shipped. This leaves no tangible drugs to look for, no familiar plastic bags full of white powder. Instead, the packaging itself is whisked away and 'cocaine laundries' are used to wash the dissolved chemicals out, before it is processed and purified into a form fit for sale and consumption.

When a Rotterdam house exploded in early 2024, demolishing a building, investigators soon found evidence that it may have been used as a cocaine laundry. Barrels of acetone and hydrochloric acid were discovered in the rubble. Such outwardly anonymous sites, whether sitting in a Rotterdam terrace or hidden among farm buildings in Noord-Brabant, can also be used for the production of synthetic drugs. All told, in 2023 the Dutch police found and destroyed a record 151 drug laboratories, a rise of 44% from the year before. Forty were in Zuid Holland, near Rotterdam itself, and 35 were among the dairy cows and buttercups of Noord-Brabant. There was also a 25% increase in the number of chemical dumps like the one in Halsteren, up to 191. Cocaine laundries and other related sites are volatile places, bringing a risk of everything from contamination and poisoning to explosions and general criminality. (If you think you might have stumbled across some form of narcotic laboratory, like Erik de Jonge getting a whiff of chemicals in his nose, your sense of smell can be a good guide to what you have found. If there is a smell of nail polish remover, it is probably cocaine, while cannabis is spicy and ecstasy is sweeter and might remind you of aniseed.)

These signs of expansion in the Dutch drugs industry are not something that can simply be blamed on the Mocro Maffia. Over the (main) Belgian border in Antwerp, the Public Prosecutor's Office said that around half of those arrested for drug-related offences in the port were Dutch, a continuing trend. The head of the office is Franky De Keyzer, a name simply begging to be used in a movie about the drugs trade. He said that an entire wing of Antwerp's prison was full of Dutch criminals, and in 2022 and 2023 six Dutch people were arrested in connection with an apparent plan to kidnap the Belgian minister of justice.

This Dutch association with drug smuggling is not a new thing. In Quentin Tarantino's 1994 film *Pulp Fiction*, the hitman Vincent Vega (John Travolta) had just returned to the US after spending time in Amsterdam, where he famously wrestled with different terminology in burger restaurants.

The international dimension of the drugs trade was highlighted by the case of Karim Boyakhrichan, a notorious drugs cartel boss arrested in Marbella, Spain in 2023 during a money-laundering operation. The following year a Dutch request for extradition led to confusion in Malaga's provincial court. Instead of extraditing him, the court authorised his release on a piffling bail of €50,000 and he promptly disappeared back into the underworld. In a separate incident a year later a convicted narcotics trafficker from Schiedam, just west of Rotterdam, Marco Ebben, was killed in Mexico in what appeared to be a shootout between rival drug cartels. In response, a rapper from Amsterdam called Djaga Djaga, currently locked up thanks to a murder conviction, posted on Instagram. 'Rest in peace warrior, Marco Ebben'.

Drugs-related headlines continue to tick by. In 2021 the police announced that they had dismantled a criminal network that had utilised the Aalsmeer flower market for cocaine trafficking. The same year 3 tonnes of cocaine and €11 million in cash was discovered in the village of De Kwakel, along with guns, ammunition and a vintage car. Drugs busts in Rotterdam port, sometimes implicating port workers, are a regular occurrence. The authorities can only scan 1% of the 14 million or so containers that transit the port, so the 60 or so tonnes of cocaine that they seize is a mere fraction of the total. In 2024 a garden gnome was discovered to be made from the synthetic drug MDMA (the key component of ecstasy). Meanwhile in 2020 a collection of shipping containers was discovered in a warehouse set in the grassy expanses of Wouwse Plantage, again in Noord-Brabant. They were sound-proofed and one boasted a dentist's chair complete with straps positioned to hold down the arms and legs of the occupant. Pruning shears and pliers were also discovered, but then again this was in farmland. The apparent torture containers did not appear to be amateur work, noted the case prosecutor grimly.

The recent serious uptick in criminality has alarmed Dutch society, from chemical dumps in Noord-Brabant to the nefarious activities of Ridouan Taghi. This was most keenly highlighted by an essay that Femke Halsema wrote in the *Guardian* newspaper, with the provocative headline, 'As the mayor of Amsterdam, I can see the Netherlands risks become a narco state'.[2]

In the article, Mayor Halsema worried about young children being drawn into the cocaine trade, and Amsterdam's role as a financial centre with money leaching out through the legal economy, into hospitality and the city's red hot property market. With the money came violence, social disruption and the deterioration of entire neighbourhoods. She was careful to state that in her mind this was not an indictment of Dutch liberal drug policies.

Nevertheless, Femke Halsema's counterpart in Rotterdam, Ahmed Aboutaleb, did pin some blame on domestic demand and the acceptance of cocaine as a middle-class narcotic. Wastewater analysis from the European Monitoring Center for Drugs and Drug Addiction bears this out. The Center's investigators plunged into the sewers of 88 cities in 24 countries, and found consistently high drug use in the Netherlands. Five of the top eight cities for cocaine use were Dutch, along with three of the top four for MDMA. Rotterdam had the highest levels of cannabis in its waste pipes, along with second place for MDMA and ketamine. Remember, though, that drugs gangs see the Netherlands more as a gateway to Europe, rather than a core market in its own right. An estimated 90% of cocaine passing through Rotterdam's port is destined for elsewhere in Europe, notably Britain.

The money generated from the illegal drugs trade is considerable. The National Statistics Agency CBS estimated that in 2021 illegal drugs, prostitution and tobacco generated around €17 billion, although it appeared to lament that most of the proceeds disappeared abroad. Europol has warned that Dutch organised crime is moving into new areas such as people trafficking, online fraud and tax fraud.

Few areas of the economy are immune, and police have even identified the Dutch cheese industry as vulnerable to criminality. In one incident 300 hefty rounds of wax-wrapped cheese were stolen from a farm in Gelderland. Each one was worth over €100, and although they carry identification numbers the authorities believe they simply disappear abroad where those numbers mean nothing.

Dutch criminality is also blossoming in unlikely areas. Police figures show that in 2023 137 Dutch nationals were involved in a total of 367 attacks on ATM cash machines. Authorities in the Netherlands have resorted to preventative measures such as glue that sticks banknotes together when an ATM is attacked, but this has simply displaced the Dutch criminals across the border into Germany.

This presents a different face to Dutch criminality. In the past some of its home-grown crooks have been thought of as loveable rogues, a bit like gangsters in the East End of 1950s London who leaned heavily on community spirit and love for their mothers. One such Dutch gangster was the charismatic Willem Holleeder, nicknamed 'The Nose'. He gained a certain notoriety after involvement in the kidnapping of the beer tycoon Freddy Heineken in 1983, and even appeared on a TV talk show in 2012 to discuss his life after being released from prison. Unfortunately for him he was to return to jail a few years later. His sister, Astrid, recorded conversations on a device hidden in her bra that showed him to be far more violent and abusive than his public celebrity allowed for. That evidence helped put him behind bars once again, sentenced to life in 2019 for ordering a series of killings. Astrid, who is now in hiding, said she did not mind when her brother was a 'mere villain', but for her murders crossed a line.

All of this feels a long way from the streets of Baarle-Nassau, which have a neat order to them despite the confusion of international frontiers. As I walked I wondered whether that confusion could make the town an ideal setting for its own gritty crime drama, with the sober brick facades of its buildings housing characters with absurd nicknames and pitiless eyes. Idle farm outbuildings in the fields and hedgerows outside the town could hide a multiplicity of criminal endeavours. The plot could revolve around the gangsters skipping across borders and jurisdictions to stay one step ahead of whoever was pursuing them. I paused as I passed a café where an older couple in cycling gear was being served a pair of small Heinekens. They smiled politely, and it was hard to imagine a less criminal scene. But the way that hardcore criminality hides behind such beguiling innocence was exactly the point of my walk around Baarle-Nassau in the leafy heart of Noord Brabant.

Crime on the scale that the Netherlands is experiencing carries the potential for real damage. Most obviously there is violence, drug use and crime. As Femke Halsema warned, it can play an insidious role, the promise of easy money eating away at families and communities, while the dirty money itself wheedles its way into all corners of the economy. The malevolent actors that sit behind the cash are not in it to contribute to society or strengthen Dutch democratic institutions. They sit firmly outside the *poldermodel*. Nobody thinks life is better when drug gangs start building torture facilities in the village down the road. Criminality is there in every society, but its impact in a small country like the Netherlands, which relies heavily on the probity of its institutions, has the potential to be outsize and dramatic.

The police are not giving up, and as ever in the Netherlands technology and innovation is being harnessed in the fight. The part of Rotterdam's port where fruit from Latin America tends to arrive will soon see every single container scanned upon arrival, with artificial intelligence employed to inspect the images for signs of anything suspicious. At the other end of the tech scale there is a crackdown on the 'collectors', the young people employed to retrieve consignments of drugs under cover of darkness.

Whatever the efforts of the police in Rotterdam port, in the bucolic depths of the Noord-Brabant countryside, or indeed in the streets where the plumber of Vlaardingen used to fix sinks and unblock toilets, the crime challenge that the Netherlands now finds itself facing is immense. The geographic inheritance that allowed the VOC to sail the world, that gave the country its golden age, and then, centuries later, allowed its tomatoes and tulip bulbs to dominate the world, is also its greatest vulnerability. The liberal revolution that allowed drugs gangs to gain a foothold on the streets of Dutch towns, and the enlightened approach to criminal sentencing encouraged them to operate in a country where the costs of being caught were lower. Some very evil people are now doing evil things in the Netherlands, and a web of cash is following them.

As I was writing this very chapter a new story appeared right at the top of the homepage of *The Times*, which I had open. It was part of an in-depth investigation, and it ran under the headline, 'Cocaine Inc: How Rotterdam is driving Britain's cocaine crisis'. There was a picture of the exact same dentist's chair that I had been writing about, sitting in patient wipe-clean expectation of the next victim, and a photo of boxes of bananas. There was also a photo of a burly fellow named Joop Gottmers, introduced as a former boxer and drug importer. He was no longer young, but his bicep looked like it could double up as a normal person's thigh. I would not want to spill his drink in a crowded bar. In the article Gottmers spoke about the ruthlessness of the gangs he used to rub along with. Then the journalist writes that they travelled near to where the torture chambers of Wouwse Plantage were found. Gottmers became nervous, even scared, and would not stop the car. If this wave of criminality is enough to scare Joop Gottmers, it is serious indeed.

But what of the walk that this chapter was built around? My walk around Baarle-Nassau was unlike any of the other nine. It was a saunter, a ramble, with no real start point, middle or end. I had to be careful to park in the Netherlands, as although my hire car carried a Belgian registration I was not allowed to take it 'abroad', which certainly ruled out Baarle-Nassau. After that I just wandered. Despite the dizzying number of borders the town seemed quite mundane, with some nice houses and some plain houses. There were pleasant flower beds, and a posse of teenage girls cycled by, giggling as they sang one of Adele's ballads in harmony. It was ordinary, full of people who did not fertilise onion fields with a mixture of manure and crystal meth waste or strap people into dentists chairs where nobody would be able to hear them scream. That is something to applaud, even if it feels like setting a very low bar. I liked it, and I racked up a dozen border crossings without even trying, all on foot. See if you can do better.[*]

---

[*] If I had really tried I reckon I could have hit 50 different borders. Twelve does look a bit scrawny.

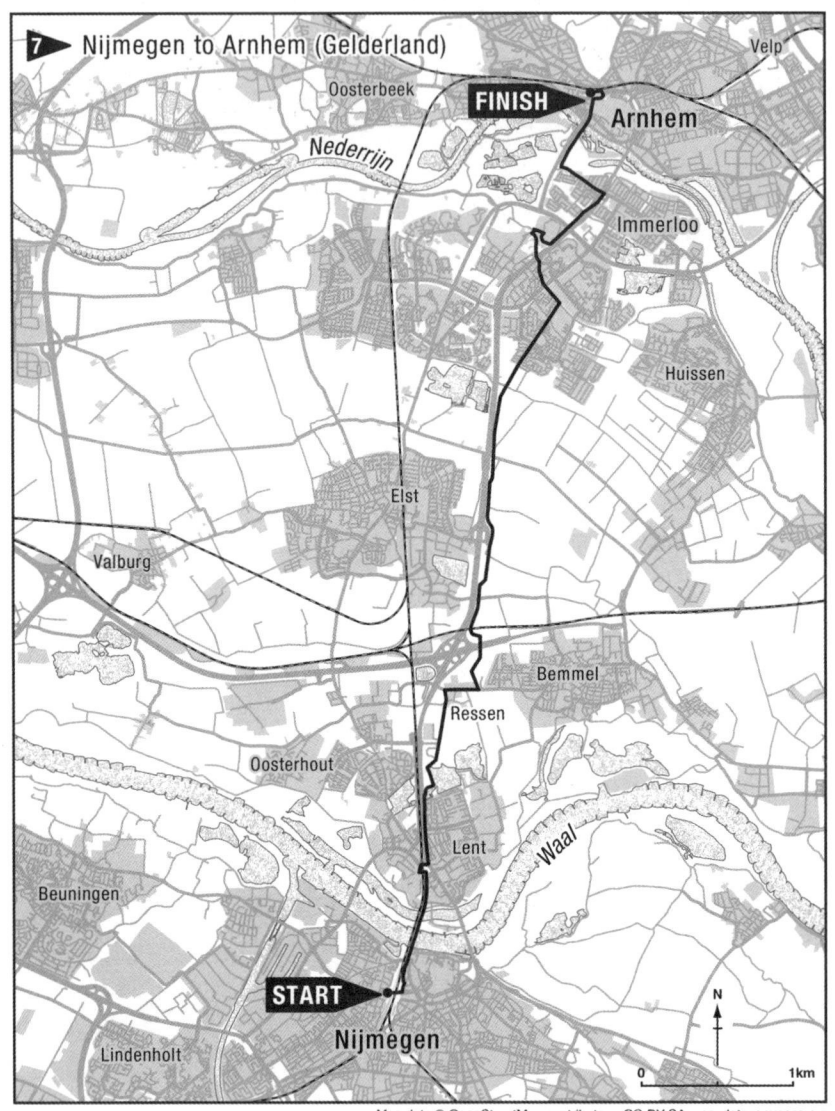

7 Nijmegen to Arnhem (Gelderland)

Velp

Oosterbeek

FINISH Arnhem

Nederrijn

Immerloo

Huissen

Elst

Valburg

Bemmel

Ressen

Oosterhout

Waal

Lent

Beuningen

START Nijmegen

Lindenholt

N

0   1km

7

NIJMEGEN TO ARNHEM
(GELDERLAND)

This is a straight line walk that starts at Nijmegen's station and finishes 16 kilometres to the north at Arnhem's station, for the quick jaunt back to the starting point. Just next to Nijmegen station is a cycle path that runs along the right edge of the train tracks directly over the Waal river. It continues through a small town, then along the N325 road before heading off slightly to the right. There is a small lake with some remarkable floating homes on pontoons and dotted with SUP boarders, then the path heads determinedly north once more. After a slight right through the village of Ressen it resumes north and tracks through countryside not far from the A325 road. My path picked its way through the rambling southern suburbs of Arnhem, past the GelreDome stadium of Vitesse Arnhem, and through a bit more countryside. It then crossed the Nederrijn river next to the train tracks. The station was a short walk further north.

* * *

'How old is your son?' asked Arnold Verschuyl, a retired doctor, our one-time downstairs neighbour in Delft, and a dear friend.

'Seven,' I told him.

'Ah, seven.' Arnold paused for a moment of reflection. 'When I was seven the Nazis invaded.'

We were in his apartment on the first floor of an old brewery on venerable Koornmarkt, one of Delft's grander canals. A medical skeleton hung just behind us, piles of books were stacked purposefully on every available flat space, and cabinets on the walls were stuffed with a lifetime of curiosities. A radio was playing in the background, picking its way through an eclectic mix of classical music and Frank Sinatra.

'We heard German aeroplanes. They were Junkers, and they made a special noise. The weather was beautiful and clear, and they jumped out with parachutes. My mother was downstairs, and I said, "Hey look!" These boys had guns. "Mama! Look, look!"'

'Was that the first that you'd heard of the war?'

'Yes. There was nothing neutral about this. Just after Delft you had a military airport, Ypenburg, then Den Haag with the ministers, the prime minister, and also the Queen. So these German boys landed and they started to shoot and there was shooting back. My father was a surgeon and he operated day and night for days on end. It was a quick examination, like "shot in here and the bullet went out there". My father walked over the little bridge with blood on his clothes. My mother was a nurse so she was gone the same moments. These Dutch boys, the German boys, they were lying in the floor and the corridors.'

Arnold paused, as if bringing his memories into sharper focus.

'There was a crashed Junkers bomber by the canal on the way to Rotterdam. The Germans had jumped out or were dead and taken away. So I went with my friends to have a look. My parents didn't know at the time.' He chuckled at his memory.

Hendrick Verton also remembered the first attacks by the Germans in 1940. He was older than the seven years of my friend Arnold Verschuyl, and lived in the town of Soest, between Utrecht and Amersfoot. At first he presumed the planes overhead were heading towards Britain. He remembered his brother telling him about dead Germans hanging from trees, their parachutes snared in the branches.*

While Arnold brought a child's perspective to the German invasion, Hendrick Verton viewed it with bitterness; not because the Nazis failed to respect Dutch neutrality, but because the Netherlands was so humiliatingly ill-prepared for the fight. His memories were of shame, of a military that lacked professionalism and equipment, of knitting committees to provide soldiers with socks and gloves, of men training with sticks because it did not have enough guns. The Dutch artillery batteries on the defensive waterline were prevented from rotating their barrels because of encroaching fruit trees, and the government refused to order branches to be cut as their budgets did not include money for compensating farmers. Verton described feeling shock and anger at the Dutch royal family escaping to Britain. His bitterness was aimed squarely at the Netherlands.

The Verton family's worldview was rooted in their pre-War experience. Hendrick Verton had been born in Zierikzee in Zeeland, which he later described as a medieval province where time stood still. During the lean years of the Great Depression his father found work in Germany, returning to the Netherlands with tales of impressive German technology, modernity and

---

* I never met Hendrick Verton, and the more I read of his autobiography the less I think I would have liked him if I had done, especially in comparison to the lovely Arnold Verschuyl. The book is *In the Fire of the Eastern Front: the Experiences of a Dutch Waffen-SS Volunteer on the Eastern Front 1941–45,* Stackpole Military History Series 2010.

excitement. It was confident, full of flags and uniforms and a sense of renewed purpose. The young boy started listening to German radio, and his sporting heroes were from the country that he saw growing in strength over to the east, like the BMW motorcycle rider George Schorsch Meier and the world champion boxer Max Schmeling. For the Verton family, the Nazi invasion was an opportunity for their country and for Europe, and a timely blow struck against the evils of communism.

During the occupation the fates of Arnold Verschuyl and Hendrick Verton followed very different paths. Arnold's father continued to work as a doctor, known for his willingness to help those opposed to the Nazis. In one instance he performed emergency surgery on a Royal Air Force pilot who had been shot down nearby, and taken in by a farmer.* The family also helped to hide a Jewish woman who was married to an engineer, thanks to a false ceiling in their large house. When he was older, Arnold followed in his father's footsteps and became a doctor with a large circle of friends in Delft and an interest in local history. He loved taking our son out for some *poffertjes* (miniature pancakes) in the splendid *Markt* in the town centre, and when we left for a new home in Italy he was the last person we said goodbye to. As a parting gift he presented Luca with an old brass gyroscope from one of his cabinets of curiosities. He was a great friend to us and a lovely man.

The decisive moment in Hendrick Verton's life was when he decided to follow his brother into the *feldgrau* of the German armed forces. He joined the Westland regiment of the Waffen SS in 1941, just months after the Netherlands fell to the Nazis.

---

* Arnold told me that the pilot had peritonitis, and died after the operation thanks to blood loss. He said that because they could not dig in the marshy ground, the unfortunate man's body was cut into small pieces and burned in a stove to avoid discovery by the Germans.

His stated motivation was to make a sacrifice for what he saw as the Europe of the future.* His wartime adventures thrust him into the horrors of the Eastern Front, although his memoirs make no mention of the brutality and war crimes that he must have (at least) witnessed. His war finally ended during the siege of Breslau in 1945, where he cut the giveaway SS blood group tattoo out of his arm with the aid of ice and a razor blade. He and his brother ended up in Germany, mining coal in the Ruhr and knowing that their names were on wanted lists back in the land of their births. Hendrick Verton remained bitter and scornful towards the Netherlands for the rest of his life.

It is commonplace to point to the Second World War as the single event that has shaped most European countries. This is certainly true for the Netherlands. In part this is because it marked such a turning point in its history, from a small and staid country with a grand global empire to a small and staid country about to lose that grand global empire after humiliations at home and abroad. This trauma forced the Dutch to reimagine who they were, and what their place was in the world. There was no escaping the various and complicated faces of occupation, resistance and collaboration. It gave them Arnold Verschuyl and Hendrick Verton, and it also gave them Anne Frank.

Now deep into the twenty-first century, the War continues to loom unusually large in the country's conscience. I was in the busy halls of Schiphol airport on Liberation Day in May 2024. Quietly, without any sense of fanfare, staff started to shut down operations in the airport's shops. By 8pm they stood, shoulder to shoulder with the light blue jackets of KLM cabin crew and a great number of travellers. At the hour of commemoration

---

* Waffen SS units were part of the Nazi Schutzstaffel (SS) organisation, but were designated for combat duties rather than duties such as internal security or running concentration camps.

there were two minutes of respectful silence, and a few quizzical looks from passengers from distant corners of the globe.* Then they started work again, getting on with their day selling bags of tulip bulbs and stacks of *stroopwafels* in cellophane wrappers.† Liberation Day itself continues to be celebrated with reverence across the entire country. The red, white and blue Dutch flag is flown across the country every May, from terraced cottages and civic buildings, farmhouses and shop fronts. But nowhere are commemorations taken as seriously as in the small city of Arnhem, right in the very heart of the Netherlands.

* * *

'When my children were the age of the boys here I took them with me and said, "Look at these stones, look at the age. You're still alive because of them laying here."'[1] In 1945 as a nine-year-old girl with her blonde hair worn in two long plaits, Willemien Rieken was charged with looking after the grave of Trooper William Edmund. The young soldier from Musselburgh in Scotland had been killed during *Operation Market Garden*, and back then his resting place in the very heart of the Netherlands was marked by a simple cross. In 2019, when she spoke to a BBC camera crew on the 75th anniversary of the Operation, Willemien Rieken was still looking after his grave. 'I feel sorry he is laying here,' she said. 'I mean he's not the only one, there's over 1,700, and I'm very, very grateful that he spent his life to liberate us.'‡

---

* In Amsterdam five people were arrested for disturbances during the two minutes of silence, including two Ugandan protesters who wanted to focus attention on their own country's plight.

† As any child who has visited the Netherlands will tell you, a *stroopwafel* is something like a cookie with a layer of caramel sandwiched between two disks of doughy biscuit.

‡ Willemien Rieken died in 2020.

The culture of remembrance is deep rooted in the Arnhem area. It was always in the background as Willemien and other children grew up. They watched every September as the comrades of those who died returned to pay their respects. You see the maroon and pale blue flags associated with the British 1st Airborne Division flying all over Arnhem. The local football team, Vitesse Arnhem, has a tradition of wearing commemorative shirts in those same colours and inviting veterans to matches. (I passed by their stadium towards the end of the walk.) It feels part of the fabric of the place.

This seventh walk ends in Arnhem, but starts in Nijmegen, a few kilometres further south. Both cities lie on the great rivers that cut across the Netherlands east to west, on their way to the North Sea. This whole region is something of a Dutch Mesopotamia, a land between those rivers. Earlier in this book I wrote about the rivers as a flood risk and as a transport artery into the centre of Europe. But to the Western Allies in 1944 they were also a barrier.

Back in June of that year the Allies had landed in Normandy, fought their way across France and Belgium, and were contemplating two enormous obstacles. One was the German border, the Siegfried Line fortified like a porcupine in exactly the place where it made sense to attack. The trouble was that any northern route around the Siegfried Line to somewhere less prickly was blocked by the second obstacle, those rivers. If only they could find a way across those rivers, allowing their tanks and trucks to trundle up to a more weakly defended chunk of Nazi Germany, success could shorten the War by a matter of months, and in doing so save hundreds of thousands of lives.

The idea relied heavily on audacity. To get across the rivers they needed the bridges, but the only way they could be secured, deep in enemy territory, was to fly over a load of lightly armed but heavily courageous soldiers. They would either parachute on to the targets or crash land gliders next to them, seize the bridges and wait. Meanwhile an armoured column of Allied soldiers and vehicles would punch its way north, one bridge at a time, relieving the airborne troops as they went. The soft heart of Nazi Germany awaited.

It did not go well. The lightly armed airborne troops had been welcomed by local Dutch people, but found themselves confronting far more German soldiers and tanks than they had expected. They clung on with the utmost bravery. But the column that was to relieve them found the going extremely tough. It juddered, eventually, to a halt. At some point, as the famous film of *Operation Market Garden* had it, Arnhem proved a *bridge too far*.

Although *Market Garden* had been worth trying, it ended up a desperate (if heroic) failure. The Allies suffered terrible losses, and many survivors were carted off into the misery of Nazi incarceration. Worse, a great number of blameless Dutch citizens were killed in the fighting. The Nazis had also observed the alacrity with which locals had welcomed the Allied troops, and responded with punitive brutality. The mass starvation of the *Hongerwinter* was one direct result. *Market Garden*'s failure also meant that the Allies faced a grim, bloody slog through the Siegfried Line and across the Rhine.

From that first bridge crossing outside Nijmegen you get a sense of how formidable the rivers were as obstacles, and the critical importance of the bridges. If you are interested in *Market Garden* (and plenty of visitors to this region are) then it can be worth taking a detour to where famous photographs of the battle were taken to see if you can match up modern reality with 1944. If you still have energy left in your legs after the walk (or a bus ticket), then head a short way west from Arnhem to Oosterbeek, the scene of some of the fiercest fighting in *Market Garden* and home to the excellent Airborne Museum Hartenstein.

Liberation took a long time to come to the Netherlands. The fighting continued into Germany, passing much of the country by and leaving it occupied by fearful, vengeful Nazi garrisons. As the War drew close to its end, an article in *Algemeen Handelsblad* from 31 March 1945 spoke of hope about the country's impending freedom, with the vivid colours of tulips and daffodils pouring out like an avalanche, dispelling the gloom from front rooms across the land. 'Yes, hunger still threatens,' it said, 'but it hurts less now that winter is over. [...] they also whisper of a future in which the darkness will disappear.'[2]

Although the Allied policy called for nothing less than unconditional surrender, the Nazi Reichskommissariat Niederlande, Arthur Seyss-Inquart, tried to negotiate a truce. He backed this up with a threat to flood vast tracts of land. An agreement was made after some carefully choreographed diplomacy, and on 28 April 1945 Ernst Schwebel, the Nazi commander of Zuid Holland, was marched by Allied soldiers into a school classroom in Achterveld wearing a blindfold. He was a 'plump, sweating German who possessed the largest red nose I have ever seen,' remembered Major-General Sir Francis de Guingand, 'the end of which was like several ripe strawberries sewn together.' On 29 April the first supply drops to civilians took place, and the actual truce was worked out a day later. Seyss-Inquart refused a full capitulation as he did not want to be remembered by history for giving up. General Walter Bedell Smith replied that he would be shot anyway. 'That leaves me cold,' the Nazi responded. 'It will,' said the General. (In the event Seyss-Inquart was hanged.) The occupation was over.

After that darkness came something of a reckoning. As well as the *Hongerwinter* there had been violence and executions, forced labour and material destruction, humiliation and misery. As the examples of Arnold Verschuyl and Hendrick Verton illustrate, there had been very many different lives to be lived in the Netherlands during the Nazi invasion, occupation and capitulation. During those dark years there was certainly heroism and suffering, but also cowardice and treachery. After the War the Dutch understandably thought of themselves largely as the victims of the Nazis, and over the years and decades their experiences were often seen through the prism of two different narratives.

The first of these narratives is the *Soldaat van Oranje* (*Soldier of Orange*), the memoir of Erik Hazelhoff Roelfzema.[3] He was one of more than 2,000 *Engelandvaarders* volunteers who voyaged across the channel after the invasion to continue the battle against the Nazis from abroad. (Erik Hazelhoff Roelfzema himself was one of 11% of this number who had roots in the Dutch East Indies.) The *Soldaat van Oranje* story resonated strongly with the Dutch public, both through the heroism of the main character but also in the compromises and challenges that it also portrayed. The 1977 film that followed the book stars Rutger Hauer in the main role, and was the most expensive Dutch film made up to that point. There is also a successful, long-running theatrical production.

The *Engelandvaarders* did exemplify a heroic response to the horrors of 1940, and they are justifiably celebrated to this day. The last of the breed was Ellis Brandon, who died at the age of 101 in 2024. She was an inveterate resister, distributing banned newspapers and stealing ration books until her own escape across the channel in 1942. To her frustration she was not sent back to the Netherlands to work as a spy, although she did keep herself busy: at one point she had a fling with the *Soldaat van Oranje* himself, Erik Hazelhoff Roelfzema. Another intrepid *Engelandvaarder,* Bram van der Stok, even managed to make the journey to Britain twice; the second time came after he had been captured, imprisoned and then took part in what became known as the Great Escape from Stalag Luft III.

Beyond the ranks of the *Engelandvaarders* many Dutch people performed acts of quiet bravery in circumstances that are quite inconceivable to subsequent generations. A network of *onderduikers* provided documents and transport to Allied agents and downed airmen.* Notably, around 10% of the Indonesians who were in the Netherlands when it was occupied became involved in the resistance.†

While some were brave, almost everybody suffered. Four hundred thousand Dutch were sent to Germany to work as forced labourers. Factories, cars, clothing and bicycles were all requisitioned and shipped east.‡ (Bridges, power plants and other pieces of infrastructure that were not requisitioned were simply destroyed later on as the Nazis retreated.) Hostages were routinely taken and often shot:§ 150 prisoners were executed in retaliation for a strike in April 1943, and 250 were killed in 1945 when the SS police chief, Hanns Albin Rauter, was wounded in an assassination attempt. The population suffered from malnutrition, typhus and diphtheria. Many were tragically caught up in fighting and Allied air raids, such as the 500 who were killed in a bombing attack on Nijmegen in February 1944. The Germans were also responsible for lots of deliberate flooding. During the Battle of the Scheldt in 1944, when the Allies tried to secure the control of the Scheldt estuary and sea access to the Belgian port of Antwerp, the Nazis destroyed dykes in Zeeland, inundating Walcheren and other islands. In a tragicomic twist, many of the Dutch men liberated during that battle were eager to pull on military uniforms to fight the hated Germans. Instead,

---

* *Onderduikers* translates as those who ducked under official life to work clandestinely against the Nazis.

† The comparative figure for the general Dutch population is estimated at 0.5%.

‡ The requisitions led to the infamous Dutch football chant to the German team, 'Give us our bikes back!'

§ The plot of one of the most famous Dutch novels about the Nazi occupation, *The Assault* by Harry Mulisch, unpicks one such incident.

they ended up being shipped off to the Dutch East Indies to fight the independence movement there instead.

The second of the narratives that frames the War years for the Netherlands was the ghastly tragedy of Anne Frank, the German-born Jewish girl who kept her teenage diary during long months of hiding with her family in an Amsterdam attic. As so many school children around the world now know, Anne and her family were eventually betrayed, and she died at the age of 15 in Bergen-Belsen concentration camp. Without doubt the Nazi-occupied Netherlands was one of the worst places in Europe to be Jewish in the Second World War. The Netherlands historically had a substantial Jewish community that largely dated back to the country's Golden Age and its unusual levels of religious tolerance. In 1796, during the Batavian Republic (a client state of revolutionary France), the Jews were emancipated and became full citizens. By the twentieth century Dutch Jews tended to be well assimilated into society and were relatively secular.

These deep roots within the Netherlands did not save them. Around 102,000 Dutch Jews were killed, and the streets of the country's towns and cities are dotted with *struikelstenen*—small, brass coloured cobble stones that mark the last place where Jews lived or worked before they became victims of Nazi persecution.* Although the suffering of the country's Jewish population is widely known and sensitively remembered, the story of Anne Frank has arguably cast the country in a more sympathetic light than is justified.

That figure of 102,000 killed translates into nearly 73% of the Netherlands' pre-War total Jewish population.[4] By comparison around 23% of French Jews were killed and 27% of Belgian Jews.

---

* The stones are also known by their original German name, *Stolpersteine*. They are the brainchild of German artist Gunter Demnig and were introduced to the Netherlands in 2007.

Meanwhile in another small neighbour of Germany, Denmark, only 116 Jews were killed, and around 7,300 out of a pre-War total of 7,500 were smuggled to freedom in an act of national heroism and defiance. In a *Financial Times* article that picked apart the different experiences of Danish and Dutch Jews, the journalist Simon Kuper (who was raised in the Netherlands) noted that the Dutch authorities were not very good at saying no to the Nazis.[5] They often looked for a compromise before being pressured by the Germans into doing what the Nazis wanted. They did this without having to actually witness massacres or the full brutality of the Holocaust. Instead, the process was bureaucratic and administrative, with relatively little Jewish blood shed on Dutch soil. This is the dark side of Dutch tolerance, where matters outside an immediate social circle go unnoticed. Some resisted, but ultimately the tough questions were avoided, few stood up in opposition to what was happening to others in their midst and 102,000 Jews were killed.

One of the most sordid administrative episodes in the story of the Dutch Holocaust was only resolved in 2024. During the occupation, the Dutch public transport company GVB routinely charged Germany for transporting Jews on special trams to the Central Station for their deportation to Westerbork transit camp. (Anne Frank and her family were among the last to be transported this way.) The author Guus Luijters, who investigated the trams, found that they had been used 900 times in total, at a cost of 10 guilders per tram in the daytime, and 12.5 guilders if it was at night time.[6] Even after the War the GVB used a debt collection agency in its efforts to pursue Germany for this money, in effect the amount they had charged the Nazis for their own tawdry logistical role in the Holocaust. In March 2024 the Amsterdam authorities announced that they would repay €100,000 in recognition of the profit it made on tram tickets for the 48,000 Jews it helped to deport during the War.

When I spoke to the journalist and historian Geert Mak he gave me a slightly different (and very Dutch) perspective. 'It was a kind of lazy collaboration, a bureaucratic collaboration,' he said. 'It was not active antisemitism like in France. A very good example is the so-called map of Amsterdam where Jews lived, ordered by the German governor in 1941. The bureaucrats could have said, "Oh no, it's very difficult, it'd take years. You can get it in perhaps '46, '47." Instead, they made this map in only two months. They didn't see how dangerous their work was.' Another example he cited was the occupation identity card, which was designed so well by the Dutch authorities that it caused problems for the resistance. 'The man who made that was not a Nazi, not at all. He wanted just to make a very good identity card.' As Geert Mak sees it, many Dutch combined a heads-down professionalism with wilful naïvety. 'People were used to safe surroundings. A lot of Jews went out by themselves. They thought, "Okay, we have to work in the east. Okay." It was a kind of innocence because the state had always been rather good with them. In Amsterdam we had a lot of Jews coming from Germany, like Anne Frank. And a lot of these people were saved. Much more sceptical!'

The grim deportations should not overshadow those genuinely heroic attempts both to resist the Nazis and protect the Jews. In February 1941 communist dockworkers led a strike in protest against the treatment of Jews. This was brutally repressed by the Nazis, who then recalibrated their anti-Semitic policies away from overt violence and thuggery and towards a more administrative approach. This created the tragedy that fused so efficiently with the mentality of some within the Dutch authorities.

Many in the Netherlands also had a residual sympathy for aspects of extreme right-wing politics, just like Hendrick Verton. Before the War the neo-Nazi NSB* was popular enough to win

---

* NSB stands for 'Nationaal-Socialistische Beweging in Nederland'.

300,000 votes in 1935 (8% of the total), with 39% support in some areas bordering Germany. In Verton's own memoirs he recalls a 1927 survey in *Algemeen Handelsblad* of the international figures most admired by Dutch people, which placed Benito Mussolini second behind the inventor Thomas Edison. More than 20,000 Dutch men joined Verton in volunteering for the Waffen SS, disproportionately far more than from other Western European countries.

Those with fascist sympathies suffered after the War, as the country sought vengeance against those who had found common cause with their oppressors. Nearly half of the 200,000 people (out of a population of just over 9 million) who were investigated for collaboration were given prison terms: 17,500 civil servants were sacked; 40 executions were carried out. Some reprisals were unofficial: *moffenmeiden*, suspected of having had sexual relations with the occupiers, were humiliated in public, and sometimes tarred and feathered.

The vengeance reached down to the children of collaborators, albeit indirectly. Some ended up in internment camps or were cruelly introduced to their classrooms as 'NSB children'. Their parents often found it hard to secure work or housing. There were particular challenges for the children of Waffen SS veterans who had been captured on the Eastern Front. Their fathers were often unrecognisable when released back home after years of toil and inhumane conditions in Soviet labour camps.* There is more sensitivity around the issue now, and although the archives on suspected cases of collaboration were opened to the public in 2025, measures have being taken to limit their accessibility.

There were peculiar blind spots in this meting out of justice. Take for instance the police, who as an institution had been

---

* The Werkgroep Herkenning foundation was established in 1981 to provide help for children whose parents or grandparents had been collaborators.

involved in general collaboration, as well as the administrative persecution of the Jews. One policeman called Jan van der Oever had refused to arrest Jews, and was sacked for insubordination. After the War he re-joined the force, but memories were long (and presumably shame was intense). He was ostracised and forced out for a second time. A similar fate was met by the only member of the Dutch police to have been an active member of the resistance. Detective Cor Verbiest was ostracised by his fellow policemen after calling for an investigation into police conduct during the War. An investigation did take place but in an echo of Dutch attitudes to war crimes committed during the struggle against Indonesian independence, the findings were suppressed and took years to surface.

In his *Financial Times* article, Simon Kuper noted that this veil of silence about the horrifyingly banal details of Dutch administrative assistance in the Holocaust only began to lift in 1965. That is when Jacques Presser published a book called *Ondergang,* the culmination of 15 years of research into everything from the stigmatisation of Jews in Dutch society through to the round-ups, the deportations, and the 102,000 deaths.* Even after *Ondergang* Simon Kuper contends that the *Soldaat van Oranje* narrative allowed most Dutch to see their country's activities during the War as fundamentally on the side of good.

Soldaat van Oranje certainly does a good job of telling a stirring story with its heroic central character. As well as good and evil it has lots in between. The other characters have varying experiences: some compromised, some tragic, some traitorous. Others simply lived through the occupation struggling with grubby everyday challenges, the negotiations and humiliations of a brutal age, ones that most of us struggle to comprehend. This mirrors the true Dutch experience of ordinary people who were

---

* *Ondergang* means 'downfall'.

somewhere in that great moral space between Hendrick Verton and Erik Hazelhoff Roelfzema.

The post-War years left the Dutch looking for a new sense of themselves, as a small European nation that had been humiliated, occupied and liberated, and then shorn of the keystone of empire. Whatever the moral murkiness associated with the occupation itself, the *Hongerwinter* had provided a dénouement with the Dutch firmly as innocent victim. They also had a black-clad evil that they could define themselves against, and the post-War period ultimately also gave them a new Europe that they could be part of.* Their sometimes-staid society had been given a firm shake, never again to settle so neatly into its pre-War form.

Few would argue against the success of the post-War Netherlands. You will see that during this walk. If the weather is warm enough, as you cross the railway bridge out of Nijmegen you will see swimmers splashing around off the beaches of the Spiegelwaal (an offshoot of the Waal river). You will pass a small lake where contented home owners sit on the balconies of the pod-like house boats that branch out over the water. You will see wind surfers and SUP boarders, and families filing into the neighbouring cinema complex. There will be llamas, sheep, cows and countless water birds: shifty-looking herons, garrulous coots and mallards forgetting how many ducklings they are meant to be looking after. Cyclists will zip by, shouting some strange vowel-infested greeting as they pass (try something like 'Oi oi oi!' or 'Hooiey!'). And then, as you head towards the bridge over the Nederrijn into Arnhem itself, you will start to see the maroon and pale blue flags. This country—good and bad and now quite comfortable for most—has its contemporary roots in those dark days in the early 1940s. The Dutch have never forgotten that.

---

* More of this post-War search for a Dutch identity in Chapter 9.

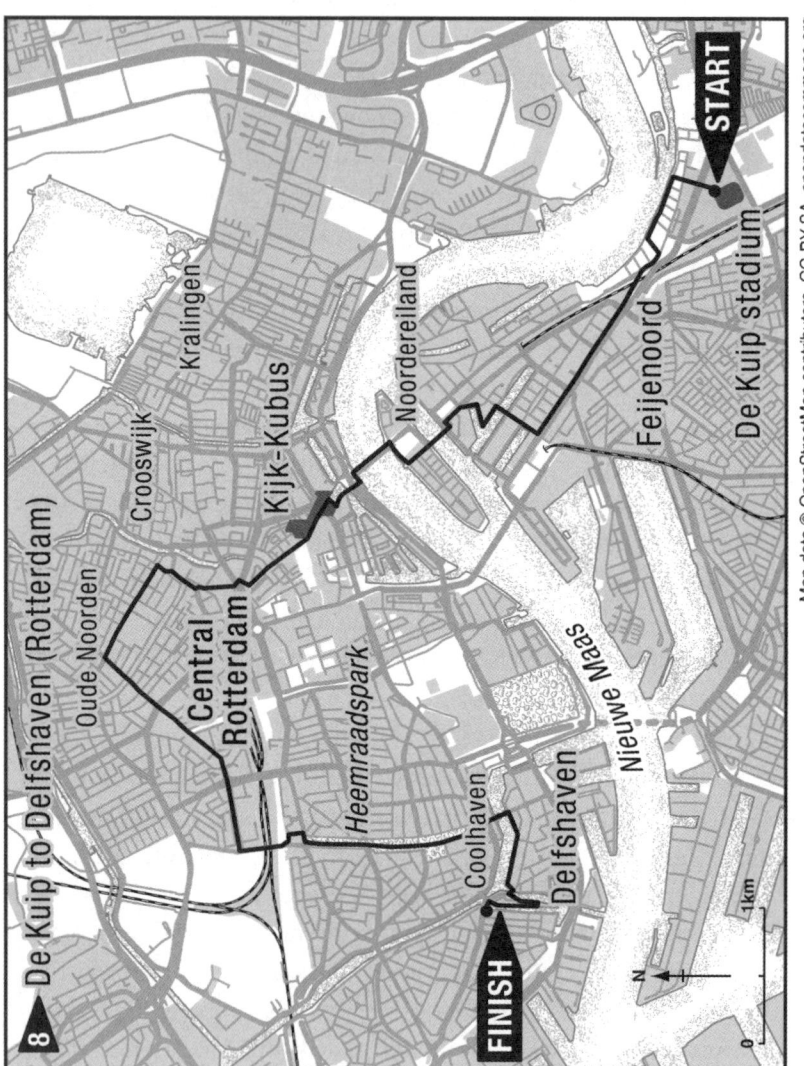

8 De Kuip to Delfshaven (Rotterdam)

START
FINISH

De Kuip stadium
Feijenoord
Noordereiland
Kralingen
Kijk-Kubus
Crooswijk
Central Rotterdam
Oude Noorden
Heemraadspark
Coolhaven
Delfshaven
Nieuwe Maas

N
0   1km

8

DE KUIP TO DELFSHAVEN
(ROTTERDAM)

This walk is a giant half-loop that starts in Feijenoord in Rotterdam's southeast, skirts the centre to its north, and then ends up in Delfshaven on the Nieuwe Maas river to its southwest. It begins at the famous De Kuip stadium. Cut through the streets opposite to see the river, then re-join the S106 road back towards the city centre. Take the Lodewijk Pincoffsweg to the river to a number of marinas and docks full of boats of every size and shape, then look to cross the Nieuwe Mass via the Noordereiland and a couple of splendid bridges. On the north bank cut through the Oudehaven to a pedestrian area ringed by some of the most famous examples of Rotterdam's modern architecture. I headed roughly north at this point, heading for the Rotte river and the main shopping street of Oude Noorden. I wandered past the shops until the street hit the Bergweg and turned southwest. After more than a kilometre this dog-legs to the right and joins the Van Aerssenlaan at the gates of the Blijdorp zoo. Turn left under the rail bridge and continue south along the watery and elongated Heemraadspark. You will reach the Coolhaven dock, and can loop around to Delfshaven in its south-western corner, one of the few bits of Rotterdam that was largely untouched by Nazi bombers in 1940.

* * *

Fans of grittier American TV cop shows might find Schilderswijk unconvincing. It sits on the trickier side of Den Haag, streets that the city's expats and internationals might only ever see from a train leaving Den Haag Hollands Spoor. It is, however, no crack-ravaged Baltimore ghetto fresh from *The Wire*. The streets are the usual orderly urban Dutch mix of cycle lanes and speed bumps, and the buildings that squat along their edges are neat, densely-packed low-rises with flat roofs. There are no broken windows, burned out cars or piles of spent cartridges. Instead, a United Nations of flags hangs in the windows: Surinam and Somalia, Brazil and Pakistan, Syria and Morocco.

'36,000 people live here, very dense,' said Mohammed el Arrag, before throwing a question at me. 'How many nationalities?' Twenty, I guessed. 'No! Between 130 and 170 nationalities and cultures. Everybody, the Jews and the Hindus, the Moroccans, Turks, Romanians, Italians, Somalians, Yugoslavs.' You have everybody here but the Eskimos, he laughed.

We were talking over a cup of coffee in Schilderswijk police station on a sunny Saturday morning. The station is an imposing corner building made from bricks the colour of dull gold and full of modern architectural flourishes: a pillar here, a grid of windows there just before a half-curved wall. Mohammed wore his weekend clothes with the tidiness typical of somebody used to looking spruce in a uniform. He still carried the air of being physically capable of breaking up a bit of disorder on the streets. His official title is Hoofdinspecteur, Cultuur en Verbinding, which translates as Chief Inspector, Culture and Connection, and his job is to make sure that those 130 to 170 nationalities and cultures in Schilderswijk rub along as happily and lawfully as possible. His story is a remarkable one.

'In 1991 the Dutch police were looking for more diversity,' he told me. He was in the Netherlands to complete his technical studies in Delft, with no longer term plans other than to find a beautiful woman who owned a cabriolet car before heading back to the Moroccan sun. A newspaper advert from the Dutch police captured his interest. 'It said don't worry if you didn't speak Dutch,' he remembers. 'And if you don't have Dutch nationality, that's also no problem, but you have to say you want it.' He leant forward with a smile on his face. 'I'm in paradise! What's this for a country!' He said he felt his application was a joke, but he sent it anyway.

Soon, Mohammed was in uniform and threw himself at the challenges he faced. 'I had the dictionary, in Arabic, in French, and in Dutch. My colleagues, they could prepare for the next day and then go to the bar. For me it was three o'clock in the night. It was not easy.' Nevertheless the work obviously suited him and he rose confidently through the ranks, learning on the job about the challenges of policing the Netherlands' increasingly multicultural communities. Then in 2017 he got the call to move to Schilderswijk. It may not have been a Baltimore ghetto, but it had its problems. Mohammed's response was to get out on to the streets and talk to people.

'Most people are good, they want to say hello. The hard bit is the ones who do not want to say hello. I'll go to the *plein*, see two or three sitting on a chair, smoking. What I like is the challenge. Maybe at this moment you do not succeed to get the contact. But maybe if you come the second time, they are thinking that they have to say something, to say hello. And that is the start.'

These were pragmatic and insightful answers that made perfect sense. Mohammed el Arrag was obviously right that this was the way to conduct policing in a massively multicultural place such as the sensitive streets of Schilderswijk. There are Schilderswijks all over the Netherlands, and each deserved their own version of Hoofdinspecteur el Arrag: so much is uncontroversial. But there were bigger questions that his answers naturally avoided, about obvious friction over multiculturalism in the Netherlands, often involving people with the same Moroccan background as his. About Geert Wilders' stunning recent electoral success, on a platform dominated by questions of migration and Islam.

The Netherlands has a long history of being a genuinely multicultural country, whether it has been the Portuguese Jews of the fifteenth century, the Moroccan and Turkish guest workers of the late twentieth century or the Syrians and Afghans of more recent times. But the country feels increasingly ill at ease with aspects of multiculturalism. This impacts both its politics and that big question of how it negotiates future existential challenges. One poll in 2024 found that 63% of the Dutch said they worried more about people coming to their country than their people leaving it, far and away the highest of the 12 European countries surveyed.*

Multicultural Netherlands is the issue that underpins this eighth walk, which is across Rotterdam. The city felt like an unlikely place for a good walk when I planned it, and on the day itself I was confronted with the grim prospect of long hours trudging past tower blocks through endless rain. I did those long hours and was utterly soaked, but the walk itself was surprisingly interesting. It kicks off from De Kuip, the stadium of Feyenoord, through the docks of the Feijenoord district and across the

---

* The next highest was Austria at 53%. The poll was from the European Council on Foreign Relations, conducted by *YouGov* and *Datapraxis*, and asked 'Generally speaking, are you more worried about people coming into your country, or your country's people leaving?' https://ecfr.eu/publication/getting-the-european-parliament-election-right/.

Nieuwe Maas over a couple of stunning bridges.* You will then see a few of the pieces of modern architecture that Rotterdam seems so proud of today, before looping through multicultural Oude Noorden. The last stretch is along the resolutely middle-class Heemraadspark and back down to the river, and Delfshaven, full of lovely old boats and a scattering of buildings that escaped the War intact.

* * *

This was not the first time I had been to De Kuip. I had taken my Italian father-in-law to a Feyenoord match there on Christmas eve 2017. Feyenoord were the defending champions, and easily put little Roda JC to the sword 5–1. I remember it for the fervent English-style atmosphere, the remarkably poor quality of the football and the blanket dismissal of Dutch football by my father-in-law, who struggles to see anything of merit beyond Sampdoria and *gli Azzurri*. I enjoyed it more than he did, and found much to appreciate in Feyenoord's evidently unpretentious blue-collar support. The club fits Rotterdam perfectly: hard-working, rough around the edges and underestimated.

The first drizzle began to fall as I began my walk by climbing the steps out of De Kuip's carpark and crossed the tram line. The Feijenoord district had the post-industrial feel of a pre-Canary Wharf Isle of Dogs, dominated by the river and indented by docks and harbours. Any geographer would find the location of Rotterdam somewhat obvious: it sits at the culmination point of the great river systems that link inland Europe with the North Sea. The barges that ploughed through the brown waters of the Nieuwe Maas in front of me were 100-metre-long monsters. They were crewed by dogged couples who lived in the

---

* In 1974 Feijenoord changed its name to Feyenoord to make it easier for foreigners to understand how to pronounce it.

handful of rooms at the stern. A small car was usually stowed on the deck, from where it could be hoisted by crane on to dry land for shopping runs. Those heading east would soon pass the city of Dordrecht before disappearing into a rabbit warren of channels, canals and rivers, seeking out destinations deep into the European landmass. To the west was central Rotterdam, then the town of Schiedam, whose patron saint Lidwina also managed to be patron saint of chronic pain and ice skating.* Beyond that lay the vast, tangled infrastructure of the Europoort, one of the world's busiest ports, connecting Europe to the world.

The morning drizzle seemed to suit Feijenoord. The post-industrial mingled with hopeful developments that were based around old docklands. Dozens more purposeful-looking barges were moored, tied up like tamed horses and with small signs of daily lives visible through their portholes. Off to my right was the iconic suspended slab of the Unilever building, a monument to peanut butter, margarine and consumer care products. I crossed over the Koninginnebrug, marvelling at the mechanised steel beauty of the neighbouring Koningshavenbrug De Hef. Ahead of me were the suspended lanes of the Willemsbrug and downstream I picked out the elegant Erasmusbrug, new symbol of the city. As a native of Newcastle I always have time for a good bridge, and a city that takes bridges seriously is one that I can relate to.

---

* Lidwina was born in 1380, and like millions of residents of these flat lands past and present skated on canals when they froze. Unfortunately she had a serious skating accident that resulted in a broken rib when she was just 15. Medieval medicine being what it was, a broken rib turned into a succession of far more serious ailments and she became ever more progressively disabled before dying at the age of 52. While biographers noted that her ailments included paralysis (other than her left hand) and bits of her body falling off, a modern suggestion is that she suffered from multiple sclerosis.

The truth is that much of Rotterdam is relentlessly and regrettably utilitarian, and the odd bridge or dock packed with old barges is a welcome break from yet more soulless tower blocks. The city was not always like this, but on 14 May 1940 it was subject to a vicious Nazi air assault that left it both physically and emotionally scarred.

The bombing of Rotterdam took place just one day before the Dutch capitulated under the Nazi onslaught. Suspicions remain that it was a needlessly vindictive demonstration of the power of the German Luftwaffe: 850 people were killed, and 25,000 homes were destroyed, along with thousands of factories, stores, workshops, offices, schools, churches and hospitals. Eighty thousand were left homeless.

The reconstruction of Rotterdam began just four days later, with the appointment of an engineer, Willem Gerrit Witteveen. His job was to earmark buildings for preservation or destruction, and draw up plans for a modern city that nodded to traditional Dutch architectural stylings. Witteveen's team slept on camp beds and worked with great urgency, fearful that the Germans would seize control of the reconstruction and turn the great port of the Netherlands into little more than a Nazi facility.

If Witteveen had had his way Rotterdam might have had a few more aesthetic flourishes than it boasts today, but that was not to be. By 1944 the disillusioned engineer had disappeared on sick leave, to be replaced by his assistant, Cornelius van Traa. The emphasis shifted firmly towards the pragmatic, and a 'Basic Plan' was drawn up that better suited the weary, grey occupation years. In 1946 the city council adopted the Plan and the city got to work. *Het Vrije Volk* heralded the news with the stirring headline, 'Rotterdam, roll up your sleeves! A major work lies before us.' An angular monument was erected, looking like it was straight out of the German Democratic Republic. It featured a muscular beefcake hitting an anvil under the illuminated slogan

'Aan den slag' (Let's get started) and 'Rotterdammers weten van aanpakken' (Rotterdammers know how to tackle things).

More recently Rotterdam has earned a reputation for some daringly modern architecture, and after I left the moorings and beer terraces of the Oudehaven behind I walked straight into a cluster of examples. There was the Kijk-Kubus, which looks like a giant toddler had thrown his enormous building blocks across a road in a fit of anger. Next to that there was a hexagonal tower block fitted with a pointy roof that makes it look like the angry toddler's 20-storey pencil. A few metres further was the Centrale Bibliotheek Rotterdam, a concrete wedding cake extruding vivid yellow guts. Across from that was the circular-roofed Rotterdam Blaak station, which like most Dutch attempts at architecture built around bicycle racks and public transport, looks fabulous.

Just as Amsterdam and Ajax football club suggest to me the tide of socially liberal policies in the 1960s and 1970s, no-nonsense Rotterdam and Feyenoord football club point to the sleeves-up pragmatism that rebuilt the nation post-War and post-empire. There might not have been much room for colour, playfulness or the architectural flourishes that Willem Gerrit Witteveen wanted, but Europe in the late 1940s was on its knees. Rotterdam embraced its functional future and put its collective shoulder to the wheel.

The giant figure in post-War reconstruction was Willem Drees, celebrated in some quarters as the Number Three Dutchman of all time.* As a politician he was very Dutch: skilled at managing a team and finding compromises and constructive ways forward. Drees was the guiding force behind the extensive welfare state that covered everything from pensions and health insurance to that scheme that paid artists who could not sell their

* His first appearance in this book was in Chapter 4, when he oversaw the decolonisation of the Dutch East Indies.

works.* His achievements in office read like a social democratic technocratic dream, regulating this and implementing that. That accolade of All-Time Number Three Dutchman was awarded for very Dutch reasons.

The future of the post-imperial Netherlands would rely heavily on leveraging its geography: it had lost the Indies, but it was still a small country with a big inheritance. It sat on the north-western edge of Europe, connected to the heart of the continent by a series of great rivers, and to the rest of the world by the North Sea. Rotterdam sat squarely at the centre of this inheritance. Money was invested in the Dutch shipping fleet, as the Netherlands looked to export both its own manufactures and those of a recovering Europe.† Rotterdam's functionality is a monument to its post-occupation rebirth, and should be celebrated.

The post-War period also brought great social change. Since the early nineteenth-century Kingdom of the Netherlands there had been institutional recognition of different groupings thanks to something called the pillar system. Groupings such as the Catholics or social democrats were organised into 'pillars' (with plenty of further sub-divisions), each provided with their own services: shops, medical facilities, schools, sports clubs and eventually print and broadcast media. The flux of the Nazi occupation undermined this entire system, resulting in a far more fluid post-War society with much more social mixing.

---

* While the Beeldende Kunstenaars Regeling was an undoubted mis-step, other parts of the welfare state have functioned with exemplary Dutch efficiency. An annual study of pensions ranked the Dutch system highest in both 2023 and 2024 (Mercer CFA Institute Global Pension Index 2024, https://rpc. cfainstitute.org/-/media/documents/article/industry-research/mercer-global-pension-index-2024.pdf).

† See Chapter 9 for more on industry, economics and the Netherlands' place in the world.

The liberalism of the 1960s sounded the final death knell for pillarisation, with the social, cultural and sexual revolutions allowing a new generation to imagine their lives. Women in particular started to play a bigger role both inside and outside the home. The burgeoning welfare state provided foundations for building more dynamic lives (and not just for fortunate struggling artists). The growth of the economy reduced migration from the Netherlands to traditional destinations such as Canada. Instead, large, urban labour-hungry centres like Rotterdam saw an influx of foreign workers who sat outside the confines of the established pillars.

Many of the new arrivals were from former colonies, for instance the Surinamese who took on Dutch citizenship after independence in 1975. Meanwhile there were also ostensibly temporary and unskilled 'guest workers', a system mirroring that of Germany. In the 1960s and 1970s many of these were from Morocco and Turkey, often from traditional societies in rural areas.* They were not expected to stay, and so they were not expected to integrate with a society that was itself trending from Christian and conservative towards liberal and permissive. As elsewhere, the government brought in new restrictions on such migration after the global economic recession of 1973. However, many of the migrants had chosen to settle and brought their families over to join them. New generations often revisited their families' country of origin for marriage. Family migration was the most common form of immigration to the Netherlands from 1976 to 2005, despite relatively high unemployment levels.[†,1] The number of second-generation Moroccans and Turks increased

---

* Significant numbers also came from southern European countries such as Spain, Italy, Portugal and Greece.

† The high unemployment levels are connected to the downturn in manufacturing and the decline in unskilled jobs, the continuing relatively

by 29.7% and 25.7% respectively between 1996 and 2000.[2] The overall pattern began to change once again from the late 1980s, as asylum seekers and refugees from a greater range of countries such as the former Yugoslavia, the Horn of Africa and the Middle East began to arrive. Beyond this there has also been a large number of more highly-skilled arrivals attracted by the highly-international Dutch economy, which as we saw in Chapter 1 has brought its own specific brand of challenges and problems.[*]

The result of these trends has been a very large increase in the proportion of Dutch residents with overseas backgrounds. In January 1972, 9.2% of the population had a migrant background, still overwhelmingly from other parts of Europe. By 1998 the figure was 16.7% and in 2018 it was 23.1%.[3] (In Rotterdam itself around 46% of residents were from an immigrant background in 2009, with the largest minority groups from Surinam, Turkey and Morocco.)[4] With many guest workers settling permanently in the 1970s and 1980s, and bringing their families over to the Netherlands, the presumption of impermanence began to change thanks to facts on the ground.

Some began to voice the unease they felt about the way the Netherlands was managing immigration. In the 1980s Hans Janmaat succeeded in winning a seat in parliament on an anti-immigration platform, but was widely ostracised and shunned by mainstream politicians when speaking in the House of Representatives. As the 1990s wore on questions were asked about how some of the newer arrivals were fitting in with Dutch social norms. For instance Frits Bolkestein, the leader of the

---

low-level of qualifications from some migrant communities, and presumed prejudice among employers.

[*] This group includes my family: my Italian wife moved to the Netherlands from Singapore thanks to her work with Unilever, and I suppose that means my son and I count as 'family migration'.

centre-right VVD* party, suggested that Muslim immigrants with several wives could not bring them all to the Netherlands. (His book *Moslim in de Polder* argues that Muslim migrants did not fit in with how Dutch society treated women as equals.) However the roots of Dutch tolerance and wariness of racism ran deep, and even the VVD's youth wing spoke out against him.†

One hangover from persisting low-level guilt over the Dutch role in the Holocaust was a tendency to interpret any form of prejudice over race or culture as a slippery slope that led to genocide. The imperative behind immigration shifted from topping up the labour market to a moral responsibility towards those trying to escape poverty or danger. Different social norms and ethnic and religious identities were tolerated, while there was a degree of structural integration into Dutch society for new arrivals. In 1996 the ruling cabinet stated that 'the debate over multi-culturality must be conducted starting from the principle that cultures are of equal value'.[5]

This began to change thanks to a slim gay man with an impeccably bald head and fiery blue eyes. Pim Fortuyn was fated to only spend a short amount of time active in Dutch national politics, but in that time he exploded like a firework in the debate over immigration and integration. Fortuyn came to political prominence later in his life, after a career that included the very Dutch profession of advisor on social infrastructure. Although he was best known for his outspoken anti-Muslim views (his view of Islam as a 'backward culture' and 'life-threatening' sums up his main policy points) he did not see himself as being from

---

the far right. Instead, his outlook framed liberalism as social tolerance rooted specifically in Western values. As an openly gay man he saw Islam as intolerant and incompatible with the *verdraagzaamheid* of the Netherlands.* Dutch tolerance of other systems tends to extend only so far, and is conditional upon those impacted having some form of escape route. For instance, strictures against homosexual teachers in fundamentalist Christian schools are tolerated as the teachers can find other jobs; rules constraining the choices available to Muslim women are not, as those women have little choice but to stay within families and communities.

This thinking led to a more generalised opposition to Muslim immigration, while any accusation of prejudice was rebutted by a firm defence of Dutch values. Pim Fortuyn's politics were further weaponised by the attacks of 11 September 2001, which focused attention on existing Muslim communities within the Netherlands. (There had been street celebrations in Ede in response to the attacks, and a magazine poll soon after found that nearly half of Dutch Muslims had sympathy with them.) That November a new anti-establishment party, Leefbaar Nederland (Liveable Netherlands), elected Fortuyn to be its lead candidate in the 2002 elections. He left them in February after proving too radical for their tastes, and formed the Lijst Pim Fortuyn in his own image. Days before the national elections, and with the promise of an electoral breakthrough in his grasp, he was assassinated by an animal rights activist.

If Pim Fortuyn was a firework, Theo van Gogh was a barrel of TNT. He was the director of a short film called *Submission: Part 1*, an incendiary critique of how Islam treats women. It was written by the Somali-born Ayaan Hirsi Ali, and was designed to provoke: in it, women with Koranic texts written on their bodies

---

* He spoke openly about having slept with Moroccan men.

told their personal stories as though speaking to Allah. The film was broadcast on public television in summer 2004, and death threats soon followed. That November Theo van Gogh was shot multiple times while cycling to work, and then had his throat slit. A Dutch Moroccan man, Mohammed Bouyeri, was found guilty of the murder.

These two assassinations are the background to Geert Wilders' politics, positioned as hostility to an alien code and culture that cannot be reconciled with Dutch values. But while Pim Fortuyn's interpretation of Dutch values emphasised tolerance and liberalism, and Theo van Gogh and Ayaan Hirsi Ali highlighted women's rights, Geert Wilders' Dutch values are the more parochial ones of 'Henk and Ingrid'. These are the names of an ostensibly average Dutch couple that Geert Wilders conjured up to explain his political position. Henk and Ingrid related to Dutch values of tradition rather than liberalism, security rather than buccaneering internationalism, clogs rather *Brand Orange*. They worked hard but felt precarious, their children found it hard to get on the housing ladder, and they bridled at the thought of surly Moroccan youths smoking weed on a park bench (even if that rarely happened in their town). Notably, Geert Wilders' polling numbers were unexceptional in the build-up to his election triumph in late 2023, until two weeks or so before the vote. That coincided with the spread of incendiary street demonstrations, involving large numbers of Dutch Muslims (among others), protesting against the war in Gaza. These may have rekindled a latent hostility in some to politically active Islam.

Geert Wilders has seemed quite happy to poke this particular hornets' nest. In 2008 he too made a film, *Fitna*, which likened the Koran to Adolf Hitler's mission statement *Mein Kampf*. Journalists report that his office door used to carry a few words in Arabic that translate as 'The Koran is poison and

Mohammed is a liar'. Inside that office was a portrait of Winston Churchill and a flag of Israel, a reminder of his time working in a *mosjav* collective settler farm on the West Bank as a teenager.* Unsurprisingly Wilders lives under 24-hour protection.

The immigration and integration challenges that the Netherlands faces, along with the electoral success of the populist right, are hardly unusual in the West. As Geert Wilders shows, the post-Pim Netherlands is also happy to approach the issue with a characteristic Dutch bluntness. A Eurobarometer survey in late 2024 found that 45% of Dutch named immigration as one of the two most important issues facing the European Union, the second highest figure in the EU and far higher than the average of 28%.[6] The Dutch police have been noticeably hasty in applying force to protests about Israel's actions in Gaza, and in 2017 Dutch commentators were quick to be outraged when the Turkish leader Recep Tayyip Erdogan attempted to organise political rallies in Turkish-origin communities in the Netherlands.

There is plenty of evidence that minority communities continue to suffer low-level prejudice and even racism. One survey found that nearly half of non-Westerners reported discrimination in the country's housing market, such as finding it harder to arrange to view properties; 70% of them did not report their frustrations as they did not think anything would be done about it. At the same time general frustrations over the malfunctioning housing market have exacerbated resentment over levels of migration. Geert Wilders' PVV has emphasised the link between housing and 'open-border' immigration. The United Nations Special

---

* He reportedly worked on the farm because he had not saved enough to travel to Australia as he had planned. After his time on the West Bank in 1980 he travelled through parts of the Arab world. See https://nos.nl/artikel/2230019-hoe-zijn-verblijf-in-israel-geert-wilders-gevormd-heeft.

Rapporteur on housing, Balakrishnan Rajagopal, visited the Netherlands in December 2023. He warned that that the 'acute housing crisis... of both availability and affordability' was feeding an 'alternative narrative' focused on an 'influx of foreigners'.[7]

Fittingly, my walk through the Dutch second city continued beyond the modern architecture of the Kijk-Kubus and the Centrale Bibliotheek Rotterdam to loop around the multicultural inner suburb of Oude Noorden. The walk along Noordmolenstraat, Zwart Janstraat and Rodenrijselaan might make Henk and Ingrid nervous, but to me the shops were full of interest. Johara Stoffen shimmered with extravagant dresses, some so heavily gilded that they looked like royal tunics from Narnia. The gold-embroidered floor length gowns in the window of Al-Noor Mode came in sage green, cerise and baby blue. Opposite was the Casablanca Patisserie and Boulangerie. The Sunnah Center promised to be 'More than an Islamic bookstore'. Huddles of young women in neat headscarves picked their way around badly parked mopeds, taking care to stay under their umbrellas. Halal chicken and kebabs were freely available, but that was hardly unusual. I had read accounts of people who had encountered friction with young Moroccan men in Oude Noorden, but when I walked its streets there was no whiff of menace. Maybe that was just the stinking weather, or maybe that is just because friction can happen and be memorable even if it is not common.

Thanks to the Dutch talent for plain speaking, some level of societal friction is often to be expected. I have had plenty of Dutch men (and it is normally men) volunteer their opinion that I am a British idiot, whether it is because I struggle with the language or that I had the temerity to honk my horn at their appalling driving. Such friction is surely even more common for non-whites. Now that Pim Fortuyn has broken the spell, you do not have to be Theo van Gogh to be blunt about how you feel various ethnic minorities are behaving.

Some attitudes towards non-whites are rooted less in malice than in a marriage of blunt speaking and viewpoints that elsewhere are 50 years out of date. Only in 2021 did the Efteling amusement park in Noord Brabant announce that it would get rid of its *Monsieur Cannibale* ride, which involved thrill seekers sitting in cooking pots that revolved around a large black African figure. The Zwarte Piet debate rumbles on every Christmas time, when the festive black-face helpers of Sinterklaas run riot with bags of sweets, insisting that they are really Spanish and are dirty from chimney soot. It was no surprise to see several Dutch supporters at the Euro 2024 tournament dressed up (and blacked up) in Ruud Gullit costumes, complete with 1988 shirt, fastidious moustache and dreadlocks.* Nathan Ake, a current Dutch player whose father is from Ivory Coast, reported that Ruud himself considered this an honour, and asked the rest of the world to 'stop making a problem out of things like this'. The lack of malice is exemplified in the story of a homeless man called Hadjer Al-Ali, who found a wallet containing €2,000 in 2024. He elected to hand it in rather than pocket the cash, and was rewarded with €30,000 in donations from well-wishers.

As in every country, some people will inevitably feel uncomfortable with change. But one major reason why the debate over Dutch multiculturalism is different from other countries goes back to the conception of the polder system. Differences are absolutely fine so long as there is a sense that everybody pulls in the same direction and Dutch feet stay dry. If a particular group is seen to be pulling away from this then it is believed to be undercutting the system.

---

* Ruud Gullit was one of the world's most talented and recognisable footballers of the 1980s and 1990s. His father was from Surinam, and Ruud was famously an advocate of 'sexy football'.

The friction and street celebrations after the September 11 attacks were not just shrugged off as a cultural difference. Neither were traditional restrictions on women and girls in some communities, in a country that prides itself on women being fully represented in higher education and the workplace. They may have said and done plenty of things that might offend, but the assassinations of Fortuyn and van Gogh were taken as unthinkable attacks on the liberal underpinnings of Dutch society. (Where would Dutch people be if they had to express their views with tact and diplomacy?) The rowdy Gaza protests before the 2023 elections were arguably part of the pattern, and certainly seemed so to enough voters to put a smile on Geert Wilders' face.

The horrendous attacks on visiting supporters of the Israeli football club Maccabi Tel Aviv in Amsterdam in November 2024 offered another invitation to Wilders. He explicitly blamed 'Muslims' and 'Moroccans' for the anti-Semitic violence. 'We saw Muslims hunting Jews in the streets of Amsterdam, a pogrom of the worst kind,' he said, with the victims 'beaten up, stabbed with knives, thrown into the water, kicked in the face'. (The coalition partners backed plans to strip those found guilty of anti-Semitism of Dutch citizenship, a move aimed implicitly at dual passport holders.) Opposition politicians cautioned Wilders about 'further' dividing the Netherlands, noting among other things that some Israeli fans had instigated the trouble. Geert Wilders did not seem to mind. Even though the governing coalition was reportedly in serious trouble of meltdown at the time, he was calculating that any new election might serve to increase his grip on power.

One revealing article in *de Volkskrant* looked at how attitudes towards migration had hardened from the point of view of the more liberal Dutch. 'The smugness is over,' wrote Loes Riejmer and Marieke de Ruiter, six months after Geert Wilders' 2023 triumph.[8] They noted that the Netherlands' self-image as 'open and compassionate' had been damaged by the election, but made worse by subsequent polling. The number of Dutch who saw a moral duty to receive foreigners had slipped from around half to 39%, with nearly 50% wanting to reimpose border controls within the European Union. Supporters of all parties wanted the EU to do more to reduce immigration to Europe, and more than half thought migrants should only have access to the welfare state after naturalisation (if at all).

On the particular day that I walked across Rotterdam the weather was so ghastly the streets were largely clear. Even Dutch cyclists were staying at home. That meant that another key—and often unspoken—feature of this debate over race and integration was missing: itinerant youths on what are called 'fat bikes'. In essence these are e-bikes that resemble a child's drawing of a motorbike, with grotesquely swollen tyres, long seats and an electric motor that can be tampered with to increase the bike's speed. Whereas a standard e-bike has a motor to back up the pedals, on a fat bike the pedals are there so it can pretend it is not a full-blown electric scooter. They tend to be imported from China (some are even smuggled in illegally) and be driven at insane speeds.

These insane speeds have turned the bikes into an urban menace, especially because they tend to be ridden by irresponsible youths that you might not normally trust with a sharpened spoon. Across the Netherlands hundreds of people are being hospitalised after fat bike accidents; sometimes the riders, and other times the poor unfortunates who were hit by one of these idiot machines. The VeiligheidNL road safety organisation found that half the people who ended up in hospital after a fat bike accident were under 16. One doctor told the broadcaster NOS that the injuries were serious: 'broken bones, cerebral haemorrhages and damage to internal organs.'[9]

The result of this carnage has been a full-blown media and political outcry, with politicians and columnists competing to condemn fat bikes in the harshest possible terms. One PVV politician summed up the public response when he said the Netherlands 'was screaming for measures to stop souped-up fat bikes... We can't go on like this.' The VeiligheidNL says it wants to raise the legal age for these machines to 16, the same as for scooters, and for helmets to be made compulsory.

In any other country this would be a simple public order issue, but in the Netherlands there are two further elements that make it explosive. First, as any foreigner can tell you, the Dutch love their bikes. In the same way that some Americans have come to associate freedom and democracy with the right to own state-of-the-art assault weapons, so the Dutch associate their own freedoms and their sense that they are all in it together on bicycles. The egalitarian nature of Dutch society and the *poldermodel* is expressed in cycling. The Dutch royal family is famously a 'cycling monarchy', and former minister Mark Rutte used to turn up to work every day on his bike, clutching a briefcase full of vital decisions about spatial planning. Nobody in the Netherlands is above getting on a bike. It is democracy and equality on two very pragmatic wheels.

The fat bike menace spits in the face of this, and not just because the latent hooliganism of many riders has made cycle paths more dangerous places. Any attempt to muzzle the *fat bike menace* necessarily undermines cycling freedoms. There is no robust definition of what a fat bike is, and so any legislation would have to be loosely drawn to hit the fast-moving target.* This is where the real problem lies. Given the outcry, the pressure

---

* There has been an explosion in sales of electric bicycles, especially among older people. In 2023, 56% of new bikes were e-bikes of various types. See 'The Dutch are cycling more, and buying more e-bikes', *DutchNews*, 7 July

to *just do something* could lead to rules that impinge upon the freedoms of other more blameless Dutch cyclists. For instance a decision that you need a helmet to ride any form of e-motorised bike would be impractical given the widespread use of e-bikes. It would also be seen by many Dutch as fundamentally illegitimate. Measures such as mandatory insurance would affect normal cyclists, but be ignored by those who are causing the problems.

Where it really gets incendiary, and why this is part of this particular chapter, is that any stroll across a Dutch town centre leads to the inescapable conclusion that a very large proportion of those who zoot around on fat bikes are from ethnic minorities. If the *fat bike menace* leads to a wider loss of cycling liberties, eroding Dutch cycling culture, there will undoubtedly be a connection in many minds with questions of integration and immigration. Taken to an (admittedly unlikely!) extreme, the fat bike scourge may yet destroy Dutch cycling culture, destroy Dutch multiculturalism, destroy the polder system, and so destroy the Netherlands itself.

I suggest you walk through Oude Noorden and make your own mind up.

When I turned left on to Bergweg I was almost too wet to care. I squelched along, wishing my jacket was more waterproof and worrying about trench foot. After Oude Noorden the surroundings seemed pretty dull and a bit anonymous. I reached Rotterdam's Blijdorp zoo, then ducked under a mammoth railway bridge, and emerged the other side on the decidedly middle-class Heemraadssingel. If your vision of Rotterdam is that it is an endless modern concrete hellhole, then this part of the walk will change your mind. A long sausage of water stretches for 1.5 kilometres between willows, grassy banks and a full complement

2024, https://www.dutchnews.nl/2024/11/the-dutch-are-cycling-more-and-buying-more-e-bikes/.

of water birds. The handsome interwar houses either side are tall, brick built and embellished with stone flourishes and a willingness to use stained glass wherever possible. There are turrets and gables, Ukraine flags and polished door steps. It is a safe bet that the staircases inside are insanely steep and that rear aspects are dotted with dozens of tiny balconies. They feel as indomitable as a family-sized Volvo.

Beyond the Heemraadssingel are more docks, which were knocked about a lot during the War. Some older buildings survive, but the post-War interruptions crammed into gaps speak of wayward bombs and demolished lives. I swung to the right next to the Coolhaven, with its array of utilitarian barges and mighty tugs. A couple more corners, and a lot more rain, saw me into Delfshaven, a little chunk of old Rotterdam that must have sat under an invisible forcefield during the dark days of the Second World War.

Delfshaven, which used to be the port for the landlocked town of Delft, around 10 kilometres by canal to the north, also has a tangential claim on a major piece of world history. In August 1620 the English religious exiles that became known as the Pilgrim Fathers set sail from its harbour in a ship called the *Speedwell*. First they sailed to Southampton in England where they joined with a second ship, the *Mayflower*, and then set off for a new beginning across the Atlantic. Alas, the *Speedwell* was less than seaworthy, and despite a couple of stops for repairs in Devon she was abandoned. Many of her passengers transferred to the *Mayflower*, and they sailed off on a miserable 65-day voyage before landing in the New World and securing their place in history. Although the Pilgrim Fathers only enjoyed a short stay in Delfshaven (they had been living in Leiden), the church near the quay where they had prayed was renamed by American visitors and is now known as the Pelgrimvaderskerk.

Delfshaven is now home to ranks of fibreglass pleasure boats and glorious old wooden barges. I could smell wood smoke hanging in the air, and the whiff of fragrant pipe tobacco. Its quaysides are darkly atmospheric, the type of place where you can imagine a murder under gaslight, or a double-crossed smuggler being coshed outside a bar. Or maybe that was just my imagination running away with itself: I was delirious with delight after having finished an enormously varied and interesting but extremely soggy trek. Delfshaven was a fitting end to the walk across Rotterdam, a tiny taste of how this great city used to be, and a reminder that it has always been a place of work, of people from different backgrounds living hard against each other. A place to ponder some of the biggest challenges facing Dutch society today. I checked the map on my phone, and squelched off to find a bus to the central station, the rain still hammering down.

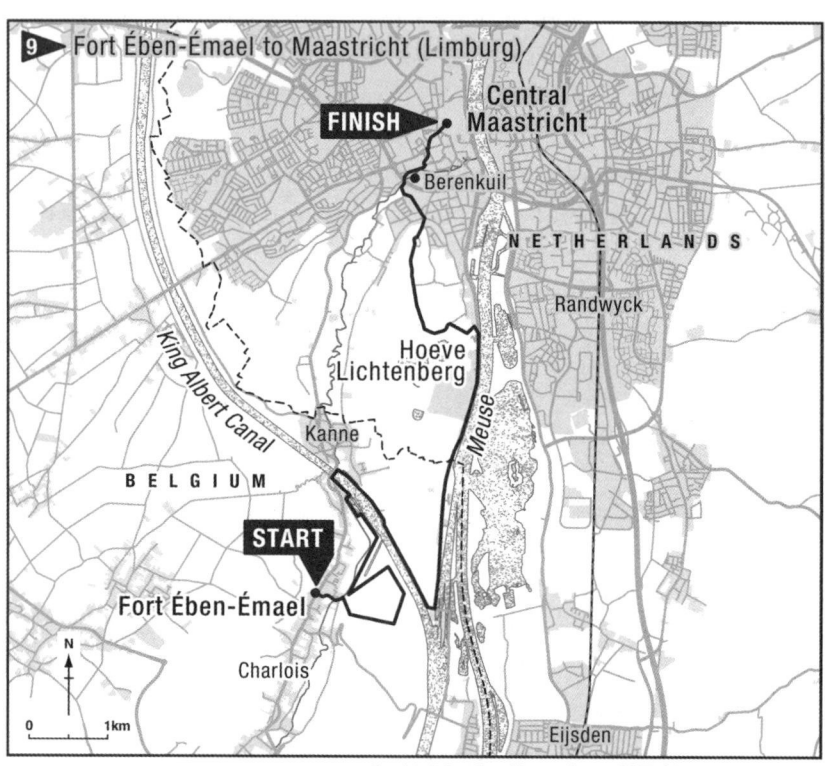

Fort Ében-Émael to Maastricht (Limburg)

FINISH
Central Maastricht

Berenkuil

NETHERLANDS

Randwyck

Hoeve Lichtenberg

King Albert Canal

Meuse

Kanne

BELGIUM

START

Fort Ében-Émael

N

Charlois

0   1km

Eijsden

9

FORT ÉBEN-ÉMAEL TO MAASTRICHT
(LIMBURG AND A BIT OF BELGIUM)

*This walk begins in Belgium, at the fort of Ében-Émael, just off the
very southern tip of the Netherlands. Once you have wandered around
the half-buried fortifications, turn north and head for a road bridge
over the large canal, into a border village called Kanne. Turn right
and walk south with the canal on your right. You will eventually
run out of land, and will turn sharply left and head due north, with
water still on your right. The Dutch border runs through some higher,
forested land, and after crossing that you will skirt some industrial
buildings, then more forest up to your left. This is where you can
peel off to inspect the caves that riddle the rocks and enjoy the clifftop
view from the Hoeve Lichtenberg fortifications. The track heads north
into Maastricht's southern suburbs, across a waterway named the
Jeker, and under the N278 road. This piece of city park includes the
Berenkuil, an unsettling life size sculpture of a young woman and
a dead giraffe. A forlorn-looking bear sits on a park bench nearby.
After this the centre of Maastricht is a short hop to the north.*

* * *

Alert readers will have noticed that the territory of the Netherlands is a flexible concept. Unlike most other countries the flexibility lies mainly with the land itself, rather than its borders. For centuries the Dutch worked hard to drain that which lay beneath their clogs, wresting it from the grip of water and turning it to productive purposes such as pastures or airports. In the 1950s and 1960s the Dutch created that entirely new province, Flevoland. Magicking up similar slices of new Netherlands is an enticing answer just waiting for a relevant question: one recent report neatly concluded that the solution to environmental challenges on farmland could be solved simply by draining another chunk of North Sea. Voilà! Back in 1945, battered, bruised and vengeful after the Second World War, the Dutch tried a more traditional approach to land acquisition, this time at the expense of their former occupiers.

Frits Bakker Schut was the president of the *Rijksdienst voor het Nationale Plan*, a particularly Dutch organisation that concerned itself with spatial planning: in essence what goes where on Dutch territory. As the Second World War came to a welcome end he interpreted calls for war damage reparations from Germany in territorial terms, coming up with plans that involved seizing impressive amounts of German territory.* The most ambitious version of what became known as the Bakker Schut Plan would have involved the annexation of cities such as Cologne and Münster, and resulted in a super-sized Netherlands that was up to 50% bigger. Echoing some of the less savoury Nazi approaches to geo-ethnic politics, the Germans living in these areas would either be deported or, if they spoke Low German dialects similar enough to Dutch, *Dutchified*. Maps that illustrate the plan make the Netherlands look obese, keeping its distinctive western and

---

* The Netherlands had asked for 25 billion guilders in reparations, but at the Yalta conference it was decided that reparations should not be monetary.

northern outline, but with a calorie-enhanced eastern edge. The Americans, struggling to deal with 14 million German refugees who had fled westwards from formerly German territories, and sick to the back teeth with European nations grabbing bits off each other, were unimpressed.

Despite Frits Bakker Schut's impressive sense of the possible, the Dutch settled for something much more modest. In 1949 the Netherlands annexed a mere 69 km² of Germany, and hastily set about painting new border posts and erecting new road signs. Most of these areas were thinly-populated countryside, but the inclusion of a couple of small towns meant that around 10,000 Germans suddenly became Dutch. The annexation did not last, and almost all of this territory was returned to West Germany after it paid 280 million marks in 1963. However, one remaining chunk of former Germany is still in Dutch hands: a small 75-metre-high hill called Duivelsberg (Devil's Mountain), now a nature reserve boasting an attractive pancake restaurant with stuffed badger and boar heads on its walls. Perhaps this is because the Dutch need all the 75-metre-high hills they can lay their hands on, especially if they can pretend it is a mountain.

That the Netherlands decided to annex even a modest chunk of post-Nazi Germany betrays the turmoil that the country was going through at the time. The late 1940s were a difficult time for the Dutch sense of place in the world. Before the War it had been seated at the high table of European colonial powers, a small country but one that could always demand respect by pointing to the vastness of the Dutch East Indies. It no longer had the Golden Age heft of the seventeenth century, but it still counted for something. Then came the Nazis, occupying the Netherlands and forcing it into numerous regrettable compromises. And then came the Japanese, sweeping through the Dutch East Indies with ease and detonating any sense of European colonial superiority.

The defeat of Nazi Germany and Imperial Japan might have held out the hope that the Netherlands could reclaim what it had lost, but that hope was soon dashed. First there were the Indonesians, rising up and fashioning that vast archipelago into a proud and independent country. However much they stated that *'Indië verloren, ramspoed geboren'* ('Losing the Indies brings disaster'), the loss of the Indies was inevitable and humbling. Then came the Americans, denying Frits Bakker Schut's hopes of grand territorial expansion: 69 km² was not nothing, but it certainly was not much. The Duivelsberg with its pancake restaurant was even less. What was next for this little country, crouching under the grey skies of north-western Europe?

This chapter is about how the Dutch sense of their place in the world has evolved since the Second World War. In previous chapters we saw how that conflict changed the Netherlands, along with its politics and its society, before its imperial heart was ripped out by the loss of the Dutch East Indies. Anybody staring off into the distance from the beaches along Texel's foreshore would no longer be dreaming of a glorious empire beyond the waves, but simply wondering if the North Sea was too cold for a dip. The Netherlands was ripe for a relaunch, ready to fall in love with American money and the comfort of a European club. Swathes of the country would double down on their internationalism, facing firmly out towards Europe and the world while at home interpreting Dutch tolerance as ultra-liberalism. Others would find that this shift to *Brand Orange* jarred with their own worldview, however parochial that was. Arguably, these tensions are at the heart of the current political divide.*

---

* The Van Dale dictionary vote for a 'word of 2024' was abandoned because of violent disagreements over their list of ten possibilities. Instead, they decided that *polarisatie* (polarisation) was the fitting word of the year.

The locations connected to this issue are scattered across the globe: from Srebrenica in the hills of eastern Bosnia to the fields of Donbas in Ukraine; from the beaches of the Dutch Antilles in the Caribbean to the Eurocratic office complexes of Brussels. The walk for this chapter, however, is (mostly) in the Netherlands, in a city that leapt into European consciousness thanks to a treaty that bore its name, signed in 1992.

The walk actually begins in Belgium, at the vast and atmospheric Fort Ében-Émael that was captured with ease by an embarrassingly small number of German airborne soldiers during the Nazi assault on the Low Countries. Despite their Low Countries brotherhood the Dutch–Belgian relationship is layered and nuanced. Many Dutch will support the Belgian football team in the World Cup if their own team has self-combusted in a blaze of orange and acrimony. However just as many Dutch will happily tell you that the border between the two is easy to spot because Belgian houses are so ugly and their roads so poor. (Belgians will counter that at least their food is edible.) From Belgium the path leads to the north, across the Maas (or Meuse), venturing over the Dutch border where you can compare the aesthetics of the two neighbours' housing stock. There is a detour into the caves that riddle the rock south of the city of Maastricht. From there it is a hop, skip and jump into that pretty city, where you can tuck into a bowl of *zuurvlees* and dream of a (slightly) Greater Netherlands.*

* * *

The fall of Fort Ében-Émael is a reminder that history has not always been kind to smaller European countries. It is a complex more than a single fortification, an incredible and vast concrete

---

* *Zuurvlees* is a traditional horsemeat stew served with apple sauce.

ant's nest, buried beneath fields of barley and wild flowers, bringing to mind Great War-era fortifications like Verdun or the Maginot Line. Great steel domes break the earth, looking like crashed flying saucers that bristle with heavy-calibre guns. They hint at the endless tunnels and dug outs that lie deep beneath your feet, nothing less than a subterranean Dreadnaught. Of course it was reputed to be impregnable. It was not, as a force of fewer than 100 German paratroopers demonstrated in spring 1940. Soon after, the Netherlands, Belgium and France surrendered to Nazi Germany.

Off to the north lies Maastricht, a city forever associated with the eponymous treaty that established the European Union in 1992. It was a decisive step towards the gradual establishment of an integrated, cooperative Europe, and away from the conflicts that led to Ében-Émael. This was a good thing for the Netherlands, giving it a new home and purpose in a post-imperial world. Maastricht itself lies in a borderland, in a 35-kilometre polyp of Dutch territory that hangs down between Belgium and Germany (and near Emperor Charlemagne's old capital at Aachen). The point at which the three countries meet is the Vaalserberg, also the highest bit of the Netherlands (a mammoth 322.5 metres above sea level). Amusingly that also makes it 329.17 metres above the lowest point of the Netherlands, in Nieuwerkerk aan den IJssel.

In the decades after the War, this more-integrated Europe prospered and modernised. The Dutch economy flourished on the back of its good geographical bones, hefty doses of Dutch ingenuity and commercial good sense. Yes, some of that prosperity was wasted on sub-standard art works and the mass indulgence of squatters, but the establishment of a strong welfare state was broadly a good thing that buttressed the newfound social fluidity. Firms like Unilever and Phillips built their international reputations, and the Dutch were able to congratulate themselves that success was built on their age-old virtues of parsimony and hard work.*

This Dutch self-image has also led to friction with some of the other countries that the Netherlands was integrating with. In an early incarnation of a united Europe, the Netherlands was one of only six members of the European Coal and Steel Community, the 1952 precursor to what is now the European Union. Decades on the European Union would reach 28 members (before mislaying Britain and shrinking to 27), which involved the Dutch rubbing shoulders with countries with a less Calvinist, fiscally responsible economic culture.† When the 2007/8 financial crisis morphed into a eurozone sovereign debt crisis the Dutch played up to a national stereotype, lecturing others about good financial housekeeping. (Some say this was always the Dutch way: a 1985 *New York Times* article noted that 'for centuries they have been known as "the people of the finger", because of their penchant for wagging fingers in people's faces, preaching to the world and to each other.')[1]

The Dutch undoubtedly like being part of the European Union, and during our years in the Netherlands I came to think of the Dutch as great joiners of clubs of all sorts. When I used to cycle to the local lake in Delft for a morning swim I passed numerous huts lined up on the edge of the forest, each dedicated to a different sport, interest or hobby. There was a shooting club, an archery club, a pigeon club, a pétanque club. There were Scout

---

* As discussed earlier, the developing Dutch economy and the need to fund a generous welfare state also generated high demand for immigrant labour from southern Europe, and then Morocco and Turkey. This too has changed the fabric of society, along with cohesion and other fundamentals of the Dutch *poldermodel.*

† Britain left the EU in 2020, after a slightly chaotic referendum in 2016 that presented the Prime Minister, David Cameron, with a result that he clearly did not expect.

huts and sports fields: rugby, hockey, football, handball, each with youth divisions and club uniforms, a smart little clubhouse and a sense of community. When joggers ran past they invariably did so in groups, often a couple of dozen strong. A few years earlier in Singapore, nobody was more amazed at the British vote to leave the European Union than our Dutch friends, who could not conceive of leaving such a club.

Despite this, my sense is that many Dutch struggle to fully trust in the future of the EU, and their country's place in it. Britain had been an annoying partner within the EU, but after Brexit the Dutch recognised that they had lost a potential ally for reform inside the corridors of Brussels. The 2024 'Draghi' report into the EU's economic competitiveness was a red flag, warning about the bloc's crippling lack of vigour and dynamism.* At the time of writing the Franco–German engine of the EU is spluttering, with one locked in a fiscal and political crisis, and the other in an intractable spiral of deindustrialisation and populist politics.† The Dutch are understandably nervous.

Europe has also been important in providing a post-imperial, post-Nazi occupation Netherlands with security. I once met a retired British military officer who had spent a hefty portion of the Cold War lurking in a top secret NATO HQ inside the caves that you can visit on this walk. There are 200 or so kilometres of tunnels under the Hoeve Lichtenberg castle. They were originally used to mine chalk, but were then used as everything from air raid

---

* The report was by the highly respected former Italian Prime Minister, Mario Draghi. It pulled no punches in detailing the EU's economic malaise, and unsurprisingly was instantly dismissed by large numbers of European politicians. See https://commission.europa.eu/topics/strengthening-european-competitiveness/eu-competitiveness-looking-ahead_en.
† Which one of France and Germany is suffering from which is open to question, and they may be freely interchangeable.

shelters to emergency storage for art treasures (such as Rembrandt's *The Night Watch*), before being repurposed as a suitable place for NATO commanders to think about the Red Army. It is also the kind of place where I could easily spend half a day, poking around chambers and rooms, climbing dusty staircases, peering into security-restricted zones, taking in the view across quarries and forests from towers and clifftops. Compared to so much of the Netherlands there is a joyous amount of simple up and down, and having a sense of height on the footpaths around the fortifications and walls of Hoeve Lichtenberg is in itself well worth the detour. It also allows you to cut inland, away from the banks of the Maas river which here can feel a bit dominated by the main road. The walk then cuts through some lush farmland towards the suburbs of Maastricht itself, which gives you more of a feel for life in this southern outpost of the Netherlands. It has a very different feel to towns and cities in the rest of the country, and not just because the land is more three-dimensional. It fits far less precisely to any conceptions of a typically 'Dutch' city. Despite the usual quota of determined cyclists, electric vehicle charging points and familiar housing stock, there is something very evidently different about it, and this gives it a sense of purpose: it crosses that provincial forcefield that you can find in the nether reaches of many countries, allowing it to break out its own personality rather than feeling utterly peripheral and a long way from the action. Landlocked Maastricht, dangling on its polyp between Belgium and Germany, also feels more interconnected with the rest of Europe than Dutch towns and cities to the northwest. The NATO role played by the caves makes a lot of intuitive geographical sense, thrust into a European border zone close to continental hotspots such as Fort Ében-Émael and even the Emperor Charlemagne's capital at Aachen. The end of the Cold War and the seemingly inexorable process of European integration took away the purpose of that NATO HQ. At the time it felt that Europe was entering a new and far more peaceful phase in its existence, with security no longer such a compelling issue. Time has sadly proved that wrong, and the Dutch were given a brutal reminder that they were living in a violent, unpredictable world before the 1990s were out, in an unremarkable town buried deep in the hills of eastern Bosnia.

* * *

I was staying at a small hotel in the town of Bratunac in Bosnia and Herzegovina when the family next door decided to kill a pig. They did it in the garden in the late afternoon, just as I was enjoying a cold beer. There were voices and a bit of grunting, followed by the sound of an animal resisting and being forcibly restrained. Then the knife went in, and the struggling pig's squeals felt more like screams. It was not quick. When it finished there was a horrible silence. The pig was dead, I was still holding my beer, and I felt completely unsettled.

I was staying in Bratunac because I was compiling a radio report on a nearby town as part of my job as the BBC's man in Sarajevo. It was a decade or so after the Bosnian War had ended, but the terrible events of those years still seeped into everything. Nowhere was that more true than in the town that I was reporting on: Srebrenica.

In July 1995 Srebrenica was at the centre of a besieged island of land in the wild hills of the east, where thousands of Bosnian Muslims had gathered under the protection of DutchBat III. This battalion of a few hundred lightly armed Dutch soldiers were charged by the United Nations with keeping the enclave's Bosnian Muslims safe, as Bosnian Serb forces under the control of Ratko Mladić closed in. The men of DutchBat failed in this mission, and 8,000 Muslim men and boys were murdered.

DutchBat's role in the horror has been relentlessly unpicked. Conditions in the enclave had been deteriorating in the months and weeks leading up to the mass murder, and starvation was starting to take hold. But eastern Bosnia is extremely remote, even now a hard drive through wild hills and endless dark forests. The media and international attention was focused on the siege of Sarajevo. DutchBat III and the thousands of wretched refugees crowding into Srebrenica felt forgotten.

When the Bosnian Serb forces launched their final assault the defences started to fold. Air strikes were requested, but the weather was closing in and they never happened. When the Bosnian Serbs threatened to kill the Dutch soldiers they had taken hostage their victory was complete. Lieutenant Colonel Thom Karremans tried to negotiate the fate of the enclave's civilians. He was firmly rebuffed, but was then filmed drinking a toast with Ratko Mladić. Even as reports started to surface of a mass killing, video footage emerged of Dutch hostages dancing the conga in celebration of their own release.

What happened at Srebrenica in July 1995 shocked a continent that was confident it had entered a new phase of history, free of the grotesque brutality and bloodshed that had blighted Europe for centuries. It also shook the confidence of the Netherlands that they could play a constructive role as a leading and enlightened European nation on the international stage.

'The whole Srebrenica drama was because the Dutch did not want to fight,' explained the journalist and historian Geert Mak during our conversation in Amsterdam. 'A Bosnian guy told me that the British soldiers really showed that they want to shoot. They prepared hospital tents, they were prepared to take casualties. That's their way. But the Dutch didn't want to fight.' He looked at me as though he was offering up an excuse as much as an explanation. 'Dutch neutrality is really strong.'

This sense of Dutch neutrality seems to me to be explained partly by the timidity of a smaller nation jammed between bigger ones, and partly by a parochial wish to stick to its own business.

There was undoubtedly an element of unworldly naïvety too, a disbelief that Ratko Mladic's men could be capable of the unthinkable crimes that they went on to commit. But, as Geert Mak had argued about the Dutch role in the Nazi Holocaust, bad things can come out of a naïve wish to avoid involvement in a messy situation. Notably, after Bosnia the Netherlands did decide to play a more active military role, from Kosovo to Iraq and Afghanistan. And now another complicated foreign policy crisis is demanding their attention.

As we were speaking in Amsterdam, at the other end of the European continent a ghastly and bloody war was rumbling on and on. The instincts of many in the Netherlands was to avoid getting drawn into the Ukraine conflict, but the Dutch government had been playing its part in materially supporting the struggle against Russian aggression. This decision was taken in the long shadow of the MH17 disaster in 2014, when a Malaysia Airlines flight from Amsterdam to Kuala Lumpur was shot down by a Buk missile fired by pro-Russian forces in Donbas, eastern Ukraine.* Two hundred and ninety-eight passengers and crew were killed, 196 of them Dutch. Three were infants travelling on their parents' laps. Outrage fuelled a potent moral clarity about the Ukraine conflict that has pushed back against instinctive Dutch neutrality.

The Dutch, and very many others in Europe and beyond, can be forgiven for wondering how they are once again having to ponder foreign policy flashpoints on their own continent. The end of the Cold War and the Soviet demise had seemed to remove the big existential foreign-policy question hanging over Europe. After that the focus was thought to be in the shape of an expanding and integrating European family, especially after the Maastricht Treaty was signed in 1992. That suited the

---

* MH17 was the name of the flight.

Dutch, who could allow themselves to be guided internationally by being a respected member of a larger club, reinforcing simple commercial interests.

Geert Mak sees this need for the Netherlands to join with others through the prism of history. Long after its heyday as a Golden Age global power the end of the Napoleonic era saw the Netherlands greatly expanded to include Belgium. In 1830, after 15 years, this ended in a messy divorce, leaving the rump of the Netherlands vastly smaller. Worse, as the Industrial Revolution gathered pace it meant it had lost those bits of Belgium that numbered among the most advanced, productive and resource-rich parts of Europe. This was sobering, even with the Dutch East Indies tucked away in the back pocket. 'After that moment the Dutch knew that we were a small part of the continent. We were always afraid of Germany, but in fact we were afraid of the continent.' He fixed me with a meaningful smile. 'We wanted to be like Great Britain,' he said. 'Kind of an island. We always needed some dream, some projection overseas. And after the independence of Indonesia it was the United States.'

'And money came from the US.'

'And money came! It is not by coincidence that we are really the most American of all European countries. American companies always try their stuff out in Amsterdam, to see how they react there. The deep frustration and fear of the Dutch is that we're the smallest country among the big countries. Sometimes we are also the biggest country among the small countries. And we are always afraid to be pushed into the oceans. That is always the fear of the small country; it is deep-rooted to look for protections.'

The question of money lies beneath any discussion of Dutch interests. The excesses of its imperium are often airily dismissed as regrettable costs associated with a wholly justifiable quest for trade and markets. The phrase 'going Dutch', meaning to divide a restaurant bill neatly in half, has been pushed to its limit by payment apps that allow Dutch friends to divide up food and drink bills with unnerving accuracy to the nearest cent. Apocryphal stories abound, such as being asked by a Dutch friend to share a miniscule parking charge after they have picked up your child from a party.

This sharp appreciation for the value of money has served the Dutch well, post-1945 as well as in the seventeenth century. Commercial interests can even be seen as the true lens through which the Dutch like to deal with the rest of the world.[*] The idea of the Netherlands as a buccaneering open trading economy ('de B.V. Nederland' or 'Netherlands Inc') goes back to the VOC's status as the world's first joint-stock company. Although back in the VOC days international competition was an amorphous concept enforced more by cannons than internationally-recognised contracts, the Netherlands' continuing emphasis on trade has served it well. The modern country has spawned multiple successful companies, and the current corporate darling is ASML. It plays a critical role in the global ultra-high end chip industry thanks to its breath-taking technological achievements.

ASML is the world's only producer of EUV (extreme ultraviolet) lithography systems, used to print the most intricate layers on microchips. In April 2024 it was valued at €360 billion, making it the highest value technology company in Europe. Its Dutch roots lie in Philips' role as a cornerstone investor in TSMC, the leading Taiwanese chip company. ASML grew rapidly alongside its supply-chain partner thanks to their interlinked products. If what it does was easy to grasp it would probably not be the only one to be doing it, but my own limited understanding of the process involves a tiny tin ball, 30 millionths of a metre across, moving at over 300 kilometres per hour in a vacuum. A carbon

---

[*] And, as discussed in Chapter 5, a keen nose for money has contributed to the Dutch tradition of tolerance.

dioxide laser warms it up and then I believe it is blasted into a plasma with a temperature of half a million degrees Celsius. This happens 50,000 times a second, producing enough EUV light to be reflected in the most flawless and smooth mirrors ever made, and this somehow results in those ultra-high end chips. If I have got any of this wrong, I apologise, and hope it does not lead anybody to build a badly-calibrated extreme ultraviolet system of their own. The machines involved are the most expensive mass-produced machine tools ever made, costing around $100 million each. Chris Miller, who understands this far better than me, explained in his excellent book *Chip War* that the EUV system is so complex that replacing just the laser would involve 457,329 parts.[2]

As well as being considered an irreplaceable link in the supply chain for those high-end chips, ASML is rightly seen as a standard bearer for the Netherlands' ability to compete at the sharp end of the global knowledge economy. Dutch governments have recognised this, and €2.5 billion of public money has been pledged for the Eindhoven region where ASML and its spin-off companies are based. It is trying to develop a cluster of knowledge-intensive industries in the region, clunkily termed 'Brainport' to match the 'Mainport' that links Rotterdam to the world's shipping lanes. ASML announced €80 million of investment into research at the Eindhoven University of Technology, funding PhD research and the construction of a new 'clean room' entirely free of dust.

However, some tensions between governmental and ASML priorities remain: although a study looking at what developing the tech cluster would mean for Eindhoven emphasised the need to build fancy homes for well-paid tech workers, government plans are heavier on social and affordable housing. ASML is also having to negotiate a febrile Dutch political landscape where Henk and Ingrid's instinctive nativism sometimes shades over into hostility towards foreign arrivals, even those clutching PhDs. Geert Wilders, never shy in spotting an opportunity, played on this when the Netherlands' population officially hit 18 million, saying simply that the country was full.* In March 2024 ASML threatened to move abroad if anything was done to curtail its access to international engineering talent and political support. Around 40% of its workforce is foreign, and its former CEO, Peter Wennink, has accused politicians of not understanding what businesses need to thrive.

* * *

As I walked into Maastricht my route took me through to the *Berenkuil*, a peculiar and creepy set of sculptures in a concrete former animal enclosure in Aldenhof Park. There you will find a sculpture of a young woman in evening dress, cradling the neck of a dead giraffe. This is as deeply unsettling a piece of public art as it is unlikely. Thankfully there is a nearby park bench where you can gather your thoughts, accompanied by a life size statue of a ruminating bear.

From the park you head up through a jumble of alleyways into the old centre of Maastricht itself. Many Dutch *binnensteden* can be charmingly disorientating, with little lanes and bridges, tiny cut-throughs and dead ends surrounded by a chocolate box assortment of houses and overflowing window boxes. What Maastricht adds to this is that it is not flat, so you get sets of steps and sloping lanes. It reminded me of the distinctive insides of

---

* The State Committee Demographic Developments 2050 established by the House of Representatives, advises that the Netherlands aim for 19–20 million people by 2050. This was accepted by the right wing government in December 2024. https://www.staatscommissie2050.nl/bijlagen-rapport/documenten/publicaties/2024/02/01/information-in-english.

old Dutch houses, which are often jumbled and full of different levels and ladders and precipitous staircases.

Maastricht has charm and personality, but even its most ardent supporters would concede that the city was an unassuming choice for that 1992 treaty. The Maastricht Treaty was meant to be far more than a transnational institutional reshuffling; rather, it was meant to be the critical moment when Europe was forged into a global force to stand shoulder-to-shoulder with the United States (at the time China barely registered). This ambition was music to the ears of the Dutch, who have long accepted that any return to greatness would only happen standing alongside a willing alliance of European neighbours, big, small and medium. The Netherlands could be a prominent mid-sized player within the EU, wielding outsize influence at the heart of this benign global force, a new type of enlightened cross-border polity for a post-Cold War world.

It has not worked out quite like that, and this is problematic. Beyond the European-level politics and its own domestic concerns, the Netherlands cannot credibly divorce its own fortunes from those of the spluttering Union. For one thing, for all my discussion of social cohesion and agility in the face of complex crises, to face down the threats of the future the Dutch state ultimately needs money. As the Draghi report points out, the economic trajectory of the EU has been flatlining (at best) since the financial crisis, and this puts Dutch prosperity at risk. Other EU countries might run out of money for over-generous pensions, subsidising theatres or fixing bridges; the Netherlands might run out of money for keeping their feet dry. A fading, inward-facing and over-regulated Europe does not suit a country that has built its fortunes on buccaneering across the waves in search of trade. But there it is, a small country in twenty-first-century Europe.

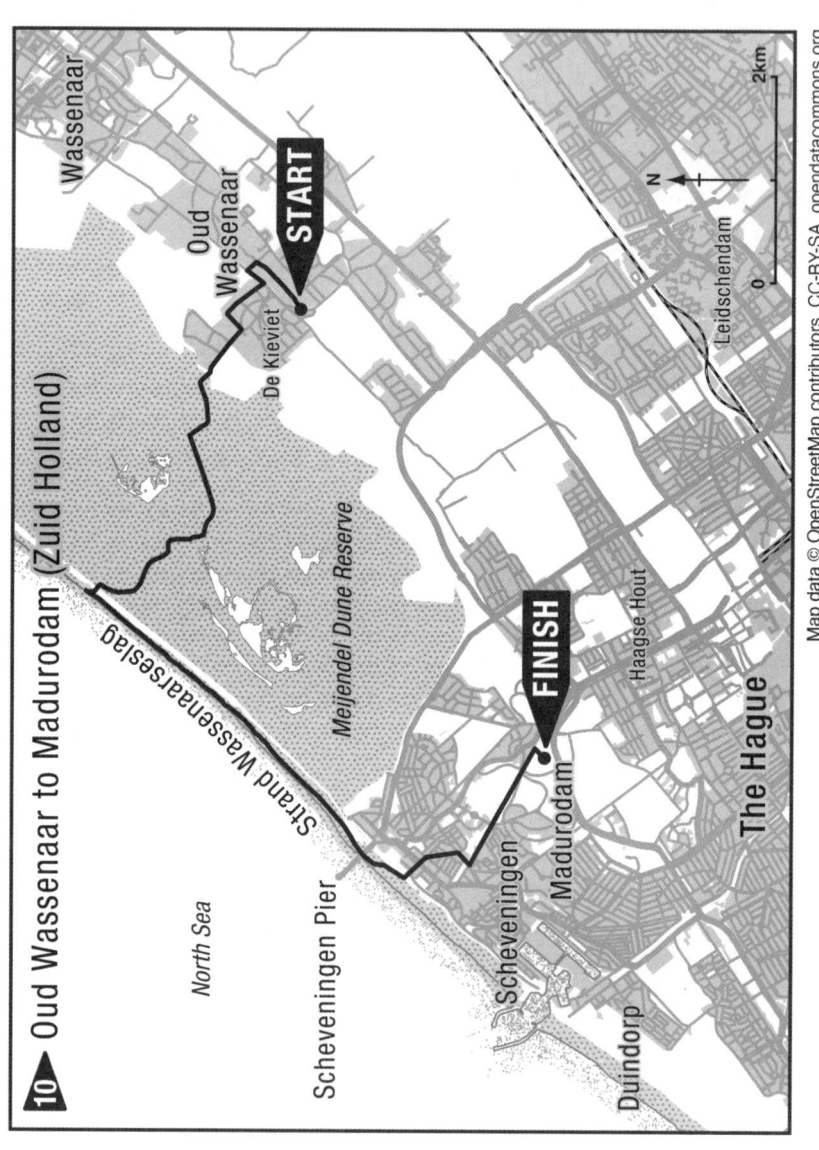

10 Oud Wassenaar to Madurodam (Zuid Holland)

START

FINISH

Wassenaar

Oud Wassenaar

De Kieviet

Meijendel Dune Reserve

Strand Wassenaarseslag

North Sea

Scheveningen Pier

Scheveningen

Madurodam

Haagse Hout

Duindorp

The Hague

Leidschendam

N

0

2km

10

OUD WASSENAAR TO MADURODAM
(ZUID HOLLAND)

This walk begins in Oud Wassenaar, where Konijnenlaan peels off the main road and disappears between the trees and mansions. I followed Konijnenlaan until the junction with Nachtegaallaan, turned left, left again and then right onto Kievietslaan. This lane turns sharp left, and you re-join a main road (Meijendelseweg) to head northwest up a slope. There is a roundabout at the top with carparks, and the footpath slides off to take you due west, then on a meander through dunes and trees. After the Monkeybos playground and a cluster of buildings you need to pick your way along paths that run through the dunes and some small lakes to the sea, roughly to the northwest. The next stretch is simple enough: you can see the Ferris wheel of Scheveningen's pier way off in the distance as you begin your hike along the sands to the southwest. Once you are there, head under the pier and if you are keen to see Duindorp, head for The Hague's harbour and around the docks to the far side, where you will find this gritty little suburb. My own track, on a ferociously windy and rainy day, took me inland in Scheveningen on Badhuiskade, past the

*Stadsboerderij 't Waaygat city farm, and directly southeast on the
Haringkade with water on my left. After just over a kilometre you
will arrive at Madurodam and the picturesque end of this final walk.*

* * *

In the tough little seaside enclave of Duindorp a gigantic bonfire
was being torched. When I say gigantic I mean *gigantic*: its base
was 20 metres squared, and tens of thousands of wooden pallets
had been used in its construction, rising up into the night sky.
In reality it looked more like an office block than a bonfire.
A similar stack blazed just to the north, piled high by the old
fishing communities of Scheveningen.

Bonfire-building competition between the two, separated by
Den Haag's harbour at Visserhaven, was fierce. These mammoth
enterprises took months of planning, and heavy machinery was
needed to put all the pallets in place. The tradition had begun
as a way to dispose of Christmas trees in the middle of the
twentieth century, but over many years the size of the bonfires
had grown. By the 2010s, rivalry had driven them higher
and higher, confirmed by official covenants on the maximum
allowable dimensions. A height of 12 metres on New Year's Eve
2014 became 35 metres by New Year's Eve 2017, on a foundation
of 15 metres squared.

By New Year's Eve in 2018 these great ziggurats of wood
and fire reached even higher into the skies above the North Sea
coast. The allowable bases were now 22 metres squared, with a
maximum height of 35 metres. But there was pressure to build
higher. In Scheveningen the pile peaked at 45.83 metres high;
in Duindorp an even more astonishing 48.66 metres. The stacks
were estimated to be around 12,000 cubic metres each, despite a
generous restriction of 10,000. Expectations for the night were
high. Unfortunately, so were the winds.

That first night of 2019 is now remembered for the *vonkenregen*, a terrifying rain of zillions of sparks and chunks of burning wood that was blown from the top of the Scheveningen bonfire and across the neighbourhoods to the northeast. Fire tornados span out of control along the beachfront. Buildings caught fire, roofs were destroyed, houses were badly damaged by the water from fire brigade hoses and bicycles melted from the heat.

This was to be expected: the Chinese may have invented gunpowder, but for the four years that we spent in the Netherlands it felt like the pyromaniac Dutch who had taken the art of exploding and burning most to their hearts. Dangerous fireworks and ludicrous bonfires are the product of several dimensions of the national character coming together: a blithe attitude to risk, an essential unruliness in the face of authority and an addiction to partying and having fun. When the Dutch do New Year, explosions fill the air, entire buildings shake, and—inevitably—fingers and eyes go missing. Hospitals report that there are generally two waves of admissions: the first on New Year's Eve, where blood-soaked revellers are whisked straight to hospital after exploding themselves; and the second a day or so later, when alcoholic stupors start to wear off and people realise that yes, they are missing their index finger.

The terrifying *vonkenregen* caused a hefty dose of soul-searching from those involved in the sea front conflagrations, then a detonation of blame and criticism. The mayor of Den Haag, Pauline Krikke, resigned later that year after a report from the Dutch Safety Board noted a litany of safety failures, including the use of unauthorised fire accelerants that had contributed to the breezy infernos.

Some obvious decisions were made, and a 10-metre height limit for bonfire towers was introduced. So far, so (kind of) sensible. And in most countries that would have been the end of it. But not the Netherlands, home of eel riots and a ferocious headstrong unwillingness to be constrained by the imposition of pesky rules.

As the next New Year's Eve crept closer, resentment grew over the restrictions. As ever, there was more at play than simple pyromania. Both Duindorp and Scheveningen are home to tight-knit fishing communities, tough places where kids were brought up to think of themselves as somewhat different to their fellow Dutch. Duindorp in particular feels isolated, its ranks of closely packed flat-roofed terraces cut off on three sides by trees and sand dunes, the other side hard against the harbour.* Inland, beyond them both was Den Haag, the international city par excellence, with its French and German and British schools and its international courts, its expat financial packages and its embassy parties. Resentment merged with identity, with a feeling of being left-behind, of being marginalised in their own land.

Alert readers of this book might predict what happened next. Yes, there were riots. These centred on Duindorp, and became known as the *vreugdevuur* ('joy of fire') riots. There were running battles in the street between youths and police. Some rioters were young: one nine-year-old boy was caught brandishing a Molotov cocktail. Journalists trying to cover the riots were bombarded with volleys of eggs. Properties were set on fire.

Unruly, blazing and explosive New Year celebrations continue to be a feature of the Netherlands. The largest and most dangerous fireworks have been banned, but autumn newspapers are full of reports of caches being discovered by police. The celebrations to see in 2024 saw 12 young people lose a hand or finger from fireworks, with over 50 people undergoing plastic surgery for their wounds. That January the Amsterdam police chief, Frank Paauw, said the only way the festival of riots, property damage

---

* Its relative isolation led to Duindorp being used as a prison camp for suspected Nazi sympathisers after the Second World War.

and attacks on emergency services could be stopped would be to ban consumer fireworks. Politicians spoke about outlawing balaclavas and classifying fireworks as illegal weapons. Jeffrey Peters of the HVLB (the association for firework enthusiasts) blamed 'antisocial bastards' for spoiling the fun for everybody else, and suggested that policemen hit by fireworks respond by firing rubber bullets. The Mayor of Nijmegen, Hubert Bruls, identified the trouble with a 'Dutch disease' where people thought they could throw fireworks at police and set fire to neighbours' fences in the name of tradition.

Whether or not there is such a 'Dutch disease' or a surfeit of 'antisocial bastards', there is an anarchic anti-authority streak running through the blood of many Dutch men and women. The Dutch do think of themselves as 'plain talking', a tendency that can translate into stubbornness, intransigence, rudeness or a propensity to riot over eels and explosions. At the heart of the Netherlands is a pact that the Dutch have made with one each other: they will come together through the communalism and cooperation of the *poldermodel* to build their remarkable country; but they also reserve the right to disagree and think everyone else is both wrong and an utter, utter idiot. Then throw a firework at them.

There is a tension involved in this, a delicate balance. The *poldermodel* works because there is a fundamental belief that the country is fair, that it is essentially equal. When the water rises and they need to pull together to plug the leak and build a bigger dyke for the future, they need to know that they are all in it together.

Yet throughout this book I have raised two reasons for wondering if the pact will hold. There will be bigger challenges facing the Netherlands in the foreseeable future, and at the same time there will be more reasons for individual Dutch people to doubt that they really are all in it together.

That is why this final walk that explains the Netherlands starts in the gilded lanes and giant mansions of Wassenaar. It then tracks south through the dunes and beachfront towards Scheveningen, its pier and Ferris wheel beckoning you forwards from many miles away. You can then head slightly further into that most international of cities, Den Haag, to little Duindorp, before tacking back inland to Madurodam. This is a theme park featuring a miniaturised version of the Netherlands, and a perfect place to sit with an ice cream pondering the future of the country.

* * *

An old acquaintance of mine returned from a posting abroad with the Dutch diplomatic service, voicing a fear that the Netherlands would be quite boring for their family. They mentioned Wassenaar, a place so respectable, so fancy, so stultifying that it seemed to represent everything they feared moving back to. The next I heard, they had moved to Wassenaar.

It may not be the liveliest corner of the Netherlands, it may even be a bit stultifying, but arguably it is one of the loveliest. And of all the grand lanes in the forested old heart of Wassenaar, Konijnenlaan is the grandest. This is the most expensive street in the entire country. In 2023 the average value of a house on Konijnenlaan (according to local council measurements) was a hefty €3.1 million, and walking along you can see why.

The road itself feels quite humble, an unmarked piece of asphalt that weaves through giant hedges and mature trees with little more fanfare than a good cycle path. Enormous piles of houses squat behind those hedges, capped with soaring rooflines of tile and great sweeps of thatch. Gardens are immaculate even by Dutch standards, if slightly larger, and there are many more flagpoles than any neighbourhood that I grew up in. Given that this is an elite area, the other surprise is that many of the driveways sit open to the road, refusing to hunker down behind forbidding fences and electric gates. I saw no private security patrols or ostentatious displays of bling.

That is as it should be in the Netherlands. One of the more striking aspects of our move from Singapore to this country was the shift in attitudes towards extreme wealth. One house we lived near in Singapore had been designed to showcase the owner's large collection of Ferraris. Eight or nine of them sat in a row for everybody to notice, slowly rotting in the moist equatorial air. Another tower block boasted a lift that plonked your car right into your apartment, so that you could admire it from your sofa on the 20th floor. The basic idea was that if you were stinking rich you had an absolute right to show it, so you did.

Not so in the Netherlands. Suddenly everybody with a six-figure salary had a Volvo. There were nice cars that cost a lot, but they were not ostentatiously expensive. There were no McLarens or Lamborghinis, Rolls Royces or Bentleys. Even the dogs of Konijnenlaan did not look like they had been bought for Instagram or looking fancy in the park. The rich ladies liked to wear clothing with a leopard skin print, but then that seemed to be just as true for all Dutch women. For a bunch of people with a keen sense of money, the Dutch are remarkably restrained when it comes to showing it off.

The underlying message of the lack of ostentation is a consensus that the Netherlands is an egalitarian society with an aversion to hierarchies. On the face of it this idea is robust: a town like Wassenaar really ought to be cluttered with half-million euro automobiles, but is not. The Dutch monarch plays along with this, seeming to have a constitutional requirement to be photographed on a bicycle every month or so. This egalitarian message is backed up by data. In 2022 income inequality in the Netherlands measured 0.285 on the Gini coefficient (where closer to 0 is more equal and closer to 1 is more unequal), a figure that has remained remarkably constant since 1990.[1] This made it the fifth most equal EU state out of the 27. Meanwhile the corresponding wealth inequality figure was a vastly higher 0.711.*

The disparity between income inequality and wealth inequality essentially means that while the Netherlands might be quite equal now, it is set to be far less so in the future. Steadily accumulated wealth will eventually win out over the pennies that drop into your bank account every month. This broadly tallies with the views of columnist and media entrepreneur Sander Schimmelpenninck. He made a Dutch television series on equality of opportunity that began with him eating soup in the kitchen of his moated castle.† 'Because I made this series about inequality, people think that I see it as an explanation for what's happening now in Holland,' he told me on a scratchy phone line. 'I don't. Holland is very rich and a land of opportunity. Inequality is growing but current voters are not really suffering from inequality, it will be their kids who suffer from that.'

Nowhere is inequality of wealth more obvious than in housing. Dutch property prices have risen extremely quickly, especially in cities like Amsterdam and the coastal strip of the Randstad.[2] House prices have been the key driver exacerbating wealth inequality year after year, harming geographical and generational equality and producing a ledger of winners and losers whose fortunes are not captured in simple income figures.

---

* Figures from the government's macroeconomic forecasting agency CPB showed that from 2011–19 the richest 0.01% had an effective tax rate of 28% thanks to non-wage income, compared to 40% for those on average incomes. https://www.cpb.nl/inkomens-en-belastingen-aan-de-top.
† Technically he is Count Sander Schimmelpenninck, and the series is *Sander en de Kloof* (*Sander and the Gap*). https://npo.nl/start/serie/sander-en-de-kloof/seizoen-1_1/de-plek-van-je-wieg/afspelen.

The geographical variation in housing favours those who were in the nicer bits of the western edge of the country to begin with, as they can draw on existing family wealth to get the younger generations on to the ladder. The children of Geert Wilders' proverbial Henk and Ingrid, living their blameless lives in the less dynamic and less international eastern half of the country, may feel aggrieved at this. If they or their friends have ever contemplated taking a job in Amsterdam, they might notice the hordes of tourists staying in short-term lets, or the masses of international students enrolled for English-speaking courses and searching for a place to live. Neither makes it easier for them and resentment grows.

Despite the inequalities of wealth created by the housing boom, the Netherlands has persisted with the *hypotheekrenteaftrek*, a regressive mortgage tax relief that hands over government cash to existing home owners. I mentioned the growing shortfall in housing back in the chapter on Amsterdam; meanwhile one in three new homes is being delayed by complaints from existing locals. This prompted the then housing minister in 2024, Hugo de Jonge, to complain that the right to a nice view was taken more seriously than the right to have a place to live.[3]

Fairness in the education pathway to a higher paying job has also been under scrutiny. Part of the focus has been on the way the Netherlands sends children into different secondary schools depending on the results of exams taken at the tender age of 11. More than half of children go straight into VMBO vocational schools at the age of 12, with 24% going to HAVO schools on the way to a further educational college and 22% to VWO schools on a university track. In 2021 the government's most senior advisory body, SER, said the education system was increasing inequality of opportunity. It called for mixed ability classes in the early years of secondary school rather than rigid demarcation of future careers at 12.

A contemporary television documentary series, *Klassen*, helped to focus attention on this issue by following 11-year-olds at school in Amsterdam-Noord. It highlighted how difficult some students found it to prepare for these crucial tests while facing struggles with their home lives and other challenges. In 2024 the government tried to ameliorate the problem by telling schools to revise their recommendations for future schooling upwards when children do better in tests. The same year the Education Minister Robbert Dijkgraaf said he wanted to move away from talking about 'high' and 'low' levels of education, as it set up an unhelpful hierarchy that did not fit with individual skills. It has been well documented that children from ethnic minorities have tended to be consistently marked down by their teachers relative to their white peers.

During our years in the Netherlands I heard plenty of talk of certain schools being 'white', where parents apparently lobbied behind the scenes to keep numbers of ethnic minority pupils low. (My son was not in the Dutch system, so this is hearsay.) As Delft is a university town I saw more visible evidence of another form of inequality every day that I stepped outside my front door. Many of the largest and (hitherto) grandest canal houses in Delft were owned by student societies. To those lucky enough to join, these provided splendid accommodation, a vibrant social life and enduring networking connections to last a lifetime. To my eye these societies always seemed to consist of the poshest looking men coupled with the best-looking women. A friend of mine told me that the student societies of TU Delft had been earmarked by her more mercenary friends as a key hunting ground for well-connected, high-earning future husbands. To my ears, those big buildings in Delft often housed some of the most obnoxious and antisocial students, who acted as though they were invulnerable to criticism about echoing late night parties and bicycles humorously thrown in canals. My impressions tallied with wider impressions about these societies: their umbrella organisation LKVV introduced a code of conduct after a flurry of headlines about sexual harassment and violent hazing rituals. One society at the University of Groningen, Vindicat, came under the microscope after two badly injured geese were discovered in one of its houses, along with a swastika sprayed on a wall.

While there may not be too many ostentatious displays of bling in the Netherlands, there is certainly obvious privilege, and obvious deprivation. As noted in previous chapters, perhaps a fifth of Dutch people are struggling financially. Eurostat is more precise, suggesting that 16.5% of the population is at risk of poverty and social exclusion. The figures are predictably worse for immigrant children, with almost 19% of those born abroad officially classed as poor. Compare that to a child who, along with his or her parents, was born in the Netherlands: only 2.5% of such children are officially poor.

Recently there have been attempts to help those in dire financial straits. In Rotterdam the super-wealthy Van der Vorm family is trying to tackle the debts of 1,000 families, provided they were caused by a life changing set-back such as redundancy or serious illness. Amsterdam and Utrecht have tried taking on the debts of young people. In 2024 Arnhem council announced that it would be clearing the debts of around 50 families in the deprived Immerloo II area in a two-year trial. Much of the money would come from charitable foundations, and there would be no repayment requirements. Reports suggest that many families were initially suspicious of the scheme, and resisted taking part.

The suspicion and resistance that lingers in some corners of Dutch society owes a lot to creeping alienation from the authorities. On the one hand there is the disquiet over the types of policies exploited by Geert Wilders' PVV, including the *spreidingswet* dispersal of asylum seekers across the entire country.* On the other is a run of high-profile scandals that make the proverbial Henk and Ingrid (and their Muslim counterparts) wonder whether the state really is on their side. Fracking for gas near Groningen delivered benefits to the Dutch industrial base, but the thousands of locals whose houses were cracked and rendered unsafe from earthquakes did not feel that their voices had been heard. A childcare benefits scandal involved tens of thousands of parents being incorrectly accused of fraud, and hundreds of children being removed from their families.† Although this led to the collapse of the then government in 2021, as of 2024 many victims are still awaiting compensation.

Such incidents undermine trust in the authorities, just as a belief in societal fairness is also taking a knock. The Dutch housing market is now acting less like a conveyor belt for mobility and more like a crooked lottery that compounds benefits for the lucky winners while preventing progress for the others. No wonder that a Eurobarometer survey in late 2024 saw 47% of Dutch respondents report that housing was one of their two main national concerns, compared to an EU-wide average of 13%.[4] Worse, its dysfunction is wheedling its way into other issues. It threatens to stymie the economic vibrancy of the densely packed Randstad on the country's west coast, and in particular Amsterdam. It also bleeds into a populist form of politics that finds room to blame highly skilled international workers and students (along with other immigrants) for exacerbating housing woes. ASML is not the only company that requires exactly those sectors for its lifeblood.

---

* *Spreidingswet* translates as the 'distribution law'.
† Parents with dual nationality, a group disproportionately including poorer parents from ethnic minorities, were subjected to extra scrutiny over their child benefit arrangements.

The Netherlands Interdisciplinary Demographic Institute (NIDI) says the housing market can even be charged with causing birth rates to fall. Between 2010 and 2023 the average number of births per Dutch woman fell from 1.8 to 1.43, echoing the catastrophic demographic decline seen elsewhere in western Europe and beyond. The NIDI estimates that between 15 and 27% of this decline is due to dramatic house price increases. Daniel van Wiki of NIDI noted that if they cannot afford good homes, 'people will either lower their standards or postpone having children. The data here suggests that, at least in some cases, it's the latter.'[5]

The Netherlands is far from the only country troubled by inequality, but there are few other places where the sense that everybody is pulling together is so fundamental to society and—ultimately—physical survival. The *poldermodel* requires a fair society where everybody, however argumentative, stands next to everybody else and faces challenges together. This is a high bar, and required of few other countries (thank goodness). Geert Wilders' political success might be less about the growth of intolerance than a signal that the Dutch social compact is no longer quite so robust, no longer trusted. The same might be said of the tractors massing on the Malieveld, the spate of riots and wilful public disturbances and the frustrated minorities feeling that they are stuck on the margins of Dutch society.

'It's wealth, decadence, boredom,' says Sander Schimmelpenninck, who believes a void in modern Dutch lives is being exploited by populist politicians. 'We have too much time on our hands, sitting on our couches, watching our phones,' he says, while those politicians exacerbate differences but offer few solutions. He sees a mismatch between the character that has allowed the Dutch to flourish for so many centuries, and the character now needed to face their future challenges. 'We are very pragmatic, we cooperate when we see a concrete problem that needs solving. But climate change is existential and global, and we are not well equipped to comprehend this kind of bigger issue. We are light spirited, open minded, good at having fun. But I'm not sure there's much more to us. We're not big thinkers, and I don't think our qualities are much needed now.'

The challenges of climate change that loom on the horizon will be considerable.* What I saw during my walks across the Netherlands left me in no doubt that the country is an elemental battleground between humanity and nature. For the best part of a millennium humans have gained enough of an upper hand to make sense of the country and propel it to extraordinary successes: in culture, art, empire, geopolitics, naval affairs, agriculture, science, economics, sport and architecture (but not necessarily cuisine). If you do not associate the flat, boring, waterlogged Netherlands with extraordinary landscapes, think again. Epic beaches, lush forests, meadows, dunes, polders and waterways of every description. Understanding how those landscapes have been shaped by that elemental battle will make you appreciate them even more.

This first half of the twenty-first century is seeing that struggle taken to new heights. Climate change is raising water levels and causing ever more extreme weather, whether storms in the North Sea or vast quantities of rain in the European heartland, draining through the great rivers that cross these low lands. At the same time, the remarkable intensity of how the Netherlands has organised itself is itself causing problems, from

---

* The challenges to the Netherlands' complex physical infrastructure are not just from climate change. I could also throw in the existence of invasive American species of crayfish that destroy aquatic ecosystems while happily destabilising the banks of canals by burrowing into them. You often see them on bicycle paths waving their claws in the air in the manner of belligerent drunks looking for a fight.

its ultra-productive farms to its urban areas and housing stock. If it fails to grapple with these challenges it could find that they become systemic, and then—at least symbolically—it all gets washed into the North Sea.

If ever a European country had a stake in mitigating climate change, putting its collective shoulder to the wheel to sort out that rising water, it is the Netherlands. After all, this is a country that is planning to build a new village of 8,000 homes a full five metres below sea level.* But it is not. As I write this, the latest Climate and Energy Outlook from the Netherlands Environmental Assessment Agency says that it is 'very unlikely' that the country will hit its target of 55% less emissions in 2030 compared to 1990.[6] Not one single sector is on track to hit its targets. On the other hand the Netherlands came second only to Denmark out of 63 countries in the 2025 Climate Change Performance Index, which assesses countries on CO_2 reductions, sustainable energy supplies and overall climate policies.[7] That represents an improvement of well over 20 places in four years. The Netherlands has obvious reasons to deal with climate change, and needs to remember them. I suspect that rather too many politicians have opted for the easy decision again and again, just as in other countries less vulnerable to climate impacts. The physical future of this geographic extremity—and future generations of Dutch men and women—relies upon it.

* * *

The footpath from old Wassenaar heads up a long slope, that reliable Dutch signifier that water is close. At the top of the slope is a car park and a glorious view over forests and dunes towards the sea. A web of footpaths and cycleways fans out through

---

* The village of Cortelande will be in the Zuidplas (Southern Pond) polder near Gouda.

hillocks of twisted oaks and sandy beaches, where rosy cheeked ladies from Wassenaar walk their Labradors and cyclists stretch their lycra-clad limbs. I passed the Monkeybos playground, little more than a straggly copse full of concrete pipes and branches for kids to adventure in. The Netherlands does playgrounds extremely well, with an assumption that mud and broken bones are all part of the plan for a healthy childhood. Unlike in Britain or Italy they also tend to be embarrassingly clean, tidy and cared for. I miss that.

The sand dunes that skirt the length of the North Sea coast feel like they were transplanted onto the edge of this ultra-organised country from the wild oceanic edge of Western Australia. They act as a living, breathing flood barrier, in addition to allowing dog walking and the peculiar sensation of actually climbing up and down slopes. They also formed part of the Nazi Atlantic Wall of defences, and halfway through the beach section of this walk you will pass a couple of grim concrete bunkers, staring hard out to sea high above a beach bar. (The Nazis also used this particular section of sand dunes on the way to Scheveningen to launch V1 and V2 rockets at London and Antwerp, and shoot people in the head.) This is where we came for our Sunday dog walks, a chance in coastal Holland to tramp around a landscape that felt wild, that felt like it had not been designed by those tall spatial planning men in dark suits.

Beyond the dunes autumn was hitting the Dutch coast with a vengeance. When I piled down the sandy slope onto the beach itself I felt the full force of the weather. I walked into the wind with my body at an angle, as Scheveningen pier slowly, very slowly, loomed closer into view. I felt like I was being sand blasted. Although the Ferris wheel at the end of the pier was still turning, the viewing gondolas were all empty; even the flexible Dutch attitude to risk thought better of being hoisted dozens of metres up above the boiling waves while the wind blasted them violently from the side. A multicultural crowd of teenagers on a school visit hung around the wave line, laughing as the wind caught in their jackets. A group of Muslim schoolgirls in their long, flapping dresses looked like elegant pawns in a game of giant chess.

I cut up towards the run of bars on the Scheveningen seafront, looking for relief from the wind in the shelter of the Zanzibar Beachclub and De Golfslag. Diners slurping lunchtime Heinekens and tucking into bowls of *bitterballen* eyed me with pity from the safety of their indoor firepits.* Maybe that was my hair, which had been shaped by the storm and the sea spray into something a 1960s Pan Am air stewardess might have attempted if they had enough hairspray. I climbed a makeshift steel bridge above construction works for new flood defences, reached the lee of an ugly apartment block and reconsidered.

My original plan had been to marry the walk through Scheveningen with a visit to Duindorp, its *joy of fire* rival on the other side of the little harbour. Duindorp's sense of embattlement was recently reinforced by a new development of swanky multi-story apartments, squeezed between it and the harbour. Even more so when the development's new residents went to court, trying to force the closure of a nearby open-air football pitch, saying it was noisy and a focus for youthful mischief. But Duindorp would have to wait for another less stormy day. I felt the first raindrops fall from the angry sky, and I had little desire to turn up for my flight home later that evening sodding wet. Instead, I dialled up Google maps on my phone, and had a revelation.

Off to the north, not far past the Stadsboerderij 't Waaygat city farm, was the good, clean, wholesome fun of *Madurodam*, where the Netherlands has been miniaturised and theme-parked

---

* *Bitterballen* are small deep fried balls of some form of liquid meat, often smothered in some gloopy sauce or other. I found it easy to resist their charms.

for mass enjoyment. In one compact area it was possible to see the marvels of the entire country, shrunk to 1/25th their real size, laid out amongst a network of paths and walkways.

Many of the sights were familiar from my odyssey around the Netherlands: there was the Maeslantkering that kept Dutch feet dry; the Nationaal Monument op de Dam from the seething heart of Amsterdam; Schiphol airport itself; and even Rotterdam's Kijk-Kubus, made from row after row of conjoined cubes. *Madurodam* was a celebration of all that was notable and magnificent about the country. There was the Basilica Sint-Jan from Den Bosch and the Rijkmuseum, Utrecht's Domtower and Delft's Prinsenhof. And then suddenly it got very, very Dutch.

If Italy, where I live, had done its own version of *Madurodam* it would have included glories such as Venice's Grand Canal, the Colosseum, the Trevi Fountain, Florence's Duomo. Justifiably so. Britain might have included a touch of popular culture, such as the set from the TV soap opera Coronation Street, and the US would surely have had the HOLLYWOOD letters on their hillside. China would have gone for grandiosity, with the Forbidden City, the Great Wall and the monumental skyline of Shanghai. And the Netherlands?

The Dutch found space to include a sewage treatment plant.

Honestly, it had a 1/25th scale sewage treatment plant, in a theme park.

And not just that: it had 1960s housing estates and industrial facilities, anti-flooding infrastructure and transport infrastructure.* Remember that this is a country where they are not ashamed to put form and function alongside that long glorious history, where housing units are purposefully designed to knit together with public transport and playgrounds that repurpose

---

* The housing estates were accurate replicas of real ones, not just something plucked from the imagination.

as flood sinks. The light industrial estates and productively optimised agriculture are there along with wind turbines and oil and gas infrastructure. This is a country that measures, analyses and acts.[*]

That miniaturised 1/25th scale sewage treatment plant sums up the magnificence of this remarkable country. It suggests that however much some might forget what has made the Netherlands what it is, there is pragmatism at the centre of the Dutch mind, a recognition that there is more to this place than clogs and *Brand Orange*. In 2024 the Central Bureau of Statistics found that 84.2% of Dutch people rated their lives at 7 out of 10 or better. CBS's chief economist, Peter Hein van Mulligen, told reporters that 'The Netherlands is a rich and happy country across the board.'[8] That is not a statement that could ever be made of a country that neglected its sewage system. The kind of mind that decided to plonk a miniaturised sewage treatment plant in a theme park is also the kind of mind that can think its way through the challenges the Netherlands faces.

'Let's be realistic,' Geert Mak told me. 'It is very well possible that most cities like Amsterdam will survive a hundred years, perhaps two hundred years. I would be surprised if I could come back after 300 years and this city would be still there.' He took a sharp intake of breath as he spoke about the probable demise of his beloved Amsterdam, but he was right; the challenges ahead are likely to be that serious.

But if there is another thing that walking around this astonishing country taught me, it is that you should never bet against the hard work, pragmatism and ingenuity of the Dutch, *if* they can stick together. Geert Mak spoke about a friend of his who recommended that they start moving Amsterdam to a safer

---

[*] In 2023 on average every Dutch resident produced precisely 456kg of waste, including increases in organic and garden waste categories.

place beyond Arnhem. That sounds like a very Dutch solution: if the water is in the wrong place, you move it; if Amsterdam is in the wrong place, you move Amsterdam.

If the Netherlands was full of any people other than the Dutch, I would be a pessimist about its future. Instead, it is full of the Dutch, zipping around on their bikes, arguing loudly, drinking Heineken, eating unidentified fried meat products and dancing to awful techno music. As it is, I give them a fighting chance.

ROUGH TIMELINE OF DUTCH HISTORY

1200s   The Dutch Water Boards are set up to organise the collective maintenance of water infrastructure

1568–1648   Dutch Revolt against Spanish rule (also the Eighty Years War), resulting in formal recognition of the independence of the Dutch Republic

1584   William the Silent, leader of the Dutch Revolt, is assassinated in Delft (the first politician to be assassinated by a handgun)

1588–1672   Approximate dates of the Dutch Golden Age

1595   The first, ill-fated Dutch voyage (*Eerste Schipvaart*) to the Indies sets off from Texel

1602   The United East India Company (*Vereenigde Oostindische Compagnie* or VOC) is established

1619   Batavia (modern Jakarta, the capital of Indonesia) is founded by the VOC in the Dutch East Indies

1621   The Dutch West India Company (*Geoctrooieerde Westindische Compagnie* or GWC) is established

1642   Rembrandt van Rijn paints *The Night Watch*

1667   The Dutch capture the English flagship *Royal Charles* during the Raid on the Medway

1672   The *Rampjaar*, or year of disaster

1688	William of Orange becomes King William III of England, Ireland and Scotland in the Glorious Revolution
1763	The Berbice slave rebellion breaks out on the northern coasts of South America
1792	The GWC is dissolved
1799	The VOC is dissolved
1815	The Kingdom of the Netherlands is established following the defeat of Napoleon, comprising of the modern Netherlands and Belgium
1825	An aristocratic uprising sparks the Java War, with victory in 1830 leading to more formal colonial control of the Dutch East Indies
1830	Belgium declares independence from the Netherlands
1860	*Max Havelaar* is published, attacking Dutch rule in the Indies as brutal and unjust
1904	The Dutch declare victory in the Aceh War in Sumatra after four decades and a cost of around 100,000 lives, although fighting continues until 1914
1914–1918	The Dutch are neutral during the First World War
1932	The Afsluitdijk is completed, sealing off the opening of the Zuiderzee and creating the IJsselmeer
1940	Nazi Germany invades the Netherlands and the occupation begins
1942	Imperial Japan conquers the Dutch East Indies
1944	Operation Market Garden fails
1944–1945	The *Hongerwinter*
1945	Nazi Germany capitulates and the Netherlands is liberated; Japan surrenders and the Dutch East Indies are returned to Dutch rule

1945–1949	The Indonesian War of Independence, culminating in the demise of the Dutch East Indies
1952	The Netherlands is a founding member of the European Coal and Steel Community, which eventually becomes the European Union
1953	The North Sea Flood
1954	Construction begins on the Delta Works projects
1974	The Netherlands loses the football World Cup final to West Germany and a nation is traumatised
1975	Surinam gains independence, and those born there are given five years to apply if they want Dutch citizenship
1978	The Netherlands loses the football World Cup final to Argentina and the trauma continues
1986	The *Oosterscheldekering* is opened by Queen Beatrix
1992	The Maastricht Treaty is signed, creating the European Union; El Al flight 1862 crashes in Bijlmermeer
1997	The Delta Works are completed
2002	Pim Fortuyn is assassinated
2002	The Netherlands legalises euthanasia
2004	Theo van Gogh is assassinated
2019	Dutch farmers begin their tractor-borne demonstrations
2021	The Netherlands is rocked by riots during the Covid-19 pandemic; crime journalist Peter de Vries is assassinated
2023	Geert Wilders' PVV becomes the leading party after general elections (and forms a coalition government in 2024)

ACKNOWLEDGEMENTS

The first two people that I want to thank for their help with this book are obvious: my fantastic wife, Ilaria, and my equally fantastic son, Luca. When we stepped off our plane from Singapore to Schiphol we saw a new Dutch life unfold in front of us, and it did not disappoint. Our years in Delft were magical, and the Netherlands never failed to delight and fascinate us. If the book captures anything of the happiness of those years it is thanks to Ilaria and Luca, and I love them both to bits. This book is rooted in all the experiences we had, the things we saw, the people we met, and for that reason I also ought to include Baffo, our Aussiedoodle dog from Breda, who helped with introductions.

In the middle of writing this book I suffered a bad accident involving a quad bike, a Scottish tree and my face. This almost (but not quite) killed me, and I am so grateful to both Ilaria and Luca for helping me recover, especially after a literal face-rebuilding operation (thank you to Professor Bernardo Bianchi). This also brings me to the team at Hurst, who were generous in allowing me to delay writing the book by a couple of months. Thank you in particular to Michael Dwyer for his green light and support, and Alice Clarke for her organisation, and her terrific and sympathetic editing.

Some of the people that we met during our years in the Netherlands either appear in the book or helped me knit the book together. Arnold Verschuyl was our first neighbour and a great friend throughout, and deserves a special mention. There is also a long list of people who have helped with everything from insightful friendship to interviews and introductions. In no particular order I would like to thank Arnout van de Rijt and Giullia Stellari, Greg Jackson, Jan Arie Groot, Tilly Kaisiepo, Henk Ovink, Klaas Jan van Calker, Marleen Reinke and Nick Phipps, Anke Truijen, Jan Kees Vis, Angela Bekkers and Arno Boersma, Stientje van Veldhoven, Janneke de Vries, Henrieke Jonker, Santiago Londoño, Alberto Pallecchi and the entire World Resources Institute office in Den Haag, Martin van Ittersum, Geert Mak and Yvette Cramer, Antonia Bayliss, John Savage, Elena Martini, Matthew Walsh, Nadine Walsh, Emanuele Fantini, Valeria Pecchioni, Kirsteen Campbell, Antoon van Welie, Eric Hendriks, Roel Jongeneel, Ken Giller, Yuca Waarts, Jan Bonjer, Sander Schimmelpenninck, Mohammed el Arrag, Jan Schippers and Kees van der Staaij. There are doubtless others that I have missed off the list, and I apologise.

I also owe great thanks to my parents, Jennifer and Stuart Walton. They brought me up to poke around places and ask questions, and also passed on to me their great love for the Netherlands. Being able to follow this up by writing a book like this has been quite a task but great fun. It is a unique, complex country and I have tried my best to make sense of it, in the hope that others will also see it in a new light, hopefully while tramping across bits of it. I have tried my hardest with the bits in Dutch, but I know from bitter experience that this is often not enough. Apologies. If there are factual mistakes in the book they are my fault and I apologise, and I trust that some Dutch man or woman will make it their mission to point this out to me. Thank you in advance.

NOTES

INTRODUCTION

1. https://www.youtube.com/watch?v=TjKmyFbh1NY&t=156s.
2. https://www.cbs.nl/nl-nl/nieuws/2024/23/brede-welvaart-nederland-een-na-hoogste-van-de-eu.
3. https://tenwalksexplain.com/.

1. EMMELOORD TO URK (FLEVOLAND)

1. 'De Cock en Baantjer zijn ongeveer een', Loes Smit, *Trouw*, 11 March 1987. https://www.delpher.nl/nl/kranten/view? query=urk+misdaad&coll=ddd&maxperpage=50&identifier=ABCDDD: 010827081: mpeg21:a0076&resultsidentifier=ABCDDD: 010827081: mpeg21:a0076&rowid=3.
2. 'The Netherlands: That Rotten Dike', *Time Magazine*, 27 July 1959. https://content.time.com/time/subscriber/article/0,33009,864749, 00.html.
3. Burgerperspectieven 2016/4, Sociaal en Cultureel Planbureau 2016 (p.25). https://www.scp.nl/binaries/scp/documenten/monitors/2016/12/30/burgerperspectieven-2016-4/web_COB_2016_4.pdf.
4. 'Studenten uit het buitenland voelen zich minder vaak welkom', Mark Misérus and Francesca Lionetti, *de Volkskrant*, 7 March 2024. https://www.volkskrant.nl/kijkverder/v/2024/veel-internationale-studenten-denken-dat-nederlanders-niet-van-ons-houden-v1034472.
5. 'Sturen op gebalanceerde internationalisering hogescholen en universiteiten', *Rijksoverheid*, 13 May 2024. https://www.rijksoverheid.

nl/actueel/nieuws/2024/05/13/sturen-op-gebalanceerde-internationalisering-hogescholen-en-universiteiten.

6. 'Waardering van het Nederlandse ondernemingsklimaat daalt opnieuw', University of Amsterdam and SEO, 9 December 2024. https://www.uva.nl/content/nieuws/persberichten/2024/12/waardering-van-het-nederlandse-ondernemingsklimaat-daalt-opnieuw.html?cb.

7. https://alternativetransport.wordpress.com/wp-content/uploads/2015/05/lexical-distance-among-the-languages-of-europe-2-1-mid-size.png.

2. WESTENSCHOUWEN TO VROUWENPOLDER (ZEELAND)

1. https://timesmachine.nytimes.com/timesmachine/1953/02/15/issue.html.

2. From *Itinerarium Mundii*, a travel log and diary that Peter Munday kept and revised in several forms through the seventeenth century.

3. HOEK VAN HOLLAND TO DELFT (ZUID HOLLAND)

1. For lots of fascinating detail about Dutch agricultural development see *Knowledge, networks, and niches: Dutch agricultural innovation in an international perspective, c. 1880–1970*, Harm Zwarts, PhD thesis. https://www.globalacademicpress.com/ebooks/harm_zwarts/.

2. 'Niet alles kan overal', *Rijksoverheid*, 8 June 2020. https://www.rijksoverheid.nl/documenten/rapporten/2020/06/08/niet-alles-kan-overal.

3. Quoted in 'Can Gouda's cheesemakers stall a sinking future?', Nina Siegal, *New York Times*, 1 June 2024. https://www.nytimes.com/2024/08/01/world/europe/netherlands-gouda-climate.html.

4. See *Embracing chaos: how to deal with a world in crisis?* by Jan Rotmans (Emerald Publishing 2023).

5. 'Klimaatverandering en de Nederlandse woningmarkt—Inzichten en beleidsadviezen', Sandra Phlippen and Bram Vendel, ABN AMRO, 21 February 2024. https://www.abnamro.com/research/nl/onze-research/klimaatverandering- en-de-nederlandse-woningmarkt-inzichten-en.

6. 'European climate risk assessment', European Environment Agency, 11 March 2024. https://www.eea.europa.eu/publications/european-climate-risk-assessment.

4.   DEN BURG TO 'T HORNTJE (TEXEL)

1.   'Empires Attitudes', YouGov 2020. https://d3nkl3psvxxpe9. cloudfront.net/documents/YouGov_-_Empires_attitudes.pdf.

2.   https://www.youtube.com/watch?v=328vqH3kVgA.

3.   From 'The Queen Looks at the Future', DBNL. https://www.dbnl. org/tekst/wilh001quee01_01/wilh001quee01_01_0008.php.

4.   'Dutch income in and from Indonesia 1700–1938', Angus Maddison, *Modern Asian Studies*, Volume 23 Number 4 (1989), pp. 645–670.

5.   Cited in *Revolusi: Indonesia and the birth of the modern world*, David van Reybrouck (translation by David Colmer and David McKay), Vintage 2024.

6.   From https://historibersama.com/interview-with-dutch-veteran-joop-hueting/. https://www.youtube.com/watch?v=K4Iz3_Y9i9w.

5.   BIJLMERMEER TO AMSTERDAM CENTRAAL (AMSTERDAM)

1.   One account of the fate of flight 1862 stands out head and shoulders above the rest, a chilling and forensic examination of the crash by Admiral Cloudberg (one of very many that she has written): https:// admiralcloudberg.medium.com/concrete-and-fire-the-crash-of-el-al-flight-1862-7f2e8fa4bee9.

2.   'Nieuwsblad van het Noorden', Groningen, 5 October 1992, p. 4. Geraadpleegd op Delpher, 12 March 2024. https://resolver.kb.nl/ resolve?urn=ddd:011020061:mpeg21:p004.

3.   'Is God het gat in de Bijlmer?', Jacob Noordmans, *Leeuwarder Courant*, 17 October 1992. https://resolver.kb.nl/resolve?urn= ddd:010622757:mpeg21:p005.

4.   'Pa Sem's wonderbaarlijke wederopstanding', *De Telegraaf*, 31 December 1992. https://www.delpher.nl/nl/kranten/view?coll= ddd&identifier=ddd:010691547:mpeg21:a0505

5.   Quoted in 'The permissive Dutch', Richard Reeves, *New York Times*, 20 October 1985. https://www.nytimes.com/1985/10/20/magazine/ the-permissive-dutch.html

6.   Jaarsverslagen 2022, Regionale Toetsingscommissies Euthanasia, 4 April 2023. https://www.euthanasiecommissie.nl/uitspraken/ jaarverslagen/2022/april/6/jaarverslag-2022.

7.   'This Dutch woman is physically healthy—and choosing euthanasia at 33', Senay Boztas, *The Times*, 14 April 2024. https://www.thetimes.

co.uk/article/a6507eff-ee89-41e4-b980-31bdc8b32432?shareToken=949ea4c483aaf7e7372e6a384c1e1569.

8. 'Dutch woman, 29, granted euthanasia approval on grounds of mental suffering', Harriet Sherwood, *The Guardian*, 16 May 2024. https://www.theguardian.com/society/article/2024/may/16/dutch-woman-euthanasia-approval-grounds-of-mental-suffering.

9. 'Which cities have the worst overtourism problem?', *The Economist*, 1 August 2024. https://www.economist.com/finance-and-economics/2024/08/01/which-cities-have-the-worst-overtourism-problem

10. https://www.amsterdam-rules.com/.

11. Klaas Knot quoted in 'Dutch central bank president argues for scrapping Affordable Rent Act', *NL Times*, 23 October 2024. https://nltimes.nl/2024/10/23/dutch-central-bank-president-argues-scrapping-affordable-rent-act.

12. 'Woningtekort weer opgelopen, ruim 400,000 huishoudens zoeken eigen plek' *NOS*, 12 July 2024. https://nos.nl/artikel/2528531-woningtekort-weer-opgelopen-ruim-400-000-huishoudens-zoeken-eigen-plek.

13. 'Nieuwe wet zet middenhuur in Amsterdam verder onder druk: elke woning trekt 450 gegadigden', Marc Kruyswijk, *Het Parool*, 4 December 2024. https://www.parool.nl/amsterdam/nieuwe-wet-zet-middenhuur-in-amsterdam-verder-onder-druk-elke-woning-trekt-450-gegadigden-b3991d67/.

14. 'Gezondheid en welbevinden Amsterdamse jongeren: Resultaten Gezondheidsmonitor Jeugd 2023', GGD 2024. https://www.ggd.amsterdam.nl/publish/pages/1053205/factsheet-gezondheidsmonitor-jeugd-2023-amsterdam-wt24_1.pdf.

6. BAARLE-NASSAU AND BACK AGAIN (NOORD BRABANT AND BITS OF BELGIUM)

1. 'Voor het eerst doet vrouw van dedreigde loodgieter haar verhaal: "Ons leven is voorgoed veranderd"', *AD*, 26 March 2024. https://www.ad.nl/binnenland/voor-het-eerst-doet-vrouw-van-bedreigde-loodgieter-haar-verhaal-ons-leven-is-voorgoed-veranderd-a85fc163/.

2. https://www.theguardian.com/commentisfree/2024/jan/05/amsterdam-netherlands-drugs-policy-trade.

7. NIJMEGEN TO ARNHEM (GELDERLAND)

1. Quotes from 'Dutch woman who tended Scots soldier's grave dies',

BBC, 29 July 2020. https://www.bbc.com/news/uk-scotland-edinburgh-east-fife-53579714.

2. 'Bloemen!, Algemeen Handelsblad, 31 March 1945', from Geraadpleegd op Delpher, 12 March 2024. https://resolver.kb.nl/resolve?urn=KBNRC01:000047177:mpeg21:p001.

3. *Soldier of Orange: the Dutch Resistance to the Nazis—a Personal Story of Defeat and Triumph, Danger and Heroism*, Erik Hazelhoff (Hodder and Stoughton 1972).

4. Figures vary, but here I am using the figures listed at https://encyclopedia.ushmm.org/content/en/article/jewish-losses-during-the-holocaust-by-country.

5. 'Delivered from evil', Simon Kuper, *Financial Times*, 21 January 2005. https://www.ft.com/content/77ed868e-6ab3-11d9-9357-00000e2511c8.

6. 'Trambedrijf GVB prober na oorlog transportkosten van familie Frank te verhalen', *NOS*, 5 March 2024. https://nos.nl/nieuwsuur/artikel/2511547-trambedrijf-gvb-probeerde-na-oorlog-transportkosten-van-familie-frank-te-verhalen.

8. DE KUIP TO DELFSHAVEN (ROTTERDAM)

1. 'The Netherlands as a Country of Immigration', R. Jennissen, M. Bovens, G. Engbersen and M. Bockhorst, in *Migration Diversity and Social Cohesion. Research for Policy* (Springer 2023). https://doi.org/10.1007/978-3-031-14224-6_2.

2. 'Migration and Immigrants: The Case of the Netherlands', Aslan Zorlu and Joop Hartog, Tinbergen Institute Discussion Paper, No. 01-042/3 (Tinbergen Institute, Amsterdam 2001) and Rotterdam. https://hdl.handle.net/10419/85952.

3. From 'The Netherlands as a Country of Immigration', R. Jennissen, M. Bovens, G. Engbersen and M. Bockhorst, in *Migration Diversity and Social Cohesion. Research for Policy* (Springer 2023). https://link.springer.com/chapter/10.1007/978-3-031-14224-6_2#Fig4.

4. 'Rotterdam, Netherlands—Intercultural City', Council of Europe Intercultural Cities Programme. https://www.coe.int/en/web/interculturalcities/rotterdam.

5. See 'Fear masquerading as tolerance', Christopher Caldwell, *Prospect Magazine*, 3 May 2009. https://www.prospectmagazine.co.uk/essays/52932/fear-masquerading-as-tolerance.

6. Standard Eurobarometer 102—Autumn 2024, https://europa.eu/eurobarometer/surveys/detail/3215.

7. https://www.ohchr.org/sites/default/files/documents/hrbodies/hrcouncil/sessions-regular/session55/advance-versions/A-HRC-55-53-Add1-AUV.pdf.

8. 'Empathie voor migranten kalft in rap tempo af, onder kiezers van vrijwel alle partijen', Loes Reijmer and Marieke de Ruiter, *de Volkskrant*, 4 June 2024. https://www.volkskrant.nl/nieuws-achtergrond/empathie-voor-migranten-kalft-in-rap-tempo-af-onder-kiezers-van-vrijwel-alle-partijen-be13ca91/.

9. 'Zorgen over jonge slachtoffers fatbike—ongelukken na "meetweek"', *NOS*, 29 October 2024. https://nos.nl/artikel/2542570-zorgen-over-jonge-slachtoffers-fatbike-ongelukken-na-meetweek

9. FORT ÉBEN-ÉMAEL TO MAASTRICHT (LIMBURG AND A BIT OF BELGIUM)

1. 'The permissive Dutch', Richard Reeves, *New York Times*, 20 October 1985. https://www.nytimes.com/1985/10/20/magazine/the-permissive-dutch.html

2. *Chip War: the fight for the world's most critical technology*, Chris Miller (Simon and Schuster Ltd 2023).

10. OUD WASSENAAR TO MADURODAM (ZUID HOLLAND)

1. 'Income inequality in the Netherlands is well below the EU average', Centraal Bureau voor de Statistik, 3 July 2024. https://www.cbs.nl/en-gb/news/2024/27/income-inequality-in-the-netherlands-is-well-below-the-eu-average.

2. See https://calcasa.nl/files/Calcasa_Jaarverslag_Miljoenenwoningen_2023.pdf

3. 'Minister Hugo de Jonge: "Boze buurmannen maken veel geluid, maar de mensen in de knel hoor je niet"', Aaldert van Soest, *Nederlands Dagblat*, 24 April 2024. https://www.nd.nl/nieuws/nederland/1221199/minister-hugo-de-jonge-boze-buurmannen-maken-veel-geluid-maar#.

4. Standard Eurobarometer 102—Autumn 2024. https://europa.eu/eurobarometer/surveys/detail/3215.

5. Quoted in 'Why rising house prices are cutting the Dutch birth rate', Senay Boztas, *The Times*, 7 July 2024. https://www.thetimes.

com/world/europe/article/why-rising-house-prices-are-cutting-the-dutch-birth-rate-8tqlsrqjl.

6. 'Klimaatdoel 2030 raakt uit zicht; extra beleid met snel effect nodig', Planbureau voor de Leefomgeving, 24 October 2024. https://www.pbl.nl/actueel/nieuws/klimaatdoel-2030-raakt-uit-zicht-extra-beleid-met-snel-effect-nodig.

7. Climate Change Performance Index Ranking 2025. https://ccpi.org/ranking/.

8. 'CBS: Nederland is rijk en gelukkig, welvaart wel ten koste van latere generaties', *NOS*, 15 May 2024. https://nos.nl/artikel/2520567-cbs-nederland-is-rijk-en-gelukkig-welvaart-wel-ten-koste-van-latere-generaties.

INDEX